Good Rabbitkeeping

Sue Fox

tfb

Good Rabbitkeeping
Sue Fox

Project Team
Editor: Mary E. Grangeia
Copy Editor: Stephanie Fornino
Designer: Stephanie Krautheim
Indexer: Elizabeth Walker

TFH Publications
President/CEO: Glen S. Axelrod
Executive Vice President: Mark E. Johnson
Editor-in-Chief: Albert Connelly, Jr.
Production Manager: Kathy Bontz

TFH Publications, Inc.
One TFH Plaza
Third and Union Avenues
Neptune City, NJ 07753

Printed and bound in China

13 14 15 16   5 7 9 8 6 4

Library of Congress Cataloging-in-Publication Data
Fox, Sue, 1962-
 Good rabbitkeeping: a comprehensive guide to all things rabbit / Sue Fox.
    p. cm.
 Includes bibliographical references.
 ISBN 978-0-7938-0663-8 (alk. paper)
 1. Rabbits. I. Title.
 SF453.F598 2008
 636.932'2--dc22

                        2008015849

The Leader In Responsible Animal Care For Over 50 Years! ®
www.tfh.com

Chapter 1
Meet the Rabbit 5

Chapter 2
Rabbit Breeds 21

Chapter 3
Where to Get Your Rabbit 79

Chapter 4
Housing and Accessories 97

Chapter 5
Diet and Nutrition 119

Chapter 6
Grooming Your Rabbit 135

Chapter 7
Health Care 147

Chapter 8
Rabbit Behaviors 167

Chapter 9
Taming and Training 181

Chapter 10
To Breed or Not to Breed 193

Chapter 11
Things to Do With Your Rabbit 219

Resources 241
Index 248

TABLE OF CONTENTS

Chapter 1

Meet the Rabbit

If you have never kept a pet rabbit, you undoubtedly have expectations as to what it would be like. The best way to have a good experience and prevent disappointment is to know as much as you can about rabbits before sharing your home with one. Knowing ahead of time how they interact with people, the type of care they need, and other noteworthy characteristics, such as their tendency to chew, will help you determine if a bunny can meet your expectations and whether you can properly care for one.

As with any pet, the decision to keep one should never be made on impulse. Choosing the right pet requires careful thought and some research. The information in this book will help you make a good choice by answering questions about the characteristics of different breeds, explaining what is required for proper care, and helping you determine how well a bunny might fit into your lifestyle and family.

NATURAL HISTORY

When undertaking the care of any domestic animal, learning about his natural history, physiology, and behavior in the wild can be helpful when interacting with him because he still retains many of his instinctual traits and physical attributes. More simply stated, the more you know about wild rabbits, the more you will understand why your pet rabbit behaves the way he does.

Rabbits Versus Hares

Rabbits and hares look the same but differ in several interesting ways. Hares differ from rabbits because they have "precocial" young who are born fully furred and with open eyes. Baby hares are able to run within a few minutes of birth. In contrast, most rabbits have "altricial" young who are born blind, deaf, and furless. Until they develop more, baby rabbits are unable to run for several weeks. Rabbits and hares have unique skulls—a joint located at the back of it allows slight movement. This unusual feature helps absorb shock to the skull while a rabbit leaps and runs at high speeds.

Origins

The pet rabbits most people keep today are the domesticated version of the European rabbit (*Oryctolagus cuniculus*). The genus portion of his scientific name, *Oryctolagus*, means "digging hare" in Latin (even though the European rabbit is not a hare), and the species moniker, *cuniculus*, means "underground passage." Originally, zoologists placed rabbits in the order Rodentia (rodents), which includes animals such as hamsters, guinea pigs, rats, and mice. For various reasons, including the fact that rabbits have two pairs of upper incisors and rodents have only one, rabbits were moved into their own order called Lagomorpha. This order is divided into two families. One family, Ochotonidae, includes only pikas, which look slightly similar to guinea pigs but have rounded ears and no visible tail. The other, Leporidae, includes both rabbits and hares.

For tens of thousands of years, the European rabbit was found only in Spain, Portugal, and southern France. Some scientists think he could not move beyond these areas because of the dense forests that covered most of Europe after the last ice age. The European rabbit does not live in forests; his habitat is open country. However, he started to increase his range after people began to cut down the forests. Even so, his way north into the rest of Europe was blocked by the Pyrenees mountain range.

Today, this single species has been introduced to most countries in the world, including Antarctica, the Australian region, southern South America, and islands off the west coast of the United States.

Wild Habitats

Wild rabbits live in a variety of habitats, including the arctic tundra, high-elevation mountain peaks, pine forests, deserts, open grasslands, and tropical forests. They flourish in a wide range of climates and are able to withstand temperatures as low as 10°F (-12°C).

Most species of rabbits are solitary. However, the European rabbit is an exception. He is social and lives in colonies called warrens, which are a series of dens and tunnels. The burrows help him avoid high temperatures and stay warm underground in cold weather. Dominant males have several females in their territories, and the females establish a dominance hierarchy among themselves. Some groups of rabbits are dominant to others and maintain larger territories.

Species

At least 49 species of rabbits are known worldwide, with 17 living in the United States. Depending on the particular species, the rabbits found in North America weigh between 0.5 and 11 pounds (0.2 and 5 kg).

One of the more interesting species is the tiny pygmy rabbit (*Sylvilagus idahoensis*). He is the only rabbit found in North America who digs his own burrow. The pygmy rabbit lives under a canopy of tall sagebrush in the western part of the United States. When eluding a predator, he quickly scampers into his burrow for protection.

Other species, such as the black-tailed jackrabbit (*Lepus californicus*), live in wide-open deserts and rest in shallow scrapes beneath bushes. To escape predators, jackrabbits can hop up to 20 feet (6 m) and reach speeds of 30 to 35 miles an hour (48 to 56 km an hour) over short distances.

Depending on the regions in which they live, wild rabbits also have an interesting array of adaptations. The snowshoe hare (*Lepus americanus*), who lives in regions with snowy winters, molts into a white coat in fall and into a brown coat in spring. His large, furry hind feet, which help him easily travel over the snow, give him his common name.

Many species of wild rabbits are good swimmers. When pursed by a predator, they will readily enter water and escape by swimming dog-paddle style with all four feet. The swamp rabbit (*Sylvilagus aquaticus*) of the southeastern United States leads a semi-aquatic life and swims in water to get from one place to another. When hiding from a predator, he may remain submerged underwater except for his nose.

Behavior in the Wild

Being herbivores at the bottom of the food chain, wild rabbits are only just above the plants they need to eat. In their natural habitat, they browse on tender new seedlings and the succulent buds and young leaves of bushes. They eat a variety of foods and select different plant species and plant parts, depending on the time of year. In the fall and winter, they usually eat the bark of bushes and trees and nibble more grass, while in spring and summer, they eat more flowering plants.

This foraging behavior poses a certain level of threat, however, because above the rabbit in the food chain is a variety of carnivorous predators, including coyotes, birds of prey, and snakes. For a rabbit, danger can come from the sky, from behind a bush, or from inside a burrow. When alarmed, a rabbit thumps the ground with his hind leg and can also sense ground vibrations caused by the thumps of other nearby rabbits. His first response to danger is to freeze to avoid detection. He then rapidly bolts into a burrow or tries to outrun the predator. If he is caught, he gives a piercing distress call. Rabbits are an important source of food for many predators, but their rapid rate of reproduction helps compensate for their high rate of predation.

Wild rabbits live in a variety of habitats. At least 49 species are known worldwide, with 17 living in the United States.

In their own social structure, rabbits are very territorial animals. They have three glands that they use to scent mark their territory, whether it be home or kin: chin glands, anal glands, and inguinal glands. Dominant rabbits mark much more than subordinate ones. Mother rabbits mark their babies, called kits, with their chin and inguinal glands, which are located in the groin; they will attack any young that smell different from their own. Rabbits also use their droppings, which are scent marked from their anal glands (similar to dogs), to mark their territory by scattering them as they hop around. Pet owners will sometimes notice their rabbit scent marking by rubbing his chin on table legs or the floor. However, people can't detect the scent this gland produces.

PHYSICAL CHARACTERISTICS

Two of the rabbit's most conspicuous features, his long ears and long, jumping hind legs, evolved to help him evade predators. A rabbit can swivel his ears to track the direction of a sound; his keen hearing alerts him to potential danger. Long ears also help a rabbit stay cool by dissipating heat. Those from cold, northern climates have small ears to help conserve heat.

The various breeds of domestic rabbit have a range of ear sizes from small to large, including lop ears that fall to the sides of the head. The domestic rabbit's ears help keep him cool, just as a wild rabbit's ears do. The only sweat glands they have are in their lips, and they are not enough to do the job.

A rabbit's long, jumping hind legs, flexible back, and powerful hindquarters allow for rapid bursts of speed and quick changes in direction. Rabbits who rely on their legs to run usually have long hind legs and live in open areas, whereas those with short legs usually live in brushy areas and bolt underground. The different breeds of domestic rabbits have varying leg lengths, although they obviously do not need to escape predators. For example, dwarf rabbits have short legs, while the Belgian hare (not a true hare) has long, slender legs typical of hares living in vast desert environments.

Unlike rodents, rabbits do not hold food in their front paws. They eat while on the ground or stand on their hind legs to nibble shrubs. Bulging eyes on the sides of their head provide them with a wide view to detect predators. However, they can't see the area below their mouths and use their whiskers and lips to find plants they like to eat.

Domestic Rabbits

Seen today in more varieties than ever before, the rabbit has retained his popularity over many centuries. Along with dogs, cats, and mice, rabbits kept as domesticated pets can be traced back as far as the 1500s.

Rabbits first appeared in recorded human history as early as 1100 BCE but were not domesticated until the 15th century.

Rabbits have six chisel-like incisors in the front of their mouth, two pairs on top and one pair on the bottom. These teeth never stop growing. Their molar teeth also continue to grow throughout their lives. (Teeth that continuously grow are termed "open root.") Rabbits' teeth can grow up to 5 inches (12.7 cm) per year. The incisors and molars are naturally worn down by chewing on tough, abrasive plants. Without continual growth, their teeth would soon wear down and be rendered useless.

Female rabbits are usually larger than males, which is the opposite of most mammals. This trait is present in most breeds of the domestic rabbit. Adult females have a large fold of skin over their throats called the dewlap. Shortly before giving birth, a female will pull fur from the dewlap to line her nest.

TOWARD DOMESTICATION

The history of the domesticated rabbit is closely tied to human conquest and exploration. About 3,000 years ago, the Phoenicians, an ancient trading people from the eastern part of the Mediterranean Sea, were impressed with the usefulness of the rabbit for meat and fur when they founded new colonies in Spain. Being seafarers, they distributed them to other locations while traveling and trading. Breeding pairs of rabbits were even released on islands where their offspring could provide food for sailors during their travels.

But the long road toward domestication did not begin until approximately 2,000 years ago, when the European rabbit was introduced to Italy. The Romans raised colonies of captive rabbits in large walled gardens called leporaria. It is thought that wild rabbits were netted and then released into the leporaria for fattening before being harvested for their meat and fur. Basically still wild, people did not control the rabbits' breeding. Some researchers think that leporaria were precursors to the warrens or game parks that developed later in the Middle Ages.

It is likely that the Romans introduced this convenient and prolific source of food and fur throughout their empire. Evidence shows that Roman sailors released rabbits in the Balearic Islands, a group of islands, which include Ibiza and Majorca, located south of Spain in the Mediterranean Sea. They reproduced so successfully there that the islanders were overrun and experienced famines because their harvests were destroyed by the overabundant rabbit population searching for available food. The people had to appeal to the emperor for help in ridding their lands of this burdensome problem.

The European rabbit was not found in Great Britain until around 1066 CE, when he was introduced after the Norman conquest. Wherever rabbits became established, they were hunted as game animals. Aside from being hunted with falcons, dogs, and from horseback, they were also captured with snares, nooses, and nets. Rabbit hunting is still a popular sport in many parts of the world.

But it was French Catholic monks who were credited with beginning the true process of rabbit domestication during the Middle Ages. Because the monks lived in seclusion, they needed an easily obtainable source of food, especially during Lent, the annual season of fasting and penitence that begins 40 days prior to Easter. Oddly enough, they began to raise rabbits because laurices, unborn or newly born rabbits, were officially classified as "fish" in 600 CE by Pope Gregory I and thus were permissible to eat during Lent, a time when meat was forbidden. Although it sounds grossly unappealing to modern people, laurices were considered a delicacy in earlier times. The monks kept the rabbits within the monastery walls and eventually in cages. Once they began to maintain them in enclosures, the process of domestication began. Inevitably, they would select and breed them for various traits and characteristics. By the 16th century, rabbit breeding spread across France, Italy, Belgium,

The difference between domesticated and wild European rabbits is apparent when orphaned babies are reared by people. Even though the wild baby may have been handled several times a day and be somewhat tame, he will become increasingly skittish and fearful as he gets older. Once he reaches sexual maturity, his behavior will usually change completely and he will lose any tame, pet-like qualities. In contrast, the domestic rabbit will tolerate and even enjoy being touched and handled. While his behavior can also change upon sexual maturity, it is not to the extent that he cannot be kept as a pet any longer.

and England. Rabbits were the last major species of livestock (which includes cattle, horses, pigs, goats, sheep, donkeys, and poultry) to be domesticated.

Beginning in the 19th century, raising rabbits in hutches became common in rural Europe and city suburbs. In summer, rabbit keepers picked fresh greens each day for their stock, and in winter they were fed hay. Raising rabbits continued to increase in popularity well into the 20th century. Today, they are commonly kept not only in Europe but also on farms, in backyards, and in homes across the United States.

Wild Versus Domestic Animals

A domesticated animal is selectively bred in captivity by people who control his breeding and food supply. Bred for generations to live in close association with people, domesticated animals differ in many ways from their wild ancestors.

Domesticated rabbits were bred to be docile, predictable, comfortable around people, and easy to handle. In contrast, wild European rabbits have strong natural instincts and will panic when kept in an enclosure. They are also afraid of people and will readily bite. Changes in the rabbit's morphology, or body shape, also occurred over time. For example, domesticated rabbits became heavier and "meatier" than their wild brethren. They also reached sexual maturity earlier and had greater numbers of litters and more offspring in each litter.

Because these captive animals were protected from predators, those with unusual coat color mutations that normally would have made them conspicuous and vulnerable in the wild survived and were selectively bred by humans. Naturally, as pets, a more conspicuous color is not a problem because the animal is not subject to predation.

As a result, selective breeding for colors that were not found in nature, such as albino, blue, and yellow, was seen by the 1700s. All domesticated small animals, including rats, mice, hamsters, rabbits, and guinea pigs, eventually developed mutations from their normal color.

Over time, through additional selective breeding, people developed rabbit breeds with different sizes, colors, and types of fur. By the late 19th century, an explosion of rabbit breeds occurred. Some were developed for meat, others for their attractive looks. People continue to develop new breeds today.

THE RABBIT'S MANY ROLES

Rabbits have played many roles in human society: They've been considered livestock when raised for meat and fur; they've been used as experimental animals in laboratories; they've been eliminated as agricultural pests in many places; they've been reared as show animals; and they've been kept as beloved pets.

Many pet owners have a hard time accepting that most rabbits were, and still are, reared as a source of meat for people to eat. Rabbits have been an important source of food in Europe, particularly during the two World Wars. Today, countries that produce and consume the most rabbit meat include France, Italy, and Spain. These nations have large farms and facilities to process the rabbits, and the meat is relatively common in stores and restaurants there.

Although the United States does not share the same history of consumption, people have raised rabbits in their backyards for food. Once seen as the food of the common man, rabbit meat was commonly available in grocery stores up until World War II. Since then, consumption has declined due in part to fewer farms and federally inspected plants willing to process the meat. Because most commercial rabbitries prefer New Zealand breed crosses

Spanning centuries of domestication, rabbit breeds of different sizes, colors, and fur types were created through selective breeding.

and pet owners prefer small breeds of rabbit, many of the older and larger meat breeds are nearing extinction.

Fancy Rabbits

About 150 years ago, people began breeding "fancy" rabbits whose purpose was purely for looks and showing. However, even these fancy rabbits weren't considered pets as we know them today. They were thought of as livestock and kept outside in hutches or in cages inside barns.

It has only been in the last 30 or so years that rabbits have been commonly kept as indoor pets and allowed to share their keepers' homes. Pet rabbits really increased in popularity during the early 1970s, when various lop-eared breeds were imported into the United States and when other much smaller breeds, such as the Netherland Dwarf, became more commonly available. Manufacturers responded by providing cages and other supplies that made it easier to keep these adorable creatures as well-cared-for housemates.

The publication of the House Rabbit Handbook in 1985 and the subsequent formation of the House Rabbit Society (HRS) in 1988 also contributed a great deal to a better understanding of domestic rabbits and more than likely to their acceptance as house pets. The ongoing mission of this organization has been to rescue and find homes for abandoned rabbits, as well as to educate people in their proper care. The group does not support their breeding or promotion as food animals or for any other commercial or exploitive interests. Its philosophy and policies promote only one acceptable way to keep rabbits and redefines their role only as companion animals. This conflicts with more traditional groups such as the American Rabbit Breeders Association (ARBA), which supports raising rabbits for show, meat, and fur.

RABBITS AS PETS

Rabbits can be affectionate, curious, and intelligent pets, and they engage in a number of endearing behaviors. Imagine having an adorable, fluffy bunny who sits up on his haunches waiting, nose twitching, for you to let him out to play. Once out of his cage, he will probably do a happy dance, twisting and leaping in midair. Always inquisitive, he may wander off to investigate his "playroom," but sometime later, he may come back to find you, nudge you with his nose for some petting, and then hop off again, looking for new adventures. Or he may just sit quietly next to you while you read a book or watch television. Your bunny may show affection for you by licking your hand or grooming your hair. Some will follow their owners around the house, getting underfoot. Many enjoy playing with toys, and a few will even play catch!

However, not all rabbits are friendly and playful. Many an owner has complained that her bunny sits in the cage like a lump of fur or that he is timid and runs away when let out to play. Some rabbits become territorial and will bite when a hand is placed inside their cage. Regrettably, many of these problems develop due to the owner's misunderstanding of what the pet requires, and sometimes the behavior is due to neglect.

Overall, a rabbit's potential pet quality depends strongly on his temperament and on the care and attention with which he is provided. Domestic rabbits are instinctively timid and easily frightened; this is because they retain their innate character as prey animals for whom danger is always present. No matter how affectionate, your rabbit will never overcome his urge to run when scared. Failure to act goes against his instincts to protect himself from being injured or killed by predators (theoretically, in the case of a pet, of course). However,

Rabbit Personality

A rabbit's personality or temperament is important to the quality of your pet-owning experience. There is a large variation in rabbit temperaments. Friendly rabbits are curious and will come up to people and seek attention. They love to be petted and will nudge you with their nose for more. If given the opportunity, they will follow you around, and some even seem to want to be picked up. Outgoing rabbits often sleep confidently on top of their nest box and are not bothered by household noises and events.

In contrast, shy rabbits might flinch when touched or consistently move away from your hand. They appear uncomfortable and spend considerable time inside their nest box. Just like cats, a shy rabbit can be encouraged to be less shy, but he will never be as easygoing as a naturally friendly individual.

Most pet owners enjoy confident, bold rabbits better than they do a shy and skittish one. Of course, other factors will also affect your rabbit's personality, such as age, gender (if your rabbit is not spayed or neutered), the environment with which you provide him, and how often you play with him.

with proper handling and some training, you can strengthen the bond between you and your pet. Once your rabbit learns to trust you and feels secure, he will want to spend time with you and will provide you with lots of entertaining companionship.

IS A RABBIT RIGHT FOR YOU?

People choose pets for a variety of reasons, but they often do so because they are attracted to the animal's looks. The new pet owner also has expectations as to what keeping the animal will be like. Perhaps a friend or a relative had the same pet—they had pleasant experiences visiting with the animal and think they know what keeping him entails.

Although it may appear otherwise to some, rabbits are interactive animals requiring a good amount of your time. They need daily exercise outside their cage. Kept locked in their enclosure, pet rabbits will become bored and unhappy and will eventually develop physical and behavioral problems. Some experts recommend at least three hours of exercise each day. While giving a fixed number is difficult, the fact remains that they must receive a substantial amount of daily activity to remain healthy.

Consider whether you have the time (and interest) to perform the daily tasks required to care for a rabbit. Besides exercise, you must provide your furry pet with two meals a day, as well as clean his litter box and cage every few days. Domestic rabbits are docile and friendly, but owners must invest time and patience to bond with them. If you lose interest, your once-friendly pet might become shy, withdrawn, more easily frightened, and less likely to enjoy your company. In turn, you will be less likely to enjoy your rabbit. If you are away from home during the day and most of the early evening, consider choosing a different pet who does not require as much daily interaction.

Rabbits have a long life span compared to many other small animals; they live about seven to ten years. If you have any doubts about making such a long-term commitment, consider adopting an older rabbit from one of the many rabbit rescue organizations. You could provide a good home and some love for a homeless animal and would also have an opportunity to see if keeping a rabbit agrees with your lifestyle.

You could also consider being a "foster parent." Many rescue groups need temporary homes for the rabbits they acquire until permanent situations can be found. Taking in a foster animal means that you will provide the same level of care you would if he were your own pet but only until he has a new home. Besides having the pleasure of doing a good deed (and perhaps even adopting one of your foster wards), you'll also have flexibility should your lifestyle change. The knowledgeable people at most rescue groups can answer any questions that arise and provide support for you in this endeavor.

Not Disposable Pets!

Rabbits are the third most popular pet in the United States after cats, who are first, and dogs, who are second. Besides joining the ranks of America's most popular pets, rabbits are also distinguished by another less noteworthy trait: They are high on the list of abandoned or surrendered pets. The phenomenon of disposable pets is no longer limited to just dogs and cats. With their increased popularity, more and more pet rabbits are being given to animal shelters and rescue groups because their owners no longer want them.

Perhaps these pet owners were not properly prepared to care for their rabbits, or perhaps their reasons for getting rid of their pets are as all-encompassing and similar to those given by people who give up their cats and dogs. Surveys performed by various rescue groups have found several common reasons why pet owners have given away their rabbits. Two issues are most noteworthy: First, pet owners could not tolerate their rabbits' adolescent behavior, and second, the owners were not prepared for the rabbits' long life span.

The best way to have a good experience and prevent disappointment is to know as much as you can about rabbits before sharing your home with one.

A rabbit's potential pet quality depends strongly on his temperament and on the care and attention with which he is provided.

Rabbits as a Child's Pet

Experts tend to agree that rabbits do not make good pets for young children. Although they may dream of holding and cuddling their bunnies, rabbits usually don't like being picked up, carried around, or held on a lap for very long. They will tolerate such interactions temporarily but will then quickly demand to be put back down. When restrained for too long or roughly handled, a rabbit can bite, kick with his strong hind legs, or scratch with his sharp nails. A child who is painfully bitten or scratched is likely to drop the rabbit, which can result in the animal incurring a spinal injury or a fractured or broken leg.

Parents should expect to be the primary caretakers of a young child's rabbit and must show her how to properly interact with any pet. Because youngsters occasionally tease animals, they must be watched while playing with them. They can sit quietly on the ground and let the exploring rabbit come to them to say hello. Petting a friendly bunny between his eyes, from his nose to his ears, and gently petting his jowls are sure ways to win his friendship.

Because children do not have long attention spans, caring for their pets can become one more chore unenthusiastically carried out once the novelty wears off. If your child is going to soon become more involved in after-school activities, a long-lived rabbit who may sit neglected is a poor choice. A better selection might be a hamster or rat, both of whom live between two and three years.

Do Your Homework

Rabbit ownership is a much bigger commitment than most people realize. Your pet may remain a member of your family for ten years or longer. Consider carefully whether you can make a long-term commitment to all aspects of his care. As a responsible owner, you should be willing to properly care for your rabbit and ensure his health and well-being throughout his entire lifetime.

Chapter 2

Rabbit Breeds

More than 180 rabbit breeds are recognized around the world, although some are only available in their country of origin. There are also different varieties within each breed. A rabbit's coat, features, shape, and size define his particular breed, while variety is determined by color variations. Some individual breeds were once just a variety of another breed, but they later developed enough of their own characteristics to get their own breed name.

Scientifically speaking, rabbit breeds are different varieties of the domestic rabbit, *Oryctolagus cuniculus*, created through selective breeding. When rabbits of the same breed are mated together, they will reproduce a breed type. Members of the same breed share a certain number of morphological traits (biological form and structure), such as ear length and whether the ears are erect or hang down. They also share physiological characteristics (biological bodily processes), such as a tendency to grow rapidly. In general, breeds are developed and maintained by people.

THE FIRST DOMESTIC BREEDS

Although it is likely that captive wild rabbits were kept as pets from the earliest times, it was not until much later that they were domesticated and bred for specific traits. Selective breeding first appeared in the Middle Ages, when rabbits were initially treated

Although it is likely that captive wild rabbits were kept as pets from the earliest times, it was not until much later that they were domesticated and bred for specific traits.

as domesticated farm animals, but it wasn't until the 1500s that records exist of color variations.

Tracing the exact history of the various breeds is almost impossible, although information is known about certain color types and sizes. For instance, the first written records of black, white, piebald (black and white), ash-gray, and gray-brown rabbits, as well as giant rabbits four times the size of normal ones, are from the middle of the 16th century. Agricola, a monk from Verona, Italy, who was in charge of his monastery's gardens and livestock, recorded his observations on the emergence of these different animals around 1595.

Besides variations in color and size, different types of rabbits were also noted. In 1606, a French agricultural scientist, Olivier de Serres, classified three types of rabbit: the wild rabbit, the semi-wild or warren rabbit who was raised inside walls or ditches, and the domesticated or hutch-bred rabbit.

Historical information may be easier to find about more unusual breeds. For example, we know that solid silver rabbits were first noted as early as 1631 in England. English sailors are credited with bringing the first Angora rabbits to the Bordeaux region of France in 1723. Himalayan rabbits were known in Europe by 1858. The "silver-plated" rabbits reported in France just prior to 1924 are believed to be the Champagne d'Argent, a breed that is now quite rare.

By the mid-19th century, animal fancy began to emerge as a hobby in Western Europe and the United States, and rabbit breeding became a fashionable pastime. Breeds were created and modified strictly for the purpose of exhibition rather than for food, fur, or wool. Today, the domestic rabbit continues to be popular as a show animal and pet, and as such, new breeds continue to be developed and recognized by breed clubs and organizations worldwide.

BREED DEVELOPMENT

Many rabbit breeds known today were originally created in European countries, such as Germany, Great Britain, the Netherlands, Belgium, and France, as well as in the United States. By using rabbits from local populations, crossing breeds, utilizing mutations in color and/or fur type, and selecting for size and body type, people developed many different varieties, each with unique characteristics. The development of some breeds is known in detail, including the names of the people involved and the rabbit breeds used, while the origins of others are lost in time. Sometimes fanciers in different countries developed similar breeds at the same time, which occurred with the Lilac breed.

Fashionable No More

Just as with dog breeds, rabbit breeds can come into and fall out of fashion due to people's preferences. In the early 20th century, the Belgian Hare was enormously popular, and thousands were imported into the United States. Almost every state had a contingent of Belgian Hare breeders and clubs, but now the breed is quite rare.

More than 50 recorded rabbit breeds, primarily known from Europe and the United States, have vanished. Some became extinct because breeders changed the breed's desired weight, making the rabbit larger or smaller, such as the now extinct Heavyweight Belgian Hare. Some old breeds, such as the Blue Imperial from Great Britain and the more recent Peruvian created in the United States, disappeared because they failed to develop a following, perhaps due to political reasons and changing markets. An interesting fact, however, is that some extinct breeds can be recreated; breeders in Great Britain have done so with the Golden Glavcot.

Regional Breeds

Some rabbit breeds have a limited geographic distribution. For example, particular breeds are found only in developing countries. These breeds have been selected to have a high tolerance to local conditions, which typically include either the hot, rainy weather of the tropics or the hot, dry weather of deserts. These types of environments are typically very stressful for rabbits and are not their natural habitat. However, through selection over time, they have become regionally adapted. Some of these breeds do not have consistent colors or patterns, but they are still considered a breed because they are of a similar type and have adapted over many years to climate extremes.

Examples of regional breeds include the Bauscat of Egypt, the Criollo of Mexico, and the Baladi (which means "native" or "local" in Arabic) of Sudan. While these breeds are typically small with low productivity, they are hardy and can tolerate harsh conditions. None of these breeds has yet developed a following in other countries, although it is possible that they might eventually find interested breeders in the United States or Europe.

Other regional breeds are now found in numerous countries around the world, such as the Champagne d' Argent, who was developed from a regional population in Champagne, France. However, many of the reasons for transporting breeds, such as for showing or for meat development, do not apply to those from developing countries.

Rare Breeds

With so many breeds constantly being developed worldwide, it becomes important to monitor and preserve older, more traditional breeds. The American Livestock Breeds Conservancy (ALBC) promotes the conservation of endangered breeds of poultry and

Rather than judging one rabbit against another, a breed standard allows an animal to be judged on his own merits according to the "standard of perfection" set forth in its guidelines.

livestock, including rabbits. These particular breeds are threatened because agriculture has changed. Many traditional livestock breeds have also lost popularity and are threatened with extinction. Modern food production favors the use of a few highly specialized breeds, such as the New Zealand or New Zealand crosses, which are selected for maximum output in a controlled environment. Traditional breeds that take longer to reach market weight, such as the Blanc de Hotot, are not suitable for today's commercial rabbit farms. Pet owners' preferences for small rabbit breeds have also contributed to reduced numbers of heritage meat rabbit breeds.

The Conservancy believes that these traditional or "heritage" breeds are an important part of America's agricultural inheritance and could contain traits that might be valuable in the future. Eleven rare breeds of North American rabbits are listed by the ALBC: American, American Chinchilla, Belgian Hare, Beveren, Blanc de Hotot, Crème d' Argent, Giant Chinchilla, Lilac, Rhinelander, Silver, and Silver Fox. If one of these breeds strikes your fancy, perhaps you could contribute to the breed's continued existence by breeding them. Although they can be difficult to obtain, with persistence, you can locate a breeder and obtain a pair.

BREED STANDARDS

The first organization devoted to rabbit breeding and showing in the United States, the National Pet Stock Association, was formed in 1910. In 1917, the group changed its name to the National Breeders and Fanciers Association of America, and in 1924, it settled on its current name, the American Rabbit Breeders Association (ARBA).

The ARBA sets the official breed standards for recognized rabbit breeds, and it is in charge of the criteria judges use to evaluate rabbits in shows, which are as formal as dog and cat shows. These standards are beneficial to breeders and anyone interested in showing because they provide a reference to the agreed-upon "standard of perfection," known as conformation, for each breed. The standard becomes a blueprint by which breeders choose their breeding stock, which is particularly important because how a rabbit conforms to the standard will determine whether he can be shown. An animal is given points based on features that make him unique and the best in his category.

The ARBA currently recognizes 47 rabbit breeds. Some breeds are old and have been recognized in Europe or in the United States for more than 75 years. Others are new, such as the Mini-Satin, whom the ARBA recognized in 2005.

Most European countries also have national rabbit organizations that host shows and promote their recognized breeds.

BREED CLUBS

National breed clubs, or national specialty clubs, are chartered by the ARBA. These clubs provide an ongoing forum that allows fanciers to learn from and help one another, often through events, newsletters, and direct access to other members. This help can consist of encouraging new members when they first show their rabbits to sharing information on health and feeding.

Another prime goal of most clubs is to continue improving their breed. (See Chapter 10 for information on what it means to improve a breed.) Other objectives might be to popularize and promote their breed. Clubs with large memberships often sponsor local, state, and national shows. Breed clubs frequently come up with a special name to describe their breed. For example, the Rhinelander is the "Calico of the Fancy," while the Dwarf Hotot is the "Eyes of the Fancy." If you have a purebred rabbit, club memberships are usually relatively inexpensive and a great way to meet people who share your passion for your chosen breed.

Creating New Breeds

Besides recreating or improving old breeds, rabbit fanciers continue to develop new ones. How does someone go about creating a new breed? First, a breeder has to have an idea of what she wants to produce and why. Then it takes years of devoted work, usually in collaboration with other breeders, before the new breed becomes a reality.

People enjoy the challenge and respect the knowledge required to produce a novel breed. An understanding of genetics is almost always necessary because problems crop up in a breed's development that must be fixed. For example, before the characteristic deep blue color was fixed in the American's coat, specimens often had undesirable brown patches or stray white hairs in the fur that needed to be bred away. Sometimes breeders take unforeseen traits and use them to develop a whole new breed, as happened with the American Fuzzy Lop. When first introduced, the Holland Lop rabbit was only available in solid colors, and some breeders wanted to add the broken pattern to the breed's gene pool. In an effort to achieve this coat variation, a wool gene was also introduced during crossbreeding, and the American Fuzzy Lop, known for his long "fuzzy" coat, was born.

Unlike dog breeders, who do not approve of outcrossing purebreds to different dog breeds or dogs of unknown heritage to improve the quality of a breed, rabbit breeders do not mind. As long as a rabbit's pedigree shows three successive generations of the same breed, he is considered whatever breed is shown on the pedigree. For example, when the Blanc de Hotot breed was first imported into the United States, breeders thought that their conformation needed some improvement. By mating the early imports with white Beverens,

The different rabbit breeds are based on size, fur type, color, color pattern, ear type and/or size, and any combination of these features. They have been developed for meat, such as the New Zealand White, who grows quickly and has big muscles; for fur, such as the Angora; and purely for looks, such as the Netherland Dwarf. Size and body type vary widely. Individuals of the giant breeds can weigh up to 20 pounds (9.1 kg), while dwarf breeds weigh less than 3 pounds (1.4 kg).

breeders achieved their goal of improving the breed's conformation while keeping the Blanc de Hotot's notable frosty white coat. The offspring of these crosses are still considered and registered as Blanc de Hotots. In contrast, a dog would not be allowed to be officially registered with a national organization such as the American Kennel Club (AKC) if he had such an outcross.

Breed Recognition

A breeder who would like to present a new breed for consideration must undertake a fairly lengthy development process. The ARBA, which supports the development of new rabbit breeds, allows its members to submit applications for breed recognition if the animals meet specific requirements. First, the breeder must make sure that the proposed new breed has distinct traits that are consistently passed on to successive generations. The new breed must be unique, not just a slight modification of an existing breed.

Once a new breed meets these requirements, one individual who is the breed's sponsor must propose a breed standard and apply for a Certificate of Development from the ARBA. After holding the Certificate for at least three years, the breed sponsor can then present the new breed for its first showing at the ARBA convention. Ninety days prior to this, she must provide the ARBA with proof that at least five other ARBA members are actively raising the new breed to the proposed standard. The second and third showings must include at least three pairs of rabbits. These two presentations must be done in consecutive years after the first showing is accepted. If the breed is approved, it is included in the ARBA Standard of Perfection and can compete in all ARBA-sponsored shows.

BREED CHARACTERISTICS

Breed standards list the specific characteristics or features required for each breed. The different rabbit breeds are categorized by body type, size, fur type, color, color pattern, fur density, ear type and/or size, and any combination of these features. Some breeds have been developed for meat, such as the New Zealand white, which grows quickly and has big muscles. Others are developed for fur, such as the Giant Chinchilla, or for wool, such as the Angora. And some are developed purely for looks, such as the Jersey Wooly. In particular cases, breeders select for exaggerated features, such as the enormously long ears of the English Lop, which are at least 21 inches (53.3 cm) when measured from tip to tip, or for extremely small size, such as the Netherland Dwarf, who weighs less than 2.5 pounds (1.1 kg).

Aside from such notable exceptions, however, rabbit breeds look broadly similar. Unlike with animals such as dogs, in which each breed has a distinct conformation, rabbit breeds don't differ in such specific terms. For example, they don't quite approach the incredible difference in size found among dog breeds: The Chihuahua is around 5 percent of a Great Dane's weight, while the Netherland Dwarf rabbit looks tiny next to the enormous Flemish Giant and is only 20 percent of its weight.

Although features such as color and fur type may be immediately noticed, more subtle differences among breeds that might not be as obvious to a new rabbit fancier may be seen in the rabbit's body type. Some breeds have high, arched backs and look like hares. Others

Different rabbits breeds are categorized by body type, size, fur type, color, color pattern, fur density, ear type and/or size, and any combination of these features.

Foreign Breed Recognition by the ARBA

Even breeds that are recognized in other countries, such as Great Britain or Germany, must go through the American Rabbit Breeders Association's (ARBA) breed recognition process. Doing so helps make sure that the breed meets the criteria required by ARBA standards. The presentation process ensures the breed's quality and also makes certain that there is enough interest in the proposed breed to warrant its recognition.

are round and plump with shoulders that are much lower than their hips. Some breeds are long and slinky with flat backs.

In general, rabbit breeds are divided into two main groups: those developed for their fur and those developed as utility breeds. Both groups come in myriad shapes, colors, and sizes. The following summarizes their overall characteristics.

Types of Fur

There are four types of rabbit fur.

Normal Fur: Normal fur is the most common. It has two layers, an undercoat and an overcoat. It is thick, shiny, and of variable lengths up to 1.5 inches (3.8 cm). Some rabbits with normal fur have what is classified as flyback or rollback fur. Flyback fur will "fly back" to its normal position when stroked from the hindquarters to the shoulders. Most breeds have a flyback coat. Rollback fur gradually returns to its normal position when stroked from the hindquarters to the shoulders.

Rex Fur: Rex fur is short; ideally, it should be 0.6 inches (1.6 cm), but it can be up to 0.9 inches (2.2 cm) in length. The fur is extremely dense and stands straight out from the rabbit's body. Rex fur looks and feels like plush velvet. It is the result of a mutation that reduces the guard hairs to the length of the undercoat.

Satin Fur: Satin fur is strikingly shiny, lustrous, and very dense with a fine texture. It is usually a solid color and the same length as normal fur. However, compared to normal fur, satin fur is finer and has a more transparent hair shell. The greater transparency makes the pigment show through more clearly so that satin rabbits appear more brilliant in color compared to normal furred breeds.

Angora Fur: Angora fur is typically called "wool" by rabbit fanciers. Depending on the breed, the wool may be from 3 to 5 inches (7.6 to 12.7 cm) long. The hair is soft and fluffy. Angora rabbits are sheared or hand-plucked. The wool is spun and used to make clothes.

Coat Colors

Agouti is the natural color of a wild rabbit's coat. It consists of gray fur on the back and much lighter or white fur on the belly. The long guard hairs (the longest, coarsest hairs in the coat that form the topcoat) are black but bluer at the base and deep black at the tips. The guard hairs are black at the tips with a yellowish band in the middle and bluish coloration at the base. The soft undercoat is tipped with yellow and is bluish at the base.

Using mutations in the agouti color, people have developed purebred rabbits in dozens and dozens of colors. Some breeds have only a few color varieties, such as the Palomino, which comes in only two colors, while others, such as the Netherland Dwarf, are available in more than two dozen colors.

Color has always fascinated breeders. Ultimately, an understanding of coat color genetics is important in the maintenance and development of a new color within a breed. Rabbit fur contains only two pigments: black and chocolate. All other colors, including agouti, that don't look black or chocolate are due to genetic modifications of these two colors. One modification is whether the color is either full (intense) or faded (dilute). Thus, the color black can become blue and the color chocolate can become lilac. Additional modifiers produce other full colors such as sable and chinchilla and other dilute colors such as opal and squirrel. Other genes modify different traits such as markings and coat patterns.

Markings and Coat Patterns

Fanciers classify the various markings and patterns found in the rabbit's coat with a variety of terms as follows.

Broken: Any recognized breed color, along with white, that is evenly distributed in patches, spots, or a blanket pattern.

Butterfly: A marking on the nose, which includes the whisker bed and upper lip, and extends up the center of the face.

Pointed White: The body color is pure white, and the markings on the nose, ears, feet, and tail are a darker color such as black, blue, chocolate, or lilac.

Self: The same color is on the body and appendages.

Shaded: The shaded pattern has a gradual transition in color, usually from dark to light. The lighter color is found on the sides and belly.

Ticked: Longer guard hairs occur throughout the coat and are a different color than the body fur.

Wide Band: The same color is on the body, ears, tail, and feet but a lighter color may be on the eye circles, inside the ears, and beneath the tail, lower jaw, and belly.

Adult Weight of Bucks and Does per ARBA Standards

BREED TYPES	WEIGHT [pounds (kilograms)]	
	Bucks	Does
Small/Dwarf Breeds		
American Fuzzy Lop	4 (1.8)	4 (1.8)
Britannia Petite	2.5 (1.2)	2.5 (1.2)
Dutch	3.5–5.5 (1.6–2.5)	3.5–5.5 (1.6–2.5)
Dwarf Hotot	3 (1.4) (maximum)	3 (1.4) (maximum)
Florida White	4–6 (1.8–2.7)	4–6 (1.8–2.7)
Havana	4.5–6.5 (2–3)	5.25–5.5 (2.4–2.5)
Himalayan	2.5–4.5 (1.2–2)	2.5–4.5 (1.2–2)
Holland Lop	4 (1.8)	4 (1.8)
Jersey Wooly	3.5 (1.6)	3.5 (1.6)
Mini Lop	4.5–6.5 (2–3)	4.5–6.5 (2–3)
Mini Rex	3–4.5 (1.4–2)	3.25–4.5 (1.5–2)
Mini Satin	3.25–4.75 (1.5–2.2)	3.25–4.75 (1.5–2.2)
Netherland Dwarf	2.5 (1.2)	2.5 (1.2)
Polish	3.5 (1.6)	3.5 (1.6)
Silver	4–7 (1.8–3.2)	4–7 (1.8–3.2)
Tan	4–5.5 (1.8–2.5)	4–6 (1.8–2.7)
Thrianta	4–6 (1.8–2.7)	4–6 (1.8–2.7)
Medium Breeds		
American Sable	7–9 (3.2–4.1)	8–10 (3.6–4.5)
Belgian Hare	6–9.5 (2.7–4.3)	6–9.5 (2.7–4.3)
English Angora	5–7 (2.3–3.2)	5.75–6.5 (2.6–3
English Spot	5–8 (2.3–3.6)	5–8 (2.3–3.6)

Medium Breeds (cont.)	Bucks	Does
French Angora	7.5–10.5 (3.4–4.8)	7.5–10.5 (3.4–4.8)
Harlequin	6.5–9 (3–4.1)	7–9.5 (3.2–4.3)
Lilac	5.5–7.5 (2.5–3.4)	6–8 (2.7–3.6)
Rex	7.5–9.5 (3.4–4.3)	8–10.5 (3.6–4.8)
Rhinelander	6.5–9.5 (3–4.3)	7–10 (3.2–4.5)
Satin Angora	6.5–9.5 (3–4.3)	6.5–9.5 (3–4.3)
Silver Marten	6–8.5 (2.7–3.9)	7–9.5 (3.2–4.3)
Standard Chinchilla	5–7 (2.3–3.2)	5.5–7.5 (2.5–3.4)

Large Breeds

	Bucks	Does
American	9–11 (4.1–5)	10–12 (4.5–5.4)
American Chinchilla	9–11 (4.1–5)	10–12 (4.5–5.4)
Beveren	8–11 (3.6–5)	9–12 (4.1–5.4)
Blanc de Hotot	8–10 (3.6–4.5)	9–11 (4.1–5)
Californian	8–10 (3.6–4.5)	8.5–10.5 (3.6–4.8)
Champagne d'Argent	9–11 (4.1–5)	9.5–12 (4.3–5.4)
Cinnamon	8.5–10.5 (3.6–4.8)	9–11 (4.1–5)
Crème d'Argent	8–10.5 (3.6–4.8)	8.5–11 (3.9–5)
English Lop	9 (4.1)	10 (4.5)
Giant Angora	9.5 (4.3)	10 (4.5)
New Zealand	9–11 (4.1–5)	10–12 (4.5–5.4)
Palomino	< 9 (4.1)	< 9.5 (4.3)
Satin	8.5–10.5 (3.9–4.8)	9–11 (4.1–5)
Silver Fox	9–11 (4.1–5)	10–12 (4.5–5.4)

Giant Breeds

	Bucks	Does
Checkered Giant	11 (5) (minimum)	12 (5.4) (minimum)
Flemish Giant	13 (5.9)	14 (6.4)
French Lop	10.5 (4.8)	11 (5)
Giant Chinchilla	12–15 (5.4–6.8)	13–16 (13–7.3)

Although there is no right or wrong choice when deciding on a family pet, size, fur type, and temperament are important factors to consider.

Eye Color

There are more than 100 different rabbit coat colors but only five eye colors: brown, blue-gray, blue, marbled, and pink (also called ruby red).

Body Type Profile

The ARBA categorizes each of the 47 recognized breeds by putting them into one of the following five body type profiles. The topline is the profile of a rabbit's shoulders, back, and hindquarters when viewed from the side, and it figures prominently in the overall classification system.

Commercial: The commercial type is characterized by a full body and firm flesh. The depth of the rabbit's body equals the width of the body. The highest point of the topline is over the rabbit's hips. Commercial breeds are usually developed for meat and fur.

Compact: The compact type is considered somewhat similar to commercial rabbits, but they are lighter in weight and shorter in body length than commercial-type rabbits. Some compact breeds are described as "bulldog-like."

Full Arch: The full-arch type looks somewhat similar to a wild hare. The arch starts at the nape of the rabbit's neck and continues in a smooth, unbroken line over the shoulders, loin, hips, and rounds down to the base of the tail. Most breeds have more depth than width of body.

Semi-Arch: The semi-arch type has an arch that starts at the back of the shoulders and follows through to the base of the tail. Breeds in this type are referred to as having a mandolin appearance.

Cylindrical: The cylindrical type has a straight topline with no arch or rise. Viewed from the side, the profile does not taper. This type has fine bones and a long, slender head.

Temperament

Although dogs differ in temperament based on breed—for example, Bull Terriers are feisty and energetic and Golden Retrievers are easygoing—similar stark differences among rabbit breeds do not exist. There are some generalizations based on size. For example, dwarf rabbits are more excitable, while large breeds are usually more docile. Plenty of exceptions exist, though. For example, the Dutch rabbit is a small breed noted for being calm, whereas the Checkered Giant, one of the giant breeds, is known for being spirited. Moreover, even within a breed, a range of temperaments is found so that some individuals are calm and friendly and others are shy and standoffish.

Besides size, body type profile can also be used to assess potential temperament. Generally, breeds that are the full-arch type are more alert and energetic, and some tend to be more inclined to nip. Large breeds, such as the English Spot, and small breeds, such as the Britannia Petite, are classified as full arch. The semi-arch types are similar in temperament but to a lesser degree. The calmest and most docile breeds tend to be the commercial and compact types. Only one breed, the Himalayan, belongs to the cylindrical group, and it is generally gentle.

Specific breed characteristics and temperament are discussed in the breed descriptions that follow.

BREED DESCRIPTIONS

It's important to be well educated in all aspects of rabbit ownership before making a choice about what rabbit will best fit your lifestyle, and part of making an informed decision includes knowing as much about your chosen breed as possible. Although there is no right or wrong choice, size and temperament are important factors to consider when deciding on a family pet. Check out all the breeds and see what their advantages and disadvantages are with regard to your personal circumstances. You can visit a rabbit show or breeder to find out more about breeds in which you are interested. Most breeders would be happy to help you come to a decision that best suits your situation. ARBA and breed club websites list upcoming shows, some of which may be in your area.

The following breeds are those recognized by the ARBA.

Small/Dwarf Breeds

American Fuzzy Lop

Weight: Less than 4 pounds (1.8 kg).
Description: The American Fuzzy Lop is recognized in more than two dozen colors that are broken down into six groups: agouti, broken, pointed white, self, shaded, and wide band. This breed's wool is slightly coarse, with well-distributed guard hairs. Juveniles need more grooming than the adults do, but plan on regular brushing sessions. Some fanciers think that American Fuzzy Lops can occasionally be excitable, but they're also curious and make good house rabbits.
Body Type Profile: Compact.
Breed History: The American Fuzzy Lop was developed using the Holland Lop, English Spot, and French Angora. The Holland Lop was only available in solid colors when he was first introduced into the United States. Some fanciers wanted the Holland Lop to also have a broken pattern. By breeding Holland Lops to English Spots, they were able to produce rabbits with the broken pattern. But the broken pattern rabbits didn't have the rollback fur that the Holland Lop must have according to the ARBA breed standard. Instead, they had the flyback fur of the English Spot. To fix this, the breeders bred their rabbits to French Angoras, who have a gentle rollback coat. Breeders occasionally found a Holland Lop with long wool in one of these litters.

Because the gene for the "fuzzy coat" was recessive, mating two fuzzy Holland Lops together resulted in some of their offspring having the fuzzy hair. One of the breeders decided to develop these rabbits as a new breed named the American Fuzzy Lop.

After spending four years developing the new breed, she was granted a working standard for the American Fuzzy Lop at the 1985 ARBA National Convention. The new breed passed at its second ARBA showing the following year. However, in 1987, the ARBA Standards Committee did not approve the breed because the rabbits were not uniform enough. A new working standard was then written and accepted. In 1988, the American Fuzzy Lop was finally approved at the ARBA convention and became a new recognized breed. If it had not passed, fanciers would have had to start the process of breed recognition all over again.

Britannia Petite

Weight: Less than 2.5 pounds (1.1 kg).

Description: This small rabbit has sleek, silky fur that is black, black otter, chestnut agouti, ruby-eyed white, or sable marten. The Britannia Petite is the same size as the better-known Netherland Dwarf, but he has a slender, long, and lean body with a racy, alert appearance. Individuals of this breed are known for having a somewhat wild temperament. They can be skittish and shy and less hesitant to scratch or nip. Because of these traits, they do not make the best pet rabbits.

Body Type Profile: Full arch.

Breed History: The Britannia Petite is the same breed of rabbit known as the Polish in Great Britain. In the United States, the Polish breed is compact. However, in Great Britain, breeders developed the Polish to look more like a small hare with a full arch and a tucked-up belly. When the British Polish rabbits were imported into the United States in the early 1970s, the breeders had to choose a different name because the ARBA already had a recognized Polish breed—hence the name Britannia Petite. The breed was recognized in 1978.

Dutch

Weight: 3.5 to 5.5 pounds (1.6 to 2.5 kg).

Description: The Dutch has six recognized color varieties: black, blue, chocolate, gray, steel, and tortoise. The markings include a white stripe down the face, a white band around the front of the body including the front legs, white on the ends of the hind feet, and one of the recognized colors over the rest of the body. This breed has a compact, well-rounded body. Its rounded head is short and stocky, with small furry ears and bold bright eyes. A Dutch's flyback fur is short and glossy. Having a panda bear appearance in coloring, he is the heaviest and most recognizable of the small-breed rabbits. Dutch rabbits are popular pets and show rabbits. Their easygoing temperaments make them great companions and a good choice for first-time owners.

Body Type Profile: Compact.

Breed History: The ancestors of the Dutch were a type of rabbit called Brabancons, which came from the Brabant district of Belgium. In the early 1800s, thousands of live rabbits were sent each week to the London meat market from the Port of Ostend, Belgium. Rabbit

Dutch

fanciers came to the market and bought rabbits they wanted to use in their own rabbit breeding. The Brabancons often had Dutch markings, and the English breeders selected those with even markings to develop further.

Although the breed is known as the Dutch, it was actually developed in England. The first written record of the breed was in 1865. It is possible that the breed's name originated during the brief period from 1815 to 1830, when Belgium was part of the Netherlands—hence the name Dutch. Dutch rabbits were exported to the United States from England at the beginning of the 20th century. They were recognized by the ARBA in 1910.

Dwarf Hotot

Weight: 3 pounds maximum (1.4 kg maximum).

Description: The Dwarf Hotot's body is pure white except for a narrow black circle around each eye that is called an eye band. This is a stocky little rabbit with no visible neck. The head is round with short furry ears. The dark brown eyes are round and bright. The rollback fur is soft, dense, and fine. These small rabbits are docile, but some individuals have a spunkier temperament.

Body Type Profile: Compact.

Breed History: Almost simultaneously during the late 1970s, Dwarf Hotots (pronounced oh-toe) were developed independently in East Germany and in West Germany. Breeders in West Germany used repeated crossings of Netherland Dwarf rabbits, while breeders in East Germany developed a Dwarf Hotot using both the regular-sized Hotot and the Netherland Dwarf. Due to their small size, the West German Dwarf Hotots were not as vigorous as the type found in East Germany. The breeders from the two countries exchanged rabbits with each other, and breeding the two types of rabbits together improved the vigor and size of the Dwarf Hotot. Rabbits from both East Germany and West Germany were imported into the United States in 1980, and Dwarf Hotots were officially recognized by the ARBA in 1984.

Florida White

Weight: 4 to 6 pounds (1.8 to 2.7 kg).

Description: The Florida White is pure white with pink eyes. He has flyback fur. This breed has a short body with well-developed shoulders and hindquarters. The ribs are slightly narrower than the hindquarters. A medium-sized dewlap is permissible in does. Florida Whites are inquisitive rabbits, but some individuals can be timid.

Body Type Profile: Compact.

Breed History: This breed was originally created in Florida in the 1960s as a small meat rabbit and white laboratory rabbit. It is generally thought that Polish, albino Dutch, and white New Zealand rabbits were combined to create the Florida White.

This breed was never popular for its intended uses; most meat rabbit breeders prefer larger rabbits, and scientists do not like to use the Florida White because his genetic background is not as well known as rabbits bred specifically for laboratory tests. However, the Florida White is a popular show rabbit. Because he only comes in one color, more of the baby rabbits in a litter are potential show candidates. The breed was officially recognized by the ARBA in 1967.

Havana

Weight: 4.5 to 6.5 pounds (2 to 3 kg).

Description: The Havana comes in three glossy colors: black, brown, and chocolate. The black variety has brown eyes, the blue variety has blue-gray eyes, and the chocolate variety has brown eyes that show a ruby-red pupil in low light. The fur is approximately 1 inch (2.5 cm) long. His neck is short and hardly visible, and his ears are short in proportion to the size of his head and body. The temperament of the Havana is variable; some individuals are relaxed, while others are more spirited, but the breed is known for its good pet qualities.

Body Type Profile: Compact.

Breed History: This breed got its start in the Netherlands in 1898. Brown rabbits appeared

Havana

in a litter from a black and white doe who was housed with common meat rabbits kept in a stable. Expert breeders then worked to stabilize the brown color. Once called the Beaver, the breed was exhibited under the name Havana in Paris in 1903. The name came from the brown variety's resemblance to the color of a Cuban cigar.

The breed was exported to numerous European countries, including France, Switzerland, Germany, and England, where it was a popular show rabbit. The early Havanas were crossed with black Tan rabbits to eliminate unwanted white feet and were also crossed with Himalayans to improve their size, shape, and fur. Havanas were imported to the United States in 1916. The blue variety was recognized in 1965, and the black variety was recognized in 1980.

Himalayan
Weight: 2.5 to 4.5 pounds (1.2 to 2 kg).
Description: The Himalayan's body color is pure white except for markings on the nose,

ears, tail, feet, and legs. The markings may be black, blue, chocolate, or lilac. The contrast between the colored markings and white fur is quite striking. The Himalayan's eyes are pink, and his long body is shaped like a cylinder or tube. He is generally docile, curious, and enjoys attention. These rabbits can make good house pets.

Body Type Profile: Cylindrical. The Himalayan is the only breed classified as cylindrical. When shown, the breed is posed stretched out.

Breed History: The Himalayan has been known for more than 150 years. The breed's country of origin, including the source of its name, is obscure. Contrary to the name, though, it is unlikely that the Himalayan came from the Himalayan mountain range, regardless of early fanciful accounts of wild Himalayan rabbits living there. Perhaps the early developers of the breed were captivated by the exotic sounding locale. The Himalayan has been known by a variety of names, including Chinese, African, Russian, and Polish.

Some of the first Himalayans were recorded in the mid-1800s. English breeders of Silver rabbits found Himalayans in their litters. In one case, the breeder noted that he obtained Himalayans from tame silver-gray rabbits crossed with wild rabbits of the same color who were kept in warrens (a structure where rabbits are kept or bred). Another account published in 1880 describes the importation of Himalayans from China. The author stated that the rabbit was found on both sides of the mountain range and was superior to the English variety. Because of the value of his skin, the Himalayan was imported and bred in many countries, including Russia, Egypt, Germany, and France. Himalayans were imported into the United States from England at the turn of the 20th century and were officially recognized in 1910.

Holland Lop

Weight: Less than 4 pounds (1.8 kg).

Description: Holland Lops are recognized in 26 colors that are broken down into eight groups: agouti, broken, pointed white, self, shaded, tan pattern, ticked, and wide band. Although he doesn't weigh much, the Holland should look massive for his size. He has a short, muscular body that is balanced in length, width, and depth. His head appears close to the shoulders without any neck showing. His legs are short and heavily boned. His ears hang down close to the cheeks, and the openings are turned toward the head.

Not all Hollands fall within the breed standard for size. Because some may be too large to show, breeders sell the larger babies as pets. This sometimes results in a pet-quality Holland Lop who is slightly larger than the breed's recognized size. These very popular rabbits are curious, affectionate, and make wonderful house pets.

Body Type Profile: Compact.

Breed History: The Holland Lop originated in the Holland region of the Netherlands. An expert rabbit breeder believed that the French Lop would be more popular if he wasn't

Holland Lop

so large. In 1950, his first crossing of a French Lop buck to a white Netherland Dwarf doe was unsuccessful. He reversed the cross the following year. Using a French Lop doe and Netherland Dwarf buck, he was able to get a litter of kits (baby rabbits) on the third try. (The size differences between the two breeds made the mating difficult.) All the kits had normal ears. In 1952, he bred a doe from this litter to an English Lop buck, which produced five young, including one with half-lopped ears. Then through a series of additional breedings between rabbits from the two different litters, he was able to increase the percentage of rabbits with lop ears. By 1964, he had developed a lop-eared rabbit weighing less than 4.5 pounds, presented as the Holland Lop. The breed was distributed throughout Europe but was not imported into the United States until 1974. It was recognized in 1979.

Jersey Wooly

Weight: Less than 3.5 pounds (1.6 kg).

Description: The Jersey Wooly is recognized in more than 20 colors that are broken down into six groups: agouti, any other variety (white with black or blue points), broken, self, shaded, and tan pattern. Because the Jersey Wooly's coat has more thick guard hairs than underwool, it is considered easier to care for than other longhaired breeds. However, the coat of rabbits younger than six months will require more frequent grooming than an adult's coat. This is because a younger rabbit's fur is fluffier and more prone to mat until more guard hairs develop with an adult coat. The Jersey Wooly is a very gentle, sweet rabbit who makes an excellent pet.

Body Type Profile: Compact.

Breed History: The Jersey Wooly got its start in the 1970s. A breeder from New Jersey wanted to create a small rabbit with easy-care wool fur specifically for the pet trade. She used the offspring of crosses between Angoras and Netherland Dwarfs to develop these cuddly, woolly rabbits. Over many years, the rabbits became even smaller, and additional crosses with Netherland Dwarfs were made. In 1984, the Jersey Wooly was introduced at the ARBA National Convention and Show. It was recognized as a breed in 1988 and has become popular both in the United States and with rabbit keepers throughout the world.

Jersey Wooly

Mini Lop
Weight: 4.5 to 6.5 pounds (2 to 3 kg).
Description: Mini Lops are recognized in more than two dozen colors that are broken down into seven groups: agouti, broken, pointed white, self, shaded, ticked, and wide band. This is the smallest breed of lop rabbits, who are known for their distinctive floppy ears. These extremely laid-back rabbits have excellent temperaments and make wonderful house pets and companions.
Body Type Profile: Compact.
Breed History: The Mini Lop was developed in Germany in the 1950s. Several breeds were used in its creation, including the French Lop, English Lop, New Zealand, Polish, Chinchilla, and Dwarf Lop. In 1973, it was first officially recognized in Germany. The breed was known as the Klein Widder, which translates as "little hanging ear." The Mini Lop was imported into the United States in 1972 and officially recognized by the ARBA in 1981.

Mini Lop

Mini Rex

Weight: 3 to 4.5 pounds (1.4 to 2 kg).
Description: The Mini Rex is available
in black, blue, blue-eyed white, castor,
chinchilla, chocolate, Himalayan, lilac,
lynx, opal, red, seal, tortoise, white, and
broken. The fur is extremely dense,
straight, and upright, with an ideal length
of 0.6 inches (1.5 cm). When touched,
the plush fur offers a distinct springy
resistance. It is velvety soft and lustrous,
and it feels smooth and even. Because of
the breed's short fur, the nails can seem
sharper and longer than those of a breed
with a regular coat. Does may have a small
dewlap. The Mini Rex is curious and
energetic but also friendly.
Body Type Profile: Compact.
Breed History: The Mini Rex was
developed in the United States during the
early 1980s. Because of the Netherland
Dwarf in the Mini Rex's background,
new color varieties consistently appeared
in litters. Crosses between the Mini Rex
and regular-sized Rex helped improve
body type and fur. These pairings led to the emergence of more than a dozen new colors,
including chinchilla, Himalayan, and chocolate. The Mini Rex, recognized in 1988, is
currently approved in 15 varieties.

Mini Rex

Mini Satin

Weight: 3.25 to 4.75 pounds (1.5 to 2.2 kg).
Description: The Mini Satin is white with a light ivory cast and pink eyes. As the name
implies, the coat is satiny smooth and soft and has a vivid sheen.
Body Type Profile: Compact.
Breed History: The development of the Mini Satin began in the United States in the late
1970s. The first known effort ended when the breeder discontinued the hobby. During
the ensuing decades, several other breeders worked on creating the Mini Satin. Most were
known to use crosses between regular Satin rabbits and Netherland Dwarfs. The road to

recognition was bumpy because many individuals worked on developing the breed only to drop out and be replaced by other breeders. The Mini Satin was recognized in one variety in 2006. It is likely that additional varieties will be added to the standard as fanciers develop the breed in other colors.

Netherland Dwarf

Weight: Less than 2.5 pounds (1.2 kg).

Description: Netherland Dwarfs are recognized in 37 colors that are broken down into five groups: self, shaded, agouti, tan pattern, and any other variety. The Netherland Dwarf is one of the smallest rabbit breeds in the world and has a distinctive appearance—a very compact body with short ears perched on top of a round head. From the beginning of its recognition as a unique breed, it was in demand and remains one of the most popular rabbit breeds. Netherland Dwarfs are gentle but energetic rabbits. Some individuals are timid and may require patience to win their trust.

Body Type Profile: Compact.

Breed History: This breed officially originated in the Netherlands. However, its emergence

Netherland Dwarf

occurred in Germany when Polish rabbits imported from England in the late 1800s were developed into a distinct white breed called Hermelin, which means "ermine" in German. Ermine is a type of weasel whose pure white coat was prized by the fur trade and symbolized royalty in Europe. Fashionable although quite expensive, ermine pelts were in great demand at the time. When German breeders realized that the Hermelin rabbit's small pelt could be an imitation of ermine fur, the breed's availability spread. By the early 1900s, the Hermelin was found in the Netherlands and was recognized as a breed in 1907.

Following this, several expert breeders who wanted to create colored dwarf rabbits crossed the white Hermelin with other rabbits of various sizes. Their years of effort were a success, and a new breed called the Netherland Dwarf was given a breed standard in Holland on May 1, 1940. However, World War II started ten days later. According to some accounts, only 17 Netherland Dwarfs remained in existence by the end of the war. After the war ended, a group of British fanciers brought Rex rabbits to the Netherlands to help the Dutch restock their rabbit herds. While at a rabbit show, they admired and desired these tiny dwarf rabbits. Two years later, the Dutch sent them nine dwarfs in thanks for helping them with the Rex. As a result, the Netherland Dwarf breed was finally recognized in England in 1950. The first exports to the United States occurred in 1965, and the breed was recognized by the ARBA in 1969.

Polish

Weight: 3.5 pounds (1.6 kg).

Description: The Polish is found in six varieties: black, blue, broken, chocolate, blue-eyed white, and ruby-eyed white. His glossy flyback fur is short, fine, and dense. The Polish has small ears that touch all the way to the tips and large, bold eyes. The breed has a reputation for being high strung, but this attitude is understandable since it was originally developed for meat. As time progressed, however, the Polish became more popular as a pet. Not ideal for small children, this rabbit's nervous nature makes him more suitable for a mature, adult home.

Body Type Profile: Compact.

Breed History: The Polish rabbit is one of several examples of a breed given a name that has no relation to its country of origin. The breed actually originated in England but was known as the Polish by the 1860s. The Polish breed is thought to have derived from common hutch rabbits. The ruby-eyed white variety was imported to the United States from England in 1912 and was officially recognized the same year. The blue-eyed white variety was created through crosses with white Beverens, and then the siblings of those crosses were mated. This variety was admitted to the standards in 1938. The black and chocolate varieties were created by mating a Havana doe with a ruby-eyed white Polish and again with a small black Rex. Pairing the black and chocolate offspring together fixed the color varieties.

Polish

Silver

Weight: 4 to 7 pounds (1.8 to 3.2 kg).

Description: The Silver comes in three colors: black, brown, and fawn. The silvering (white or white-tipped hairs) is very bright and distinctive due to an abundance of white guard hairs that are evenly distributed throughout the rabbit's coat, including the head, ears, feet, legs, and tail. The silver contrast is most noticeable on black rabbits. Silver kits are solid in color and do not begin to show silvering until they are approximately three weeks old. Silvers have a short, snappy flyback coat. White spots and dewlaps will cause a Silver show rabbit to be disqualified from competition. These rabbits are athletic and strong and can be excitable. They need a large cage with plenty of room to move about. Although generally not aggressive, Silvers may not be the best breed for a new rabbit owner or small child and are more suited to the experienced owner.

Body Type Profile: Compact.

Breed History: The Silver is one of the oldest domestic rabbit breeds, and records of its existence are more than 350 years old. Many experts have guessed as to the breed's origins.

It is possible that rabbits with silver hairs first appeared as black mutations in the European wild rabbit. Some accounts state that the Silver rabbit was found in large numbers in Thailand. Sailors brought them to Portugal, and from there, they were exported to other European countries, including England. According to one expert, it is possible that Sir Walter Raleigh, who died in 1618, introduced silver-gray rabbits to a warren in northern England. These rabbits were then distributed to other warrens throughout England. Gervaise Markham, a writer on English country life in the early 17th century, mentioned silver-gray rabbits in his famous book titled *The English Hus-Wife*, a best seller defining the virtues of the perfect wife, which included cooking.

The first fawn-colored Silvers appeared in the 1870s. The Silver brown was developed in the 1880s from a cross between a Belgian Hare buck and Silver fawn doe.

Silver rabbits were one of the earliest breeds found in the United States; they were already present during the Belgian Hare fad during the late 1890s. The Silver is considered a "threatened" breed by the ALBC because there are fewer than 100 annual registrations in the United States and an estimated global population of fewer than 1,000. The breed was recognized by the ARBA in 1910.

Tan

Weight: 4 to 6 pounds (1.8 to 2.7 kg).

Description: The Tan has four color varieties: black, blue, chocolate, and lilac. The rabbit's tan underside, which includes the chin, chest, belly, and tail, is a deep shade of mahogany with a brilliant reddish tint. Other markings are the triangle (a small area behind the ears), collar, nostrils, eye circles, pea spots (two spots at the inside base of the ears), and lacing on the inside edge of the ears. The coat is very glossy, which enhances the contrast between the tan markings and the bright, lustrous body color. The Tan has a short coat and snappy flyback fur. This breed has long front legs and a deep full arch. When moving, the Tan is fluid and graceful. Most Tan rabbits can be friendly, although the breed was originally described as flighty, perhaps due to its wild rabbit blood. Despite their spunky personality, they are also social and lively and can be lovable pets.

Body Type Profile: Full arch.

Breed History: The Tan rabbit got his start in the county of Derbyshire, Great Britain. The first known examples of the breed appeared in a warren in 1887 after a reverend released some Dutch rabbits and common hutch rabbits into his warren, which contained the wild European rabbit. These black rabbits with pale yellow bellies were very attractive and were shown for the first time in 1888. The original Tans were much larger than the modern Tans. Later, the blue Tan was developed at the turn of the 20th century and the chocolate Tan was created around 1920. The chocolate was suspected to have come about by crossing a black Tan and a chocolate Havana, although the variety's creator insisted that they were solely

Tan

from mutations in his black Tans. By pairing the chocolate and blue varieties together, the lilac was created. The Tan arrived in the United States in the early 1900s. The breed was recognized by the ARBA in 1910.

Thrianta

Weight: 4 to 6 pounds (1.8 to 2.7 kg).

Description: The Thrianta (pronounced tree-aan-ta) is a striking orange red. He has a small, compact body with a thick, dense coat that has a silky texture. The belly and underside of the tail are slightly lighter than the coat on the rest of the body but should be as dark and as close to the main color as possible. Thriantas are inquisitive and lively.

Body Type Profile: Compact.

Breed History: The Thrianta was developed in the Netherlands. The breed is believed to have been created using the Tan, Havana, and an orange self-colored English Spot. The breed was recognized in the Netherlands on May 1, 1940. During World War II, it didn't fare well during the German occupation. Many rabbits were eaten to prevent starvation, and the Thrianta was almost extinct by the war's end. Nonetheless, some managed to survive, although the breed faded from official Dutch recognition by 1966. An East German breeder is believed to have imported most of the remaining Thriantas to improve the color of his Sachsengold rabbits, a breed that is smaller and not as brightly colored as the Thrianta. In the late 1960s, a Dutch breeder imported some of the Sachsengold rabbits. Because East German residents lived under strict laws regulating movement, a clever smuggling plan was used to move the rabbits back into the Netherlands. Dutch breeders crossed the two breeds, but the results were mixed. The Dutch breed was first recognized under the name Sachsengold in 1971, but in 1979, the name was changed back to Thrianta. Most of Europe recognizes the Sachsengold and not the Thrianta. Beginning in 1996 and through 2003, various rabbit fanciers imported the Thrianta from Holland and England into the United States. Early efforts in 2001 and 2002 to get the Thrianta approved by the ARBA were unsuccessful, but after much work, the breed was finally recognized in 2006.

Medium Breeds

American Sable

Weight: 7 to 10 pounds (3.2 to 4.5 kg).

Description: The American Sable's color is rich sepia brown on the ears, face, back, legs, and upper side of the tail. The rest of the rabbit is a paler shade of brown. The sable's fur is sensitive to light, and the fur of rabbits exposed to direct sunlight turns a rusty color that lasts until their next molt. Some breeders think that American Sables bred in warmer climates have lighter-colored fur compared to those from cooler climates. This breed is relaxed, friendly, and enjoys attention.

Body Type Profile: Commercial.

Breed History: Sable rabbits were first recorded in England in the offspring of Chinchilla rabbits imported from France. In 1924, five years later, the first American Sable originated from offspring of purebred Chinchilla rabbits in California. Two color varieties, the Siamese Sable and the Silver Sable Marten, were recognized when the American Sable was recognized as a breed by the ARBA in 1931. Over time, the breed declined in popularity. The Siamese Sable was deleted from the ARBA Book of Standards in 1976, and only one Sable was shown at the 1981 ARBA convention. The breeder who exhibited this rabbit undertook an effort to save the breed. Using a few other specimens he located, as well as importing some from England, he and other interested breeders crossed the American Sable with sable Silver Martens, sable Rex, Havanas, Californians, and Standard Chinchillas. Other breeds were added into the mix, including Palominos, Harlequins, and white New Zealands. A new breed club was formed the following year. With the enthusiasm of the recruited breeders, the American Sable was saved from extinction.

Belgian Hare

Weight: 6 to 9.5 pounds (2.7 to 4.3 kg).

Description: The Belgian Hare is a brilliant, rich, deep red of a tan or chestnut shade over a slate blue undercolor. His belly, as well as the area beneath his jaw, is a contrasting color of cream to red. The ears are laced with black. The tail is long and straight. The top of the tail is the same color as the body, but the bottom of the tail is white. The Belgian Hare has light-colored circles around brown eyes and thin, erect ears. The fur lies close to his body and has a stiff texture. Although texture refers to the "feel" of the fur, it also refers to the ability of the fur to offer enough resistance to return to its normal position when stroked toward the head. Protruding patches of hair or hair that stands upright does not have the right texture. The Belgian Hare has a slender, arched body, with long hind legs. He is considered fine boned and should be housed on a solid cage floor. The inquisitive Belgian Hare is active, energetic, and can move quickly. Considered high strung by some, he is not a good choice for a first-time rabbit owner.

Body Type Profile: Full arch.

Breed History: The Belgian Hare originated in Great Britain and Belgium from meat breeds in the late 1800s. The breed originally came from Belgium, and further development occurred in Great Britain from specimens imported in early 1873. Because the Belgian Hare

Belgian Hare

looked so much like a real hare (except for the color), many people believed that the breed really was a cross between a rabbit and the European hare. However, he is a true rabbit and was merely bred to resemble the wild hare.

Belgian Hares were first imported into the United States in 1888. They became incredibly popular, and clubs devoted to the breed were established in nearly every major city. From 1898 to 1901, thousands of Belgian Hares arrived in the United States. In one year alone, a single British company shipped more than 6,000 Belgian Hares. Speculators became involved, and the Belgian Hare was the source of "get rich quick schemes." Belgian Hares were sold for hundreds to thousands of dollars. A record price of $5,000 was paid for one male in 1900. Famous millionaires such as the Rockefellers, Duponts, and Guggenheims even became involved because of the rabbit's money-making potential. The mania came to an end once the market became flooded. Prices for a good show rabbit dropped to less than $25.

By the 1940s, Belgian Hares were no longer commonly exhibited at rabbit shows. Since then, the breed has continued to decline in both the United States and in other countries. However, dedicated fanciers have kept the breed from becoming extinct. The Belgian Hare is now one of the rarest rabbit breeds in the United States. It is considered "threatened" by the ALBC because there are fewer than 100 annual registrations in the United States and an estimated global population of fewer than 1,000.

English Angora

Weight: 5 to 7 pounds (2.3 to 3.2 kg).

Description: The English Angora comes in more than two dozen colors that are broken into six groups: agouti, pointed white, self, shaded, ticked, and wide band. When a show English Angora is properly groomed and posed, he resembles a round ball of fluff. The length of the wool can vary from 3.5 to 5 inches (8.9 to 12.7 cm). The wool covers the feet all the way to the end of the toes. The English Angora has "furnishings," which are long wool on the ears (fringes and tassels), bangs (top of the head and sides of the ears), and sides of the head. This breed has more undercoat than guard hairs. English Angoras are considered personable rabbits, probably because they have had to adapt over the centuries to intense grooming done primarily by hand. Although the English Angora is gentle, he requires the highest maintenance of all the Angora breeds. His fine wool is easily matted and needs almost daily grooming. This breed is gentle and calm.

Body Type Profile: Compact.

Breed History: English Angoras were developed in England over a period of 150 years. Their ancestors were the French Angoras. English Angoras have very soft, silky wool. Imported into the United States in the early to mid-1800s, this was one of the first breeds recognized by the ARBA in 1910.

English Spot

English Spot
Weight: 5 to 8 pounds (2.3 to 3.6 kg).

Description: The English Spot is white with a complicated pattern of either black, blue, chocolate, gold, gray, lilac, or tortoise markings. The head markings include a butterfly on the nose, circles around the eyes, cheek spots, and colored ears. The spine marking begins behind the base of the ear and runs along the back to the tip of the tail. The edges of the spine marking are ragged, an effect called herringbone. Colored spots are found along the rabbit's sides beginning at the nape of the neck and continuing toward his hindquarters. The spots increase in size from his neck to the hip. The flyback fur is short, dense, and fine in texture. The short guard hairs give the coat a high luster. The English Spot can be an energetic breed.

Body Type Profile: Full arch.

Breed History: Spotted rabbits were recorded in England more than 200 years ago. Fanciers began to develop them into the breed that would be called the English Spot around the mid-1800s. Breeders were captivated with the rabbits' interesting markings, and the standard for what was acceptable evolved over time. In 1889, Germany imported the breed, and from there it was exported to other continental European countries. The English Spot was brought to the United States in the early 1900s and was recognized as a breed shortly thereafter.

French Angora

Weight: 7.5 to 10.5 pounds (3.4 to 4.8 kg).

Description: The French Angora is recognized in more than two dozen colors that are broken down into seven groups: agouti, pointed white, self, shaded, ticked, wide band, and broken. The breed's dense wool is coarse in texture and should be evenly distributed over the entire body, including the back and belly. Regular fur is found on the rabbit's hind feet and on the front feet to at least the ankle bone. The ears may or may not have a tuft of fur on their tips. The ideal wool length is 3.5 to 4.5 inches (8.9 to 11.4 cm). Because the wool contains more guard hairs than undercoat, the French Angora needs comparatively less grooming than other Angora breeds. Like other breeds of Angora, the French Angora is generally calm and friendly.

Body Type Profile: Commercial.

Breed History: The French Angora was first recorded in 1723, when British sailors introduced it to France. It is believed that the French Angora most closely resembles the original Angora rabbit. This breed is considered the ancestor of all the other Angora breeds (eight breeds worldwide, of which four are recognized by the ARBA). In 1920, French breeders exported the French Angora to Japan, and in 1932, to China. French Angoras were first imported into the United States in 1932 and were officially recognized in 1939. Hobbyists keep this breed to produce their own wool, but it is also widely kept in Europe as a commercial wool rabbit.

Harlequin

Weight: 6.5 to 9.5 pounds (3 to 4.3 kg).

Description: Harlequin rabbits come in two varieties: Japanese and magpie. Within the two varieties, the color may be black, blue, chocolate, or lilac. Describing the markings is best done by using one of the varieties as an example, in this case the black and orange. One side of the rabbit's head is black, while the other side is orange. The ear on the black side of the face is orange, while the ear on the orange side is black. The four legs alternate colors: one leg is black, the other orange. Beginning at the chest, five to seven bands or bars of color alternate along both of the rabbit's sides. The chest is evenly divided into black and orange. The black half and leg are underneath the orange half of the face, and the orange half and leg are underneath the black half of the face.

A magpie Harlequin is similar except the orange color is replaced with white. Harlequins are generally docile and curious, and they like attention.

Body Type Profile: Commercial.

Breed History: The Harlequin was originally known as the Japanese rabbit. Although some accounts state that the breed did not originate in Japan, evidence exists that Harlequin-like rabbits (parti- and tricolored) were bred and shown in Japan in the early 1870s. Well-marked rabbits soon became worth exorbitant sums, spurring crime related to the rabbit trade. To crack down on this, the Tokyo government taxed rabbit keepers, and in so doing, ultimately caused the demise of the fancy rabbit hobby due to the excessive tax. Japan had diplomatic and trade relations with Western countries during this period, and it is possible that the Harlequin-like rabbits were imported into France.

Harlequin

The Harlequin was first recorded in France around 1894, and some authorities believe that France is the breed's country of origin. Several accounts state that the Harlequin arose from crossing a Dutch Tricolor and a common rabbit of France. Descendents of the Brabancon breed, who were from the Brabant district of Belgium, as well as crosses of a black rabbit with a russet red rabbit, were also cited as possible origins of the breed in France.

The Harlequin was first imported into the United States in 1917. How the breed got its first name, Japanese, which fanciers in the United States and Great Britain used, is not known, unless the breed did truly originate in Japan. Both countries changed the name from Japanese to Harlequin during World War II. The British Rabbit Council (BRC) referred to the breed as the Harlequin because it looked like a court jester. Thereafter, the Japanese name was used to refer to the orange color group, and the magpie was used to refer to the white color group. (The rest of the world still uses the name Japanese for the breed.) The blue, chocolate, lilac, and magpie were produced in England in the mid-1940s. The magpie was developed by crossing the Harlequin with the Chinchilla.

Lilac

Weight: 5.5 to 8 pounds (2.5 to 3.6 kg).

Description: The Lilac's color is a uniform dove gray with a pinkish tint on the surface. The eyes are blue-gray and glow ruby red in subdued light. The dense rollback fur is soft and about 1 inch (2.5 cm) in length. The Lilac is considered reasonably docile and sweet once trust has been established.

Body Type Profile: Compact.

Breed History: The Lilac rabbit was developed at about the same time in two different countries: England and the Netherlands. Three different strains were created in England between 1913 and 1922. The rabbit breeds used in the creation of two of the strains are known. One was developed using Blue Imperials (a breed that is no longer in existence) and Havanas, while the second strain crossed Blue Beverens and Havanas. All three British strains eventually merged, and the dove-gray rabbits became known as Lilacs. Meanwhile, in 1917, a fancier in Gouda, Netherlands, created a lilac rabbit using the same breeds as those in the second British strain. The results of this breed combination were larger than those found in England and were called the Gouda.

The Lilac rabbit from England and the Gouda from Holland were imported to the United States around 1922. The Gouda never developed a following and soon vanished in America. (It is an extinct breed worldwide.) Lilacs in America have never been a popular breed. They are considered a "watch" breed by the ALBC because there are fewer than 200 annual registrations in the United States and an estimated global population of fewer than 2,000.

Rex

Weight: 7.5 to 10.5 pounds (3.6 to 4.8 kg).

Description: The Rex is available in black, black otter, blue, Californian, castor, chinchilla, chocolate, lilac, lynx, opal, red, sable seal, white, and broken. The fur is extremely dense, straight, and upright, with an ideal length of 0.6 inches (1.5 cm). The guard hairs are almost the same length as the undercoat. The lustrous fur feels smooth to the touch but is not silky in texture. When pressed down, the unique plush fur offers a distinct springy resistance. His "velveteen" coat quickly made this rabbit a favorite and contributed to his growing popularity among breeders and pet owners. The Rex is a graceful, personable rabbit. Some individuals are more energetic but still friendly and playful. They are said to be the most intelligent of all the rabbit breeds.

Body Type Profile: Commercial.

Breed History: The Rex breed got its start in France in 1919, when two rabbits with a peculiar coat were given by a farmer to an abbot in his village. The abbot housed the rabbits outdoors and ultimately in a barn, where they bred together and were eventually crossed with regular rabbits. However, because the abbot was unfamiliar with genetics, these crosses did not produce many rabbits with the rex coat. By 1924, there were about 150 Rexes, but they were in poor condition with features such as long crooked feet and patchy coats. Finally, the president of the French Rabbit Federation purchased a trio of the rabbits

Rex

for approximately $1,000. In consort with another expert, several Rex of various colors, including chinchilla, white, and blue, were produced. One of the original trio died, but the expert proceeded to breed them and obtain more Rexes.

When exhibited at the International Show in Paris in 1924, the Rex won numerous awards. The breed was imported into the United States in 1924. The prices at the time were quite impressive, with pairs going from $350 to $1,500. By 1927, the breed was found in numerous other countries, including Belgium, Germany, and England. However, the early Rex was not always consistent in appearance, and some looked very shabby. Over time and through careful selection, the Rex has become a refined and vigorous breed. It has been bred to numerous other breeds to produce rex-coated rabbits.

Rhinelander

Weight: 6.5 to 10 pounds (3 to 4.5 kg).

Description: The Rhinelander is white with a complicated pattern of black and orange markings. Six to eight spots are found on each side and hindquarter. The spots can be black, orange, or both colors. Each spot must be completely surrounded by white. The spine marking is narrow at the base of the neck, widens at the shoulder, and then narrows again at the base of the tail. The top of the tail is colored. The Rhinelander's head markings include circles around the eyes, colored ears, cheek spots, and the butterfly marking on the nose. Although not recognized in the United States, this rabbit can be found in a blue and fawn color combination in Germany and Sweden. His flyback fur is short, dense, and silky. Junior rabbits can look brindled because their fur is not yet short and silky. After junior rabbits molt into the adult fur, their colors are typically clean and sharp.

The topline is smooth with rounded hindquarters. Because the shoulders, midsection, and hips are the same width, the Rhinelander has a sleek appearance. He has moderately long legs, which give him an elegant look and allow him to move easily and gracefully. Until the breed is mature, a full arch is sometimes difficult to see in some junior rabbits.

The Rhinelander is alert and springy but can also be skittish. With lots of sensitive care, he can develop into a loving, responsive pet. Some fanciers report that it is a one-person breed.

Body Type Profile: Full arch.

Breed History: The Rhinelander was developed by a postmaster in North Rhine-Westphalia, Germany, around 1900. The breed got its start from a cross between a Harlequin buck and a common gray-checkered doe and from a separate pairing between a Harlequin buck and Checkered Giant doe. Using a buck from the first cross, who resembled a Rhinelander, and a doe from the second pairing, the breeder began to develop his vision. He bred the best examples from each litter and crossed the best does back to Harlequin bucks. In so doing, he succeeded in producing the Rhinelander, and in 1905 the breed was given a standard in Germany. The Rhinelander was first brought to the United States in 1923 and was recognized as a breed in 1924. By 1932, he was no longer found in the United States. Some experts have speculated that the breed died out due to the difficulties in breeding a rabbit who met the breed standard or because people preferred the more popular Checkered Giant. Rhinelanders were again imported into the United States in 1972, and in 1975, the breed was once more accepted into the ARBA Book of Standards. The Rhinelander is considered a "watch" breed by the ALBC because there are fewer than 200 annual registrations in the United States and an estimated global population of fewer than 2,000.

Satin Angora

Weight: 6.5 to 9.5 pounds (3 to 4.3 kg).

Description: Satin Angoras are recognized in more than two dozen colors that are broken down into six groups: agouti, pointed white,

Satin Angora

self, shaded, ticked, and wide band. This breed's wool is finer than that found on other Angora breeds. The soft, silky wool is ideally 3 inches (7.6 cm) in length. The Satin Angora has no tassels, ear fringes, bangs, or head side trimmings—this makes him easier to groom than the English Angora. However, Satin Angora wool is finer than the wool of other Angora breeds. Because of its finer texture, the wool appears less dense but requires frequent grooming. Gentle in nature, Satin Angoras make good pets but are not recommended for those who do not want to groom their animals.

Body Type Profile: Commercial.

Breed History: The Satin Angora was developed in Canada in the 1980s. A rabbit with a satin woolly coat appeared in a litter of copper Satins. This likely happened because Angora rabbits are sometimes bred with shorthaired rabbits to improve the quality of the coat. The breeder took the satiny woolly rabbit and bred him to a fawn French Angora. Satin Angoras showed up in the second generation. The breed was approved in 1987. The same varieties that are approved in the French and English Angora breeds were also recognized for the Satin Angora. The breed was imported into Europe in 1998.

Silver Marten

Weight: 6 to 9.5 pounds (2.7 to 4.3 kg).
Description: The Silver Marten has four color varieties: black, blue, chocolate, and sable. The black variety has brown eyes, the blue variety has blue-gray eyes, and the chocolate and sable varieties have brown eyes with a ruby cast. The silvering consists of evenly distributed silver-tipped guard hairs that run from the silver-white belly up to the rabbit's sides and rump. The back does not have any silver tipping. Other markings include a silver triangle at the base of the neck that connects to a narrow silver white collar running around the neck and under the jaw; silver circles around the eyes; and white nostrils. These playful and lively rabbits make great pets, although they may be a bit more timid than some of the large-breed rabbits.
Body Type Profile: Commercial.
Breed History: The Silver Marten breed is the result of a color mutation in the Standard Chinchilla, which originally came from France. To improve the Chinchilla's coat and color, earlier breeders had bred black Tans with their Chinchillas. This resulted in the Tan pattern genes being carried by the rabbits' offspring, and thus the color mutation. The black and silver mutations all occurred about the same time in the early 1920s in Europe and the United States. When the rabbits with the color mutation were bred together, their offspring were also black and silver. The black and blue varieties were recognized by the ARBA around 1930. Within five years, the sable and chocolate Silver Martens were recognized. The Silver Marten is not recognized in other countries. However, in Australia, New Zealand, and Great Britain, the Silver Fox is the same breed as the Silver Marten.

Standard Chinchilla

Weight: 5 to 7.5 pounds (2.3 to 3.4 kg).
Description: The Standard Chinchilla has dense, fine fur that is bright, smooth, and glossy. The rollback fur's ideal length is 1.25 inches (3.2 cm). Colored similar to a wild chinchilla, the undercolor is a dark slate blue, pearl, and black. Jet black guard hairs of uneven length occur above the

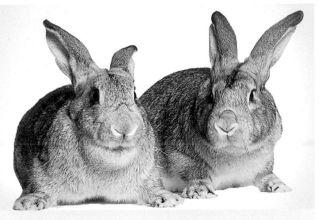

Standard Chinchilla

undercoat. Light pearl-colored circles are found around the eyes, which can be any color but pink (although brown is preferred). The underside of the tail is white, and the top is black with interspersed white hairs.

Body Type Profile: Compact.

Breed History: A French engineer developed the Standard Chinchilla around 1913. Various accounts are given as to the breeds he used, including a blue doe, a wild buck, and a Himalayan doe. A black Tan was later bred with the offspring to improve the quality of the fur. The Standard Chinchilla was exported to Great Britain in 1917, and a British sailor brought the breed to the United States in 1919, where he exhibited it at the New York State Fair. After the fair ended, the rabbits were purchased by two American breeders. These attractive rabbits became very popular, and the American Chinchilla Rabbit Breeders Association (ACRBA) was formed in 1923. After that, an enormous fur industry was established around the Chinchilla rabbit. According to one expert, the breed contributed to the development of more rabbit breeds worldwide than any other breed of domestic rabbit. However, the Standard Chinchilla is no longer a popular breed, and it is reared by fewer fanciers primarily as a show rabbit.

Large Breeds

American

Weight: 9 to 12 pounds (4.1 to 5.4 kg).

Description: The American has two color varieties: blue and white. The blue color variety has blue-gray eyes, and the white has pink eyes. The blue variety has the deepest blue color of the North American breeds. This is a docile, hardy breed.

Body Type Profile: Semi-arch.

Breed History: The American rabbit is a multi-purpose breed that was developed for its lean meat and fur. Many breeders in the early 1900s were working to develop a blue rabbit, but a California breeder was given the credit for creating the breed. It is not known exactly what breeds he used to create the American blue because he did not share information on its development. However, it has been hypothesized that the blue Vienna (an Austrian breed that is no longer recognized in the United States), blue Beveren, blue Imperial (a now extinct breed), and blue Flemish Giant were used to develop the American. When the breed was first recognized in 1918, it was called the German Blue Vienna, but because of World War I, its name was changed to American Blue. The white variety recognized in 1925 was produced using mutations from the American Blues, who were then bred to white Flemish Giants.

The American became a popular rabbit breed, and people throughout North America enthusiastically bred it. Furriers paid very high prices for a good pelt; the price for a

American

breeding-age doe started at $25. Both the blue and white varieties were popular for meat and fur through the 1940s. However, the American declined in popularity in the 1950s. It is now one of the rarest rabbit breeds in the United States and is considered a "critical" breed by the ALBC because there are fewer than 50 annual registrations in the United States and an estimated global population of fewer than 500.

American Chinchilla

Weight: 9 to 12 pounds (4.1 to 5.4 kg).

Description: The American Chinchilla's color is a bluish-gray with an interspersion of lighter and darker hairs. When the fur is blown into, four distinct bands of color appear. The ears are the same color as the body, except that their upper tips have a narrow black lacing on the edges. The American Chinchilla is medium boned with broad shoulders, and he tapers slightly from his well-rounded hips to the shoulders. The back forms a gradual arc beginning at the base of the ears, extending to the high point at the middle of the hips and continuing down to the base of the tail. Does may have a medium-sized dewlap. The American Chinchilla is gentle, calm, and friendly.

Body Type Profile: Commercial.

Breed History: The American Chinchilla is a multipurpose breed that was developed for its lean meat and fur. It was developed in France and shown for the first time in 1913. People were very enthusiastic about the new breed because its coat and color were similar to the chinchilla, a small South American rodent that is still highly prized for its soft, dense gray fur. The Chinchilla rabbit was imported into Great Britain in 1917 and was shown by a British exhibitor at the New York State Fair in 1919. After the fair, the Chinchilla rabbits were sold to several American breeders.

The original imported Chinchillas were small and weighed 5 to 7.5 pounds. Through selective breeding, the American breeders increased the Chinchilla's size and developed a rabbit more suitable for meat and pelts. The larger rabbit was the same color and similar in shape to the smaller Standard Chinchilla. In 1924, the American Chinchilla became a recognized breed.

The American Chinchilla was very popular from the 1920s through the 1940s. With the demise of the rabbit fur industry in the late 1940s, the American Chinchilla's population also declined. The American Chinchilla is found only in the United States. It is now one of the rarest rabbit breeds in the United States and considered "critical" by the ALBC because there are fewer than 50 annual registrations in the United States and an estimated global population of fewer than 500.

Beveren

Weight: 8 to 12 pounds (3.6 to 5.4 kg).

Description: The Beveren comes in three color varieties: solid black with dark brown eyes, solid blue with blue-gray eyes, and solid white with brilliant blue eyes. The fur has a gentle rollback, and the coat is dense and glossy. The Beveren's fur is rather long, between 1.25 and 1.5 inches (3.2 and 3.8 cm). He has a mandolin body shape: The body begins to arch at the back of the shoulders rather than at the nape of the neck. The ears are long and carried in a "V" shape. Some Beverens are spirited, while others are docile and enjoy being petted.

Body Type Profile: Semi-arch.

Breed History: The Beveren is a multi-purpose breed produced for both meat and fur. It was developed in the late 1800s and was named after the town of its origin near Antwerp, in western Belgium.

Noted for his silky hair of several shades of blue, the blue Beveren's color was eventually fixed at light lavender blue, which was the color preferred by furriers. Blue Beverens were imported into Great Britain and exhibited for the first time in 1905. By the 1920s, the Beveren was the most popular fur breed in Great Britain. The breeders who formed a club to promote the breed eventually recognized other breeds of fur rabbits. The organization's name changed from the Beveren Club to the British Fur Rabbit Society. Eventually, the name was changed again to the British Rabbit Council (BRC).

Because breeders in Great Britain could not agree on a weight for the Beveren, two types were founded: the standard Beveren and the giant. Both types were imported into the United States around 1915. The white Beveren with blue eyes was imported in 1933. This variety

Beveren

was developed in England from a color mutation in the blue rabbit in 1916. The breed was recognized by the ARBA in 1918.

The Beveren has never been a popular breed in the United States. It is considered a "watch" breed by the ALBC because there are fewer than 200 annual registrations in the United States and an estimated global population of fewer than 2,000.

Blanc de Hotot
Weight: 8 to 11 pounds (3.6 to 5 kg).
Description: The body color is frosty white except for the dark brown eyes that are rimmed in black. The breed has large, long, flaring ears, similar to a jackrabbit, which enable it to cool itself in hot weather. It has a compact body with a deep loin. This docile rabbit makes a good pet but requires regular and careful grooming to keep his white coat spotless; he has a striking appearance when cared for correctly.
Body Type Profile: Commercial.

Californian

Breed History: The Blanc de Hotot (pronounced oh-toe) is a dual-purpose breed used for meat and fur. It was developed in the Hotot-en-Auge region of northern France, and its name translates to "the white rabbit of Hotot." A French baroness who owned a large rabbitry of Flemish Giants and Checkered Giants developed the Blanc de Hotot. Her goal was to produce a large white rabbit with black eyes who could be used for meat, fur, and shows. She began her breeding program sometime around 1902 by crossing Giant Papillons (a French breed) with various white rabbits, including white Flemish Giants and white Viennas. Her initial results were not what she wanted, so she switched to using only the lightly marked Papillons. Through years of dedicated work and more than 500 recorded matings, she achieved her goal.

The Blanc de Hotot almost became extinct in France during World War II. However, it thrived in Switzerland, where it had been imported in 1927. Although the baroness tried to eliminate the dark eye bands on the Hotot, the Swiss breeders decided to keep them.

Blanc de Hotots were first imported into the United States in 1978. They were recognized by the ARBA in 1981. The Blanc de Hotot is considered "threatened" by the ALBC because there are fewer than 100 annual registrations in the United States and an estimated global population of fewer than 1,000.

Californian

Weight: 8 to 10.5 pounds (3.6 to 4.8 kg).

Description: The Californian has a pure white body color with dark, Himalayan markings on the nose, ears, feet, and tail. The eyes arc pink. Hair that regrows in shaved areas may grow back as black instead of white. Black, blue, chocolate, and lilac varieties are recognized by the British Rabbit Council (BRC) but are not recognized by the ARBA. This breed is characterized by short legs and a firm, plump body. The back rises gradually from the nape of the neck to the high point over the hips. The shoulders are slightly lower than the hips. The Californian is generally calm and relaxed.

Body Type Profile: Commercial.

Breed History: This rabbit breed was developed in California around 1923. It was created as a meat and fur rabbit from crosses that included New Zealand Whites, Chinchillas, and Himalayans. To improve the quality of the fur, Angoras were also used. The Californian was recognized by the ARBA in 1942. The Californian is the most widely spread breed and is found around the world. It has been bred extensively in developing countries for food and fur in addition to being used to improve local meat rabbit breeds.

Champagne d'Argent

Weight: 9 to 12 pounds (4.1 to 5.4 kg).

Description: The body color is bluish white with interspersed longer black hairs. The undercolor is dark slate blue. When viewed from a distance, the black hairs give a silver effect to his glossy coat. The nose and muzzle are slightly darker than the body color and form the breed's characteristic butterfly marking. The Champagne d'Argent has a plump body with well-furred, erect ears. The shoulders are slightly narrower than the hips and form a slight taper. The Champagne d'Argent is generally calm and relaxed, and although very large, can make a good house pet.

Champagne d'Argent

Body Type Profile: Commercial.

Breed History: The Champagne d'Argent originated in the Champagne region of France. ("d'Argent" means "silver.") Benedictine monks are believed to have developed the breed from a regional rabbit population in Champagne. This is an old breed created for both fur and meat; it was first recorded in 1631. The breed was very popular because of its high productivity—quick growth and good meat quality. Although no longer as popular, it is still raised on rabbit farms in France. Scientists have researched the Champagne d'Argent for its intensive breeding potential. The breed was first imported into the United States in 1912 and was sometimes known as the French Silver.

Cinnamon

Weight: 8.5 to 11 pounds (3.6 to 5 kg).

Description: The color is rust or cinnamon with uniform smoke-gray ticking across the back. Midway on the side, the color blends into smoke gray and becomes darker on the belly. The undercoat is orange and the eyes are brown. The feet are darker colored, and he has a dark nose. The fur is flyback. The Cinnamon is considered a fairly calm breed.

Body Type Profile: Commercial.

Breed History: The Cinnamon was developed in the United States by a Montana family in the 1960s. The breed's ancestors include the Chinchilla, New Zealand, and Checkered Giant. The family's children initiated the Cinnamon's development while breeding crossbred meat rabbits for their 4-H project. The road to the breed's recognition by the ARBA had some mishaps. One such problem included a dog breaking into their rabbitry and killing three of their presentation does. But the Cinnamon was eventually recognized in 1972.

Crème d'Argent

Weight: 8.5 to 11 pounds (3.6 to 5 kg).

Description: The Crème d'Argent is creamy white in color with an orange cast carried throughout the fur of the body. The undercoat is bright orange, and this color carries to the skin. The entire coat is interspersed with orange guard hairs. The Crème d'Argent is a docile and friendly breed.

Body Type Profile: Commercial.

Breed History: The Crème d'Argent was developed in France during the mid-to-late 1800s. It is not known exactly what breeds were used to create it, but it is likely the Champagne d'Argent, the oldest of the seven Argent rabbit breeds, was used. The first record of the breed's exhibition occurred near Paris in 1877. It became very desirable because its fur was used for trimmings on fashionable clothes.

Sometime around 1924, the first Crème d'Argent was imported into the United States by several breeders in New York. These first importations were bred to each other and also crossed with other breeds, such as the golden Palomino. In the United States, breeders "Americanized" the Crème d'Argent by selecting for larger size and a more muscular build (to have a meat or commercial body type). The breed was first exhibited in 1936. A working standard for the breed was written in 1938, and the breed was officially recognized several years later.

The Crème d'Argent has become very rare and is currently found only in the United States and Great Britain. It is considered a "watch" breed by the ALBC because there are fewer than 200 annual registrations in the United States and an estimated global population of fewer than 2,000.

English Lop
Weight: 9 to 10 pounds (4.1 to 4.5 kg).
Description: English Lops are recognized in more than 20 colors that are broken down into six groups: agouti, broken, self, shaded, ticked, and wide band. The ears of an English Lop are stupendous—when measured from tip to tip, the breed standard requires that the ears be at least 21 inches (53.3 cm). The ideal length of the ears is as long as possible provided the

English Lop

width is approximately one quarter the total length of the ear. The English Lop's ears stop growing when the rabbit is about four months old. They must also be checked and cleaned regularly. The toenails must be kept trimmed, especially those on the hind feet, because the ears can be accidentally cut when scratching. This breed is fairly easygoing, playful, and affectionate but requires special care due to its long ears.

Body Type Profile: Semi-arch.

Breed History: The origin of lop-eared rabbits is full of speculation. Countries from all corners of the world, including North Africa, Patagonia, China, and England, are cited as the country of origin. It is even possible that rabbits with lop ears originated in more than one region at a time. Lop-eared rabbits are an old breed. They were mentioned in a British book published in 1822 on the care of farm animals. In the mid-1820s, lop-eared rabbits were the first and only breed allowed to be exhibited at agricultural shows in England. Over time, the British developed the English Lop to have the longest ears of all rabbit breeds.

Giant Angora

Weight: 9.5 to 10 pounds (4.3 to 4.5 kg).

Description: The Giant Angora is only available in ruby-eyed white. The wool is composed of three types of fibers and ideally is 4 inches (10.2 cm) in length. The ears have long tassels on their tops and are lightly fringed. Tufts of hair are present on the forehead and cheeks. The feet are covered with wool that extends beyond the end of the toes. Giant Angora rabbits typically do not release their wool readily. Because plucking is not effective, the fur usually needs to be clipped. In between clippings, they must be groomed. Giant Angoras are known for their gentle disposition.

Body Type Profile: Commercial.

Breed History: The development of the Giant Angora began in the early 1980s with the importation of the German Angora into the United States. This German breed was developed in Germany from the English Angora for increased wool production. An attempt to get the German Angora recognized was unsuccessful in 1985, as the ARBA Standards Committee felt that the breed was too similar to the English Angora. A committee member required that the German Angora's cylindrical body, which allows rapid shearing, be modified to the commercial type and that the breed be increased in size. By crossing German Angoras with French Lops and Flemish Giants, the presenting breeder was able to satisfy the requirements. The breed was finally recognized in 1988.

New Zealand

Weight: 9 to 12 pounds (4.1 to 5.4 kg).

Description: The New Zealand has three varieties: black, red, and white. The black variety has dark brown eyes. The white variety is the most common color and has pink eyes. The red variety has bright, golden-red fur and brown eyes; it was the first variety that was developed.

The New Zealand is a docile pet and a good choice for a first-time owner.

Body Type Profile: Commercial.

Breed History: The New Zealand was created for meat, fur, and showing in the United States during the early 1900s. Why it was named the New Zealand is unclear and the subject of numerous fanciful stories. According to some experts, rabbits with New Zealand traits appeared in multiple litters throughout the United States. However, California breeders are given credit for improving the breed. The New Zealand was recognized by the ARBA in the early 1920s. This breed has been introduced around the world for meat production. Either alone or when crossed with local breeds, the New Zealand has a fast growth rate.

Palomino

Palomino

Weight: 9 to 9.5 pounds (4.1 to 4.3 kg).

Description: The Palomino is available in two color varieties: golden and lynx. The golden has a glossy, gold color over a cream to white undercoat. The underside of the tail, belly, foot pads, and jaw is light cream to white. The eyes are brown. The lynx color variety is a medium pearl gray that blends to a dilute orange-beige intermediate color over a cream to white undercolor at the base of the hair shaft. As with the golden, the underside of the tail, belly, foot pads, and jaws is light cream to white. The eyes are blue-gray. The Palomino has flyback fur. Rising gradually from the nape of the neck, the body topline arcs smoothly along the back before sloping down to the tail. When properly posed for showing, the Palomino's back looks like a rounded half circle. This breed has an easygoing temperament that makes it a good choice as a pet.

Body Type Profile: Commercial.

Breed History: The Palomino was developed in Washington state beginning in the 1940s. It is not known what breeds were used to create the Palomino. The breeder used rabbits he obtained from children who were rearing meat rabbits as members of Future Farmers of

America (FFA). By selecting and breeding rabbits with yellow-brown color mutations, he was eventually able to obtain litters in which all the baby rabbits had the preferred color. The breed was presented at an ARBA convention for the first time in 1952 and was finally recognized as a distinct breed in 1957.

Satin

Satin

Weight: 8.5 to 11 pounds (3.9 to 5 kg).

Description: Satins come in 11 varieties: black, blue, California, chinchilla, chocolate, copper, otter, red, Siamese, white, and broken. The fur is silky, fine, and feels very dense when touched. A Satin's coat has a distinct, glossy, lustrous shine. The ideal length is 1 to 1.1 inches (2.8 cm), but the fur can be 0.9 to 1.25 inches (2.3 to 3.2 cm). The undercoat is fine, soft, and dense. Slightly coarser guard hairs are thickly interspersed above the undercoat. Most Satins are very calm due to years of being bred for good temperaments to make proper grooming easier.

Body Type Profile: Commercial.

Breed History: The first satin mutation occurred in Indiana in 1934. A breeder who was inbreeding his Havana rabbits to improve their color and fur noticed shiny kits in his rabbits' litters. Breeders learned that the Satin mutation was recessive and could be used to create a satin coat on other breeds. The Satin breed is recognized throughout the world and was recognized by the ARBA in 1956.

Silver Fox

Weight: 9 to 12 pounds (4.1 to 5.4 kg).

Description: Young Silver Fox rabbits are born solid black and begin to show silvering at about four weeks. The silvering process takes about four months to complete. During the 1970s, a blue variety that was included in the original standard was dropped because too few were being shown. The Silver Fox has dense fur that is 1.5 to 2 inches (3.8 to 5.1 cm) in length—much longer than that found in a normal-coated rabbit. When the fur is slowly stroked from the rump toward the head, it stands up straight until it is stroked in the opposite direction. The Silver Fox is known for being docile and gentle. Breeders purposely do not breed any aggressive individuals.

Body Type Profile: Commercial.

Breed History: The Silver Fox was developed in Ohio. Although no one knows exactly what breeds were used to create the breed, experts guess that the Checkered Giant, Champagne D'Argent, and American Blue might have been used. It is thought that the self-colored Checkered Giant gave the Silver Fox his size, while the Champagne D' Argent contributed the silvering, fur length, and meat qualities. The American Blue might also have been used to improve the meat-producing qualities and the blue color.

The breed was recognized and a standard approved in 1925 under the name American Heavyweight Silver. In 1929, the name was changed to the American Silver Fox and later to its current name, the Silver Fox. Developed for both meat and fur, the breed has a deep loin (the portion of the back between the ribs and hips) and is known for providing a high percentage of meat for its body weight. The Silver Fox is considered a "critical" breed by the ALBC because there are fewer than 50 annual registrations in the United States and an estimated global population of fewer than 500.

Giant Breeds

Checkered Giant

Weight: More than 11 pounds (5 kg).

Description: The Checkered Giant is white with a complicated order of blue or black markings. On the head, each cheek has a round spot of color and each eye has a circle of color. The nose and lips are marked with a butterfly, and the ears are solid in color to their base. Two spots or two groups of spots are found on each of the rabbit's sides. The spine marking is a line of color running from the base of the ears all the way to the tip of the tail. The heavy-set ears are close together. The Checkered Giant's fur is short and dense. Considered a spirited rabbit with a strong sense of self, this breed is not recommended for beginning rabbit owners.

Body Type Profile: Full arch.

Breed History: The Checkered Giant originated in Germany in the early 1900s. His ancestors include the Flemish Giant and French Lop. Other spotted white breeds might also have been used because spotted rabbits were noted in France and Germany beginning in the mid-19th century. The breed was imported into America in 1910 and has since been developed into a type distinct from European Checkered Giants. The European rabbits are much larger than the American breed. The breed was recognized by the ARBA in 1910.

Checkered Giant

Flemish Giant

Weight: More than 13 pounds (5.9 kg).

Description: The Flemish Giant comes in black, blue, fawn, light gray, sandy, steel gray, and white. This breed has a long, broad body with massive hindquarters and good muscular development. The body, feet, and legs are strong and powerful. The ears of a full-grown rabbit are erect and should measure at least 6 inches (15.2 cm). The does may have a large, full dewlap. Known as "gentle giants," these rabbits are friendly, responsive pets. However, this is a demanding breed because individuals require a large cage, a lot of food, and a lot of attention.

Body Type Profile: Semi-arch.

Breed History: The Flemish Giant originated in Belgium. It is uncertain which breeds or types of rabbits were used in its development. One scenario entails Dutch traders bringing giant Patagonian rabbits from Argentina to Europe during the 16th and 17th centuries. However, according to another expert's research, there were no giant rabbits in South America, and it is most likely that the Patagonian was just another Belgium breed of giant rabbit.

Weighing about 14 pounds (6.4 kg), the early Flemish Giant was an impressive rabbit who, according to some fanciers, had long ears with bent tips. By the 1850s, numerous clubs for the giant rabbits existed in the Flemish region of Belgium. The breed was found in only two colors, gray agouti with a white belly and iron gray with a dark belly. In the late 1800s, new colors were developed and the rabbit no longer had bent ear tips. The giant rabbits were exported to other European countries, including Germany and Great Britain. Flemish Giants were first imported into the United States from Belgium and Great Britain during the 1890s. The breed was recognized by the ARBA in 1910.

French Lop

Weight: More than 10.5 pounds (4.8 kg).

Description: French Lops are recognized in more than 20 different colors that are broken down into six groups: agouti, broken, self, shaded, ticked, and wide band. Their ears fall down 16 to 17 inches (40.6 to 43 cm) along the sides of their heads. They have wide, muscular bodies and big heads. These unique and irresistible rabbits are affectionate and playful, although some say that they can be irritable and affectionately refer to them as "the bulldog of the rabbit world." Nevertheless, this larger than large breed is easily recognized and remains popular.

Body Type Profile: Commercial.

Breed History: The French Lop was primarily developed as a meat rabbit. To create the

French Lop

breed, it is thought that English Lops obtained by a French breeder in 1852 were successively bred with unknown giant breeds found in France and perhaps with the now-extinct giant Andalusian from Spain. Although the French Lop was exported to Germany and Switzerland in 1869 and 1899, it was not recognized in France until 1922. The breed was imported into the United States in the early 1970s. Although it is the largest breed of lop, it is still a popular pet. The breed was recognized by the ARBA in 1910.

Giant Chinchilla

Weight: 12 to 16 pounds (5.4 to 7.3 cm).

Description: The Giant Chinchilla's color resembles the bluish gray of the real chinchilla. These are gentle rabbits, but they can be energetic at times. Because of their large size, special care is required.

Body Type Profile: Semi-arch.

Breed History: The Giant Chinchilla was developed in Missouri in 1921. The breed was produced by an individual who bought some of the first Chinchilla rabbits to arrive in the United States. This breeder knew that the Chinchilla rabbit would be very popular with the American fur industry, but he also knew that a larger rabbit would be more profitable. While other breeders developed the Chinchilla into the larger American Chinchilla breed, the Missouri breeder had bigger ambitions and decided to create an even larger breed.

Using the basement of his house as a rabbitry, the Chinchilla was crossed with numerous other breeds, including white New Zealands, white Flemish Giants, and blue Americans. It took various crosses to ultimately produce the chinchilla color, and many of the pairings that intuitively seemed right, such as using the steel Giant Flemish and Champagne d' Argent, were unsuccessful. Progress toward larger size and good coloration continued. On Christmas morning, 1921, a Giant Chinchilla doe whom the breeder considered ideal was born. He named her the "Million Dollar Princess," and she was shown for the first time in the fall of 1922.

A standard for the breed was proposed and recognized in 1928. The Giant Chinchilla is considered a "watch" breed by the ALBC because there are fewer than 200 annual registrations in the United States and an estimated global population of fewer than 2,000.

Popularity Contest

The American Rabbit Breeders Association (ARBA) records the total number of registrations by breed each year. While the annual ranking of the top ten rabbits might change from year to year, the same breeds tend to show up in the top ten every year. The breed rankings in the lowest ten are more variable.

Top Ten ARBA Breed Registrations for 2006/2007

Mini Rex	3,306
Holland Lop	2,659
Netherland Dwarf	1,390
Mini Lop	1,005
Dutch	982
Polish	903
Jersey Wooly	781
Californian	674
Rex	610
English Lop	569

Lowest Ten ARBA Breed Registrations for 2006/2007

Rhinelander	36
Lilac	33
Giant Chinchilla	27
American	27
American Sable	25
Belgian Hare	23
Giant Angora	20
Cinnamon	20
Beveren	10
Blanc de Hotot	5

Chapter 3

Where to Get Your Rabbit

Now that you have done your homework and have decided that you would like to bring a rabbit into your life, the time has come to search for the perfect bunny companion. Although you may already know which breeds you are interested in, you may not know where to find them. You also may not be sure which characteristics other than breed type to consider in making your choice, such as gender and age. No matter where you get your rabbit, some basic guidelines should apply.

Knowing what to look for and what to ask are the first steps in beginning a good relationship with the lucky little bunny who will be part of your family for the next seven to ten years.

OBTAINING YOUR RABBIT

You can obtain a rabbit from a breeder, animal shelter, rescue group, pet store, or from an individual who advertises in the newspaper or some other forum, such as the Internet. Wherever you obtain your rabbit, consider asking for a health guarantee that the animal can be returned within 48 hours of sale if your veterinarian deems him unhealthy. Although a visit to the vet is an additional expense, doing so can help prevent a potentially larger medical bill and heartbreak down the road if a condition that is not obvious to you is detected. The vet can also confirm whether the rabbit is a female or male.

The Found Rabbit

What if you find a domestic rabbit hopping around your neighborhood? You can usually tell that such a rabbit is not wild by his color, size, and body type. If there are any patches of color on the rabbit's coat (including white), he is domestic. Wild rabbits are small, ranging from 2 to 4 pounds (0.9 to 1.4 kg); if the rabbit is bigger than that, he could be a domestic rabbit. Wild rabbits also have very long slender legs and a wedge-shaped head. Their ears are very thin at the tips and narrow at the base. Domestic rabbits have a more dome-shaped forehead and more prominent, chubbier cheekbones.

If the rabbit is not particularly afraid of you, he is probably domestic. Wild rabbits, even if raised in captivity, often have a natural fear of humans when mature. Some pet rabbits who have escaped or been turned loose by their owners are relatively easy to catch, but others can be difficult to capture. You can try tempting a runaway bunny with food, but your best bet is to contact a local rescue organization. You can usually find one in your area by searching the yellow pages, the Internet, or the ARBA website at www.arba.net.

Volunteers from the group can help you catch the rabbit. Animal control agencies might offer help, but many are too busy for the potentially time-consuming task. If you do catch the rabbit, you are obligated to advertise him as found before keeping him, just as you would with a dog or cat. It is also prudent to take him to a veterinarian for a checkup before making him a permanent member of your family.

You can obtain a rabbit from a breeder or a pet store, or you can adopt one waiting for a good home from a local animal shelter or rescue organization.

Breeders

You can locate breeders of purebred rabbits through the American Rabbit Breeders Association (ARBA). Information is available on its website, www.arba.net, or by e-mail or telephone. (See Resources.) Breeders might specialize in only one breed of rabbit, but many rear several different breeds. Some raise rabbits in their homes, while others have large-scale operations housed in outdoor barns. In any case, your best bet is to choose a vendor who selectively breeds for friendly rabbits and who regularly handles the babies so that they are socialized and not skittish.

Many breeders affiliated with the ARBA also compete in rabbit shows, so you may be able to get some helpful information by attending any events that take place in your area. Youngsters involved in 4-H and Future Farmers of America (FFA) clubs breed and show purebred rabbits as well. Local groups such as these can usually be contacted through agriculture extension offices. If you want to get involved in showing, you'll need to obtain a

If You Adopt...

Expect to be questioned by a rescue volunteer if you apply to adopt a foster rabbit. These people are professionals and experts who want to be sure that they place their animals in the right homes. They also want to ensure that you are making a long-term commitment to prevent putting the bunny through another traumatic upheaval in his life. This process works both to your advantage and his.

If you decide to go through a rescue organization, they will screen you quite thoroughly about why you want a rabbit, what kind of home you can offer him, and whether or not you understand the responsibilities involved in owning a rabbit. Only after you have answered these questions to their satisfaction will they begin the steps to match you with the perfect pet. Don't be upset by this probing interview—remember, their rabbit charges are their first priority. Your wants and needs come second to making sure the rabbit finds a good home.

Here are the type of questions you will likely be asked:

- Describe what food you plan to feed and why?
- How will you choose your veterinarian?
- Describe your rabbit's cage and the accessories for it.
- Where will this cage be placed?
- How many hours a day will your rabbit be inside his cage? How many hours loose inside your home?
- How will you rabbit-proof your home?
- What kind of toys do you think are suitable for a rabbit?

show-quality rabbit. Expect to pay more for a purebred show-quality individual compared with a purebred pet-quality one. It should be noted that there is nothing wrong with a pet-quality rabbit. He might have an incorrect color or other features that would make it difficult to compete successfully in shows. However, these show faults do not affect the rabbit's overall appeal or his ability to live a long, happy life as a pet.

Keep in mind that although reputable dog breeders will often take back a puppy they bred if you can't keep him at any time in his life, a rabbit breeder may not do likewise. However, some breeders might be able to help you find a new home for your rabbit.

Animal Shelters

Animal shelters and humane societies often have rabbits available for adoption. As with dogs and cats, these animals are turned in to shelters because their owners no longer want them and not because they haven't been good pets. You are likely to be able to select from a variety of ages and breeds, including mixed breeds. Sometimes entire litters of weaned baby rabbits are surrendered.

At some facilities, staff members handle the rabbits each day and socialize them with other rabbits. This is useful because they might become familiar with each rabbit's personality and may be able to guide you in making your selection. In addition, some shelters neuter the rabbits before releasing them for adoption, which can ultimately save you money because the cost to adopt the animal is less than the cost of the surgery. While animal shelters may not always have rabbits available all the time, rescue groups almost always do.

Make sure that the rabbit you select is in good physical condition. Healthy rabbits are alert and active, and their eyes, ears, and coats should be clean.

Rescue Groups

Rescue groups obtain rabbits from various sources: shelters, animal control agencies, rabbits found abandoned, and occasionally from individuals. The House Rabbit Society (HRS) is a well-known nationwide volunteer organization that has numerous local chapters devoted to rehoming rabbits. There are also many other independent rescue groups with members who perform similar functions. Rescue group members temporarily "foster" rabbits so that they are not euthanized. If homes cannot be found, they commit to providing them permanent places in which to live out their lives. All rabbits are given necessary medical care, including spaying or neutering.

Rescue groups have an application process to carefully screen potential adopters. Their members put a lot of time, care, and money into each animal and want to make sure that they will be provided with a good permanent home. Volunteers will help match you with the best fit in terms of rabbit personality. They are knowledgeable and will answer any questions that arise later.

As with animal shelters, a variety of rabbits are likely to be available for adoption. There is a fee, but it is much less than you would pay to purchase a rabbit from a pet store or breeder, plus the added cost of spaying or neutering. If for some reason your choice does not work out, the group usually requests that you return the rabbit. For some prospective owners, there is a potential drawback to getting a rabbit from a rescue group. Namely, most groups will only adopt rabbits out to people who keep them inside the house, not outside in hutches.

Pet Stores

Pet stores are convenient, and most full-line outlets sell rabbits as well as the supplies needed for their care. Both purebred and mixed breeds are offered for sale. Typically, the quality of the purebred rabbits sold at pet stores is not the same as those obtained directly from a breeder. In other words, do not expect to buy a show-quality rabbit from a pet store. Pet stores often obtain mixed-breed rabbits from local individuals whose rabbits accidentally had babies or who purposely bred rabbits of unknown breeds. A mixed-breed rabbit is just as charming as a purebred rabbit; the only caveat is that you might not know how large the rabbit will be when he is full grown.

If you live in an area with numerous pet stores, shop around. Choose one that is clean and well managed. Large chain stores do not usually have personnel with specific knowledge of rabbits, but they should at least be able to help you purchase the necessary supplies. Try to go to the store when it is not busy so that you can take your time while you evaluate the rabbit's health and personality.

Other Sources

If you check the pet section of a newspaper or various Internet forums, you might see one or more advertisements for "rabbit with cage and supplies." Usually, the rabbit is an adolescent just under a year old, and he and his supplies are offered at a low price because the seller just wants to be rid of him. Or he may need a new home because of a family move, divorce, or lack of time. However, what is most likely is that the rabbit has become sexually mature and has begun to exhibit some ornery behaviors. Such behaviors can diminish if the rabbit is spayed or neutered. (See Chapter 8.)

Do be cautious. You don't want a rabbit who has been ill-treated or neglected because he is unlikely to be friendly and might even be mean. Although the rabbit might have a charming character just waiting to blossom, most beginning rabbit owners lack the expertise

Choosing a Friendly Rabbit

Besides the obvious advice to avoid bringing home a rabbit who is aggressive and tries to bite, scratch, or struggle frantically when held, or one who runs away from your hand, how can you select a rabbit with a more friendly character?

Friendly rabbits are curious and will come up to people to seek their attention. They love to be petted and may nudge you with their nose for more. If given the opportunity, they will follow you around, and some even seem to want to be picked up. Regardless of where you purchase your rabbit, try to spend at least 30 minutes getting to know your choice before deciding whether to bring him home. In an enclosed, relatively quiet space, allow the rabbit time to explore his new surroundings; any sounds or actions you make during the first 15 minutes that cause a reaction are not very indicative of his character. He will be spending that time thoroughly investigating and marking his territory. After he has finished, a friendly rabbit will be curious and come up to you for petting, whereas a shy rabbit will run away from your offered hand, no matter how gently you talk to him. Naturally, there are rabbits with in-between personalities who might initially be afraid, but they will eventually be inquisitive and sniff your hand.

Of course, other factors will also affect your rabbit's personality, such as the environment you provide and how often you play with him. But you can at least increase the likelihood that you are buying a rabbit whose temperament may more closely match what you desire.

Keep in mind that the personality of an adult rabbit is likely to be more "fixed" than that of a baby rabbit. If the animal you want is young and exhibits shyness, you may be able to socialize him to be friendlier with training.

Before making a final decision on a bunny of your choice, ask the seller lots of questions. A rabbit's potential pet quality will depend greatly on the care and attention you will need to provide.

to help a mean rabbit become a good pet. The person selling the rabbit should be able to take him out of his cage and handle him without being bitten, kicked, or scratched. Once out of his cage, the rabbit should be calm, not frightened and skittish. Never purchase a rabbit without first seeing and handling him in person.

WHAT TO LOOK FOR

It is always important to select a healthy animal who will be able to give you and your family a good start to years of mutual enjoyment. Never choose a sick animal because you feel sorry for him, because you will both likely be at a disadvantage. No matter where you purchase your rabbit, carefully examine your choice for signs of poor health.

To begin, the eyes should be clear and bright, with no crusty matter in the corners or

When you hold a rabbit, he should feel robust and solid, not bony or frail. Use your hands to examine his body.

wet, stained fur due to tears. The nose should also be clean of any secretions. Just as some people may wipe their noses on their sleeves, sick rabbits will wipe their noses on their arms. Look at the inside of his front feet and check to be sure that the fur in these areas is not wet or matted. Also, look inside his ears and be sure that they are clean and do not emit noxious smells.

Next, check the rabbit's teeth to ensure that they are not misaligned, a condition called malocclusion, which typically requires ongoing veterinary treatment. When the rabbit's lips are pulled back, you should be able to see the front teeth, or incisors. Properly aligned top incisors will meet or slightly overlap the lower incisors. In a rabbit with malocclusion, the upper incisors curve inward and the lower incisors grow forward, almost like tusks. Hereditary malocclusion is sometimes not detectable in young rabbits. Even if the teeth appear normal at first, changes that make malocclusion more likely occur as the rabbit grows. Some rabbit breeds with shortened facial bones, such as dwarfs, are more likely to have hereditary malocclusion.

A healthy rabbit should also have dense, shiny fur that is not matted or stained. If he is molting, he may look a bit shabby, but the new hair growing in should still appear glossy. There should be no scabs, bald areas, excess dandruff, or patches of red skin. You can check by running your hand against the direction of the fur. Evidence of flea droppings (which look like black specks and turn red in water) is an indication that the rabbit has not received good care.

When you hold the rabbit, he should feel robust and solid, not bony or frail. Use your hands to examine his body. An adult should have padding over his bones but not feel like he is fat. Make sure that there are no lumps that might indicate cysts or tumors. Also, if the rabbit is calm enough, it can't hurt to listen to the side of his chest to be sure that he has no rattling breathing sounds, which may indicate a respiratory illness. He should also appear lively and alert and should not limp or appear awkward. Never bring home an animal with obvious symptoms of ill health, no matter how sorry you feel for him or how cute he is. Also, do not choose a rabbit who is housed with or near another sick-looking one. It is likely he has been exposed and might also become ill.

Always select your rabbit from a clean, uncrowded cage. Rabbits who come from a dirty, crowded environment are less likely to make good pets and are more likely to be unhealthy. The cage should not be grimy or have offensive smells. Unless recently weaned, males and females should be housed in separate cages. If juveniles are kept together and their genders have been incorrectly identified, there is a good possibility that a female could be pregnant.

WHAT TO ASK

Before you acquire your rabbit, learn as much as you can prior to making a final decision or signing an agreement on a bunny of your choice. A good breeder or rescue organization will be happy to answer any questions you may have and to provide you with information about proper care. For example, it's a good idea to ask what the animal has been fed, how often to feed, what type of bedding is best, etc. It is also important that you are comfortable handling your rabbit before you leave the breeder, rescue, or pet store, so ask to be shown how to do so properly. This will be crucial to his overall well-being while he is in your guardianship.

If not offered, request a written guarantee of the animal's health and which vaccinations (if any) he has been given, as well as a copy of any medical records available. You should also receive a bill of sale that not only shows the sale price but also the age and gender of the rabbit and any known problems. Be careful with whom you choose to do business, and be sure to keep the best interests of the rabbit in mind at all times.

HOW OLD?

Baby rabbits are so cute they are almost irresistible. If you have your heart set on a baby rather than an adult, you must exercise some caution. Do not purchase a baby rabbit who was just weaned. Weaning, as well as going to a new home and eating an adult diet, are stressful events that can cause a baby rabbit to get sick. Baby rabbits are usually weaned from their mother when they are between four and six weeks old. The earliest age a baby rabbit can leave his mother is eight to ten weeks. Although the newborns will tug at your heartstrings, a slightly older baby bunny will be hardier and just as cute. Because baby rabbits of the correct age will vary in size depending on their breed, you will need to rely on the honesty of the seller as to their age.

Baby Rabbits Versus Adult Rabbits

Because a young rabbit's small size and endearing nature make him easier to handle, he becomes tame more quickly and makes a better pet than an older one who has been infrequently handled. However, a tame adult rabbit who has been regularly handled is highly recommended. This is because his temperament is relatively fixed, and you will not need to contend with his less pleasant adolescent behavior as he becomes sexually mature. In particular, if you are buying from a breeder or obtaining your rabbit from a rescue group, you will have an opportunity to choose an individual with a temperament that better meets your expectations. Moreover, with an adult rabbit, you will know exactly how big the rabbit is.

MALE OR FEMALE?

Males and females make equally good pets. Until they become sexually mature, there are no significant differences in behavior or personality. Mature male rabbits sometimes spray urine to mark their territory. Spraying is most common in young adult males and in homes where more than one rabbit is kept, especially an intact female; it is less common in homes with a single rabbit. Any differences between males and females are eliminated if they are neutered or spayed.

Selecting a specific gender is really only important if you decide to get a second rabbit, in which case you should have your veterinarian make sure that the rabbit's gender was accurately determined. Be aware that a female might be pregnant if she was not separated soon enough from any males, so try to buy your rabbit from a facility in which the females are kept separate from the males. Depending on the breed, female rabbits can first breed around four months of age.

Determining Gender

A male rabbit is called a buck and a female rabbit is called a doe. To determine the sex of a rabbit, turn him or her over onto his or her back on your lap. Using your thumb and finger, gently move the fur away from the anus and genitals. In females, the genital opening extends like a slit toward the anus. In males, the opening is shaped like a point. Once males become adults, between the fourth and eight month of age depending on the breed, the testicles will also be visible. The differences between males and females are difficult to detect in baby rabbits. As a result, many rabbits are wrongly given a boy's or girl's name.

MORE THAN ONE?

Rabbits are social animals, and when properly introduced, enjoy each other's company. Two rabbits will groom each other and play and rest together. However, if you have never had a rabbit, it is probably best to keep just one. Get to see what keeping a pet rabbit is like before deciding to obtain another one. A second rabbit will require either another cage or your two rabbits must be housed in a correspondingly larger cage. Don't forget that two rabbits will take more care, which demands extra time and work.

You should get more than

Both purebred and mixed-breed rabbits make wonderful pets. Choose a breed whose looks and personality appeal to you.

one rabbit if you plan to keep your pets outside in a hutch. Because outdoor rabbits tend to have less interaction with their owners, they need the additional companionship. Opinions vary as to which combination of genders works best. Two males or two females can be kept together. As babies, most rabbits will get along, but once they reach sexual maturity, they are likely to fight, which can become serious, resulting in wounds that require expensive veterinary care. Problems can be reduced if the rabbits are altered.

If you decide to keep a male and female together, you can expect your female to constantly have babies unless she is altered. The reproductive life of a rabbit depends on the breed but is about five to six years for a buck and three years for a doe. Consider whether you will be able to find homes for all the babies born. Pet stores might be interested, but they might not always need them when you are ready to find a new owner for your weaned bunnies. Because there are so many rescued animals in need of homes, it is best to leave breeding to knowledgeable, professional individuals.

PUREBRED OR MIXED BREED?

If you want a purebred rabbit, you should choose a breed with looks that appeal to you. Although there are some differences in breeds, coat type and the rabbit's adult size should be the overriding criteria. Longhaired wool breeds such as the Angoras require daily grooming that can't be neglected. Large rabbits require large cages that take up a lot of space, they eat more (and defecate more), and they can be heavier to lift and handle. Within the breed you want, try to find a breeder who breeds for friendly rabbits.

Again, there is nothing wrong with mixed-breed rabbits; they make wonderful pets. However, if you don't know the size or breed of a rabbit's parents, you are unlikely to know how large he will be as an adult.

BRINGING YOUR RABBIT HOME

Once you have decided on which rabbit to purchase, you'll surely be anxious to bring your new pet home. Before doing so, however, you must have everything ready for him when he arrives so that he can immediately feel comfortable and secure. You will want to make his homecoming pleasant and be able to provide for all his daily needs. (Find out more about the supplies your rabbit requires in Chapter 4.)

Ideally, you should have already purchased a carrier in which to transport your pet. Plastic and wire travel cages made for dogs and cats work well for rabbits. A travel carrier will be invaluable throughout your pet's life because you will need it to safely transport him to the veterinarian and anywhere else he may need to go.

The carrier should be large enough for your rabbit to turn around in but not so big that

No Bunny's Perfect

An important part of being a responsible pet owner is to be able to accept and love your pet for all his qualities—for the good ones, and despite the bad ones.

Just as there is no perfect human, there is no perfect rabbit. Each will have personality and behavior quirks that make sharing a home with him a challenge at times. Just be sure that those quirks are going to be things you can live with.

No matter where you decide to purchase your rabbit, be sure that you know the upside as well as the downside to owning a rabbit: that you are committed to being his best friend and to creating an atmosphere in which he can live happily and safely. By seriously considering these issues before bringing a rabbit home, you can make certain that you are not going to add to the worsening problem of homeless and unwanted rabbits across the country. As long as your bunny companion is well loved and you respond to his needs, there is no problem you can't work through together.

he can circle frantically about. Placing a handful or two of the old bedding on which he was kept into the carrier will help him feel less anxious during the trip to his new home. Be careful not to expose your rabbit to any temperature extremes. Generally, the temperature in your car will probably be comfortable for him, but don't let a heater or air conditioner vent blow directly on him. If your trip is long, water should be made available in a gravity-fed water bottle.

ADJUSTMENT TO THE NEW HOME

Upon arrival, keep your rabbit in his carrier while you set up his new home. Place fresh bedding in the cage (as well as the old bedding from his prior home), provide fresh food and water, and don't forget to set up a corner of the enclosure for his litter box. Then let him settle in for the first few days. He will spend time smelling his new cage and possibly marking it with his scent glands. Some rabbits are more nervous than others and might not eat much the first day.

Usually, by the second day, many rabbits are more comfortable in their new surroundings and will respond well to your friendly attempts. You can offer your pet some of his food in your hand, but if he seems shy or nervous, talk soothingly to him or leave him alone for a while longer. In a few more days, his nervousness should wane and he will be less shy. Sometimes partially covering half the cage with a cardboard box will help a rabbit feel more

Rabbit ownership comes with many responsibilities. Be sure that you can make a commitment for the lifetime of your pet before bringing him home.

secure and less vulnerable because he will detect less motion around his enclosure.

Although it can be hard to do, it is often best to wait several days before letting your rabbit out of his cage. Allow him to first get used to the sounds and sights of your house and become confident in his cage. You will be able to tell when he has adjusted because he will be less skittish in his cage and more curious whenever you approach him. Nonetheless, a seemingly confident rabbit can suddenly bolt if something frightens him, so take your time. (See Chapters 8 and 9 on how to interact with your rabbit.)

Congratulations! You are now the proud parent of a wonderful pet who will bring you many years of companionship and affection.

When You Cannot Keep Your Rabbit

For various reasons, some people are unable to provide a "forever home" for their pet. If you can't keep your rabbit, try to find him a new home by asking friends or your veterinarian if they know someone who may want to adopt him. Also, try advertising in the newspaper. If that doesn't work, relinquish your rabbit to a humane society or shelter. Do not release him into the wild in the mistaken belief that he will have a better chance at a happy life. He will most likely be eaten by a predator such as a coyote, killed by a car, or slowly die from an illness. The following organizations will accept rabbits and work to find them proper new homes:

House Rabbit Society (HRS)
(510) 970-7575
www.rabbit.org

Friends of Rabbits
(703) 627-7892
www.friendsofrabbits.org

**Rabbit Welfare
Association & Fund (RWAF)**
44-08700-465249
www.houserabbit.co.uk

Chapter 4

Housing and Accessories

Just as with humans, moving and adjusting to an unfamiliar environment can be a stressful experience for a pet. When your rabbit arrives at his new home, you should have everything ready so that he has a comfortable and safe place to settle into. If you are still in the process of preparing a permanent spot for your pet, his homecoming will be a miserable and anxious time because he will continually have to adjust to changing situations.

Being able to provide for all his needs and wants upon his arrival will help make him feel secure and more likely to bond with you sooner.

INDOORS OR OUT?

Rabbits can be kept indoors in cages or outside in hutches. Some fanciers are adamant that pet rabbits only be kept indoors as "house rabbits." They believe that the type of bond you form with an animal kept in your home is different from one who is kept outdoors. For example, a house rabbit can be taken out of his cage in the evening after work or school. You can visit with him while relaxing, watching television, or reading a book. When kept inside, he has the opportunity to express his personality in a way not possible when he is kept outdoors. In turn, you will develop a more enjoyable relationship with him because you will spend more time with him.

There are other good reasons to keep your rabbit indoors. He will be safer, and because he is kept in the home as a family member, he is less likely to be neglected. Although an outdoor rabbit is still enjoyable, the time you have to interact with him is limited to daylight hours. Unpleasant weather also reduces the amount of time he can spend playing outside his hutch and limits the opportunities you are likely to have visiting with him. But with a commitment to his care and company, an outdoor rabbit can still be a fun pet.

INDOOR HOUSING AND ACCESSORIES

The type of enclosure you need depends on where your bunny will live. Indoor rabbits are generally kept in cages. This doesn't mean that your bunny should be kept a prisoner, however. He will need to have time out of his enclosure every day to exercise and play. And because his cage will be his home for the greater part of the day, it should be comfortable and spacious enough to give him room to romp about, as well as a place to which he can retire if he is in need of privacy. Luckily, although the cage is the most expensive piece of equipment you will need to buy, it's a one-time expense that should last for the lifetime of your pet.

Cages

Cages are available in many shapes, sizes, and styles. Indoor rabbit cages are usually made of galvanized steel, with a metal or plastic tray at the bottom. Some trays are attractively colored and can be coordinated to match a room's decor. They either slide out or snap off for quick cleaning.

Because rabbits are not natural climbers, a cage that provides maximum floor space

Home Sweet Home

When you first bring home your new rabbit, you might want to keep his cage in a fairly quiet location until he adjusts to his new surroundings. You can then move it to a more active, family-centered location. Alternatively, temporarily covering half of the cage with a cardboard box will increase your rabbit's sense of security and decrease his sense of vulnerability.

rather than vertical height is best. Although they might look spacious and fun, the large two- and three-story cages sold for ferrets are not recommended. However, rabbits do enjoy surveying their domain from an elevated lookout, and some enclosures provide raised platform shelves just for this purpose.

Most manufacturers label their cages for specific kinds of small pets. By choosing a cage designed for rabbits, you can assume that the size of the wire, called the gauge, is suitable and that the spaces between the wire mesh are not too large or too small. The wire mesh that composes the body of the cage should feel strong and durable, not soft and flimsy.

Regardless of what style you choose, a few general guidelines can help you in finding the right home for your pet. You should be able to easily reach into the cage to perform daily tasks such as cleaning the litter box and supplying fresh food. Whether a cage has both a top and front door or a single large front door, at least one of these doors should be big enough for you to comfortably reach all areas within the cage. (And of course, the door should be big enough to easily remove your rabbit!) Make sure that the cage has no sharp metal edges. Doors should latch securely and be stable enough that a persistent rabbit cannot push them out or bend them in at the corners. Because a rabbit's cage is large and can be difficult to move, one or more handles can make transporting it easier.

Never keep your rabbit in a glass or plastic aquarium. This type of housing does not provide sufficient ventilation and can allow heat and ammonia to build up to dangerous levels.

Cage Floor

You will find that rabbit cages come with one of three types of floors: wire mesh, slat, or solid. All three styles of flooring are suitable. However, each provides particular benefits and may require different levels of effort in cleaning and maintenance to keep your rabbit healthy and happy.

A wire floor is the most effective way to assure that the cage stays clean because it allows

The cage you purchase should be large enough to accommodate your rabbit, his nest box, food bowls, water bottle, and toys.

the rabbit's droppings and urine to fall through the mesh. Before litter boxes came into popular use with rabbits, wire was the preferred floor style. Now that litter boxes made for rabbits are commonly available, wire floors are no longer absolutely necessary. However, they are still very useful, especially when first introducing the rabbit to a litter box.

Wire floors have one major drawback: Because rabbits have tender feet, animals housed on exposed wire floors can develop sore feet, a condition called ulcerative pododermatitis. Preventing this condition is relatively simple—you can provide a piece of solid floor that has a large enough area for your rabbit to comfortably sit. A piece of untreated wood or cardboard can be used, but your rabbit will chew these materials. They will need to be replaced occasionally, particularly the cardboard. A piece of tile will help your rabbit stay cool in summer. Some rabbit owners use a piece of carpet or a towel, but these are generally not recommended because a rabbit may chew and swallow fibers, and they are difficult to keep clean.

Cages with a slat bottom were designed to alleviate sore feet and are more comfortable. However, it's still a good idea to provide a piece of solid flooring. The spaces between the slats will allow any excrement to drop below your rabbit's living space.

Solid floor cages provide excellent footing for a rabbit but are unsanitary unless he has a litter box. Rabbits produce a lot of urine and droppings; even regular cleanings are insufficient to keep a solid floor cage healthy unless the rabbit knows how to use a litter box.

Cage Size

Rabbit cages should be at least 3 feet (0.9 m) long, 2 feet (0.6 m) wide, and 18 inches (0.5 m) high. This is the absolute minimum-size enclosure necessary—even a dwarf rabbit needs a cage this large. Larger breeds require even bigger cages. If you purchase a baby rabbit, remember that the cage you get should be sized for an adult rabbit, even though it may seem large when he is young; otherwise, you will need to buy a new cage to accommodate him when he matures. The general rule of thumb is that the cage should be high enough that your rabbit won't bump his head when he stands on his hind legs. If he is a mixed breed and you don't know how large he will get, it is best to play it safe and buy the largest cage you can afford.

Your pet will spend a lot of time in his cage, so try to make it a comfortable, roomy home for him. It should have enough space for a litter box, eating area, and nest box and still provide hopping room. Ideally, your rabbit should be able to move at least three hops along the enclosure's length without running into any cage furniture.

Many people buy a small cage on the assumption that they will regularly allow their rabbit to play outside the cage. This often turns out to be a mistake; lifestyle changes and unanticipated events in life can make it very difficult to devote meaningful time to the pet. An unhappy rabbit is then stuck in a too-small cage. If you buy the biggest cage you can afford, it will be easier to keep clean and there will be a smaller risk of abnormal behavior due to confinement.

Litter Box

Your rabbit's home requires a bathroom called a litter box. Litter boxes made specifically for small animals such as rabbits and ferrets are sold at pet stores. Some are similar in design to those made for cats, and others are triangular in shape and fit into a cage corner. Most are plastic, but some are constructed of metal and wire mesh.

Bigger is Better

Do not buy a small cage on the assumption that your rabbit will always be allowed time outside of it. Lifestyle changes and unanticipated events can temporarily create situations that result in less play time, causing your rabbit to be stuck in an area that is too small. Whether in or out of the cage, daily stimulation and exercise are necessary for his well-being and longevity. In addition, a cage that is too confining will become dirty and smelly more quickly and can lead to abnormal behaviors. So, buy the biggest one you can afford.

Bedding is a critical component of a healthy environment for your rabbit. It is used to absorb moisture, reduce odor, and provide a warm, dry place to rest and sleep.

The litter box you select should be large enough for your adult rabbit to comfortably sit and turn around in. For this reason, corner litter boxes, which tend to be small, work best for dwarf rabbits. Unlike cat litter boxes, small animal litter boxes have a dip in the front wall that makes it easy for a rabbit to enter and leave. If you are unable to find this size and style, you can modify one for cats. If your rabbit kicks the litter out of the box, try using a deeper litter box with higher sides. (For information on how to train your rabbit to use his litter box, see Chapter 9.)

The litter box should be placed at one end of the cage, and the nest box, food dishes, and water bottle should be placed at the other end

Litter

A disposable absorbent material, litter, is needed for the litter box. The most common litter material used for rabbits is wood shavings, typically from pine, aspen, spruce, or pine treated with chlorophyll for odor control. Straw is suitable, although it has low absorbency. Other suitable litter materials include cat litters made from recycled newspaper (most newspaper inks are now vegetable based, not petroleum based, so they are not harmful) or compressed sawdust.

Keep in mind that rabbits will taste and sometimes eat whatever is put in their home, including the litter in their litter box. For this reason, clumping cat litters are not recommended. Purposeful or incidental consumption of this type of litter can lead to a gut impaction and risky, expensive surgery. Experts also disagree on the suitability of clay cat litter due to the risk of dust irritating the respiratory tract. As long as it is dust-free and unscented, it is considered acceptable for use with rabbits. However, it too may cause impaction if ingested. Because other suitable litters are readily available, it is probably best to avoid clay litters altogether.

Corncob litter is sometimes suggested, but because it does not absorb liquids well or control odors, it is not the best choice. Moreover, if you wait more than a few days between cleanings, you might find mold growing on it. Concern over possible gut impaction if ingested is another good reason not to use it.

Some owners use alfalfa pellets. Although they work fine, they are not recommended because they are a familiar food source and your rabbit may be tempted to nibble on them. Adults should always be fed a known quantity of pellets to prevent obesity, and snacking from the litter box can increase your pet's calorie intake.

Litters vary in price, absorbency, and odor control. If you use a less absorbent material such as straw, you should expect to change the litter box at least every day. With more absorbent products, cleanings can often be performed every other day.

Bedding

Bedding is another critical component of a healthy environment for your rabbit. It is used to absorb moisture (from urine as well as water from the occasional leaking bottle), to reduce odor, and to provide a warm, dry place to rest and sleep. Even if you have a litter box, the cage floor should still be covered with some type of bedding. The same litter used in the litter box can be used as bedding on the cage floor.

The ideal bedding is dust-free; too much dust can irritate a rabbit's respiratory system or aggravate an existing respiratory ailment. In general, paper pulp and recycled paper products tend to be lower in dust compared to wood shavings.

Odor control is also a consideration when choosing bedding. Some types naturally contain odor-masking agents such as chlorophyll, which is used in wood shavings. Many manufactured materials now contain additives specifically designed to control or eliminate odor. These specially designed beddings, often made of materials such as recycled paper, do

The Shavings Controversy

Shavings made from softwoods, which include pine and cedar, are still the most common type of bedding for small pets. They are popular because they are relatively inexpensive and are often fragrant smelling, particularly cedar shavings.

The pleasant smell associated with these materials is due to the aromatic compounds found in wood. However, cedar shavings have been implicated as both causing and aggravating respiratory problems in small animals. Few controlled scientific studies have documented these problems; more common are reports that when a pet was removed from cedar shavings, his symptoms of poor health disappeared (such as breathing distress). A few studies have shown that cedar shavings affect liver function in rats and mice, although the effect is so minute it is only of concern to research scientists. Although not all experts agree that cedar shavings pose a risk, it has become common practice to recommend against using them for small pets such as rabbits.

Some hobbyists also argue that pine shavings are harmful. However, there is no scientific evidence supporting this assumption. Research facilities across the country still house small animals on pine shavings. If there were any detrimental effects, scientists would be the first to switch beddings because they cannot afford to have their research animals harmed.

If you wish to avoid the issue completely, you can use shavings made from hardwoods such as aspen and spruce. However, they tend to be more expensive than pine and are not available throughout the country.

not just mask odor but are designed to reduce it by controlling the formation of ammonia. Such beddings promote a much healthier environment for small pets.

If you have a wire floor in your rabbit cage, only a thin layer of bedding is necessary in the tray underneath the cage floor, just enough to absorb any accidents. Alternatively, the tray can be lined with newspaper, but this will do little for odor control. If your rabbit is housed directly on the cage floor, place enough bedding on it to cover the surface and provide traction. The sides of the plastic tray should be high enough to prevent your rabbit from kicking any bedding out.

Nest Box

Rabbits use a nest box for sleeping and security. You may not have seen a nest box in the enclosures at the pet store; they are often not provided to allow you to see the animals at all times. Because a rabbit is likely to be in the pet store for a brief time, no harm is done. In his new home, however, a nest box is essential. It gives your rabbit a safe hiding place to which he can retreat from loud noises or disturbing activity outside his cage. Try not to pull your rabbit out of his nest box unless absolutely necessary. Instead, call him and let him come out on his own terms. His nest box is his refuge.

This "hideaway" should be large enough for your rabbit to comfortably stretch out in, with an opening that allows easy entry. You can purchase one made of metal, wood, or plastic. The metal ones are the most durable, but metal also tends to stay cold when it is cold and warm when it is warm. Unless the nest box is lined with wire mesh, your rabbit will chew it. However, chewing wood helps keep teeth trim and should not be discouraged. A chewed, unlined wood box will just need to be replaced more often. It is also best to remove a plastic nest box if your pet chews on it to reduce the risk of indigestible pieces being swallowed. Any commercially made nest box should have a large opening for easy cleaning. You can also make a nest box from a cardboard box. Once the box becomes chewed or smelly, you will need to replace it. Place comfortable nesting material such as straw or pine shavings in it.

Feed Containers

Your rabbit will need two dishes for food and a rack for hay. One dish will hold dry foods, while the other should only be used for moist foods. Rabbits will play with everything in their cage, so choose sturdy ceramic or heavy-duty, durable plastic dishes that can't be easily tipped over. Unless they clip to the side of the cage, a rabbit can easily move a lightweight dish and strew the contents all over the floor. Some may chew plastic dishes; if this is the case with your rabbit, switch to a ceramic dish.

Your rabbit will need two dishes for his food, one for dry foods and another for moist foods. Choose heavyweight dishes that won't tip over.

Dry foods can also be served in a hopper (typically J-shaped) that clips securely to the cage. Hoppers hold large quantities of food and work best for rabbits fed unlimited quantities, such as babies. Adult rabbits, whose food intake must be closely monitored, should not be fed by loading a large hopper whenever the food runs out. Be aware that your rabbit might defecate in his food bowl. This is nothing to be concerned about, but you can prevent this behavior by using a dish in which your rabbit cannot sit.

Place a daily ration of hay in a hay rack attached to the side of the cage. The rack's height can be slightly above ground level or as high as your rabbit can stand. You can also place hay on the cage floor, but some will be wasted because your rabbit will trample it and might defecate on it. Burrowing and playing in hay seems to be a pleasurable experience for rabbits, so consider placing some on the floor if you have an inexpensive source of quality hay.

Water Bottle

Your rabbit must always have clean water available. Gravity-flow water bottles commonly sold in pet stores work best. The sipper tube should be placed at a comfortable height for your rabbit, typically a bit higher than his head. Do not place the water bottle over a food dish in case of accidental leakage. To prevent leaks, the tip of the bottle should not touch the cage bedding or any cage furniture.

Buy the largest bottle specifically made for rabbits. Choose one with hatch marks (or make your own with an indelible marker) to help you monitor intake because water is essential to your rabbit's good health. Ideally, you should empty and refill the bottle every day, although most owners fill it every other day.

Toys

While in their cages, rabbits require some form of entertainment or they become bored and depressed. Toys give them something to do and keep them content, which will make them more enjoyable pets in the long run.

Rabbits enjoy playing with almost anything put in their cage. Because their play can

Water Bottle Versus Bowls

Don't give your rabbit water in a bowl, not even in a heavy clay crock that won't tip. His normal daily activities will quickly cause it to become dirty. Cage bedding and rabbit droppings will also foul the water. When your rabbit hops around, water will splash out of the bowl, creating a moist environment in which bacteria and mold can thrive. Moreover, rabbits with dewlaps (the large fold of skin beneath the chin) tend to get them wet when they drink. This continual wetting can lead to moist dermatitis and bacterial infection.

involve chewing and often the destruction of toys, offer only safe items. A hard block of wood, cardboard tunnels, pine cones, and cardboard boxes are good choices. Shredding a pile of newspapers or chewing apart an old telephone book can also provide entertainment. Just be sure that the covers have been removed and that the pages are not covered with a glossy coating.

Many wooden toys made for large parrots are also suitable. Wood chews keep rabbits busy and active. They also provide a hard surface to gnaw, which helps keep teeth in good shape. Tree branches from alder, willow, maple, ash, and apple are also safe if they haven't been treated with chemicals of any kind.

Roll-about balls made for hamsters and larger pets such as ferrets are not recommended. Most rabbits are too large for these toys and become stressed or even panicked if left in a confined space with them. Moreover, their natural gait is a hop, which is incompatible with these balls.

To maintain your rabbit's interest, provide him with a variety of toys; he'll have more fun, and he will be more fun to watch. However, don't overcrowd the cage because he needs to have enough room to move about freely. You can offer variety in his playthings while keeping the cage uncluttered by alternating them regularly, a trick that dog and cat owners use. By switching toys frequently, your rabbit will stay active and interested in exploring his environment. Regular activity will also help keep him physically fit.

Indoor Exercise Pen

Because your rabbit needs exercise and play outside his cage to stay healthy, it's a good idea to give him roaming privileges in one room of your house. (Of course, make sure that it is rabbit-proofed.) If this isn't possible, you can provide out-of-cage time in an indoor exercise pen. Portable pens that fold away for easy storage are sold at many pet stores.

Why Rabbits Need Toys

Rabbits have curious personalities; they love to check things out. Although they may be content to sit quietly during the day, they naturally become more active at dawn and dusk. Although rabbits in the wild forage for food and nesting materials, house rabbits don't have those needs and so enjoy having something to do. If you do not provide your pet rabbit with toys, he is likely to pick his own.

Free Toys

I save empty oatmeal boxes (the round ones) for my young rabbits who are just graduating from their nest box. They give them a place to huddle and snuggle while they are getting used to life outside the nest. But I often find that Mom plays with the boxes more than the youngsters do. Any type of cardboard box makes a great toy for rabbits. Small boxes may be tossed around, while larger ones can be explored.

I have seen breeders stuff empty toilet paper rolls with hay, partly to keep the hay neat and partly to give their rabbits an activity. Their rabbits really seem to enjoy it. I just give my rabbits the roll. It's not a permanent toy, but they have a lot of fun with it.

Limbs from fruit trees that have not been chemically treated may provide a pleasant diversion as chew toys and can help rabbits wear down their teeth at the same time. Collect some limbs during your next pruning.

You can also grow an edible garden for your pet by planting a small amount of grass, wheat, or herbs in a shallow container. If you plant one every month, he can have an occasional back-to-nature nibble whenever the mood strikes. Although this idea is not exactly free, it's close.

Borrowed Toys

Items that you may already own can often make good rabbit toys. For example, very hard plastic baby teethers are great as chew toys. I use a tough plastic alphabet toy for my rabbits. Stay away from the water-filled beads, though—a rabbit's teeth are sharper and longer than a baby's teeth.

Cat toys with a disc on either end held together with a series of spindles, rather like a little cage, provide lots of fun. The spindles are the perfect size for a rabbit's mouth. They love to lift them and throw them or put them inside other objects (their bowl, for instance). Many have a bell on the inside, so they must be made of a sturdy plastic to prevent a rabbit from chewing through and swallowing it.

Hard cat or dog balls also make wonderful rabbit toys, but avoid those that break or shred easily, and pick a size that your rabbit can handle without difficulty. Also avoid thin plastic balls with bells inside. A rabbit can break them and possibly ingest a small piece. Rubbery squeaky toys are not sturdy enough for a rabbit either. Avoid fabric-covered toys for the same reasons.

Rabbit Toys You Can Purchase

I especially like rabbit toys that are made of safe wood and are meant to be chewed. Toys like this won't last forever, but your pet rabbit will have a really good time with them while they last.

One of my rabbits' favorite store-bought playthings is made of wood sticks. Inside is a walnut. If the rabbit can figure out how to remove the sticks (or just nibble through them) and disassemble the nibbler, he can reach the nut inside. It comes in two sizes. The smaller version fits in the palm of your hand, and the larger one fits in your entire hand.

Storing Your Rabbit Toy Collection

Once you have gathered your free, borrowed, and purchased rabbit toys, keep them in a basket in or near your rabbit's cage or play space. Rotate the toys from time to time to keep his interest high.

You can either use a pen made exclusively for small animals or the variety sold for dogs or puppies. Just make sure that the space between the bars is not so large that your rabbit can escape. The pen should be 3 feet (0.9 m) high for small breeds and 4 feet (1.2 m) high for large breeds to prevent escape by jumping.

Placing a tarp under the pen will protect the floor from accidents or from destructive behavior such as scratching and digging. Provide toys and a litter box, and change them frequently. Your rabbit can play while you do chores or schoolwork. Keep in mind that a rabbit will eventually become bored and less active in an unchanging environment, so move the pen around a little if possible. Many are large enough for you to get inside.

If you have a backyard lawn, a portable grazing run provides an enjoyable means for your house rabbit to exercise and graze on fresh grass during nice weather.

Portable Grazing Runs

If you have a backyard lawn, a portable grazing run provides an enjoyable means for your rabbit to exercise and graze on fresh grass during nice weather. Most are lightweight and can be moved each day to a new grazing area. Never let your rabbit graze on a lawn that has been treated with pesticides or weed killers. Also, a portion of the run must remain in the shade during the time your rabbit is outside. Because of sensitivity to hot weather, only place him outside when temperatures have cooled below 85°F (29.4°C).

For security, most rabbits appreciate a nest box in their run. Rather than taking the nest box out of your rabbit's inside cage, a cardboard box can be used outdoors. To prevent a gut ache from eating too much grass, only allow your rabbit a 10- to 15-minute outing per day. If he does not develop diarrhea, slowly increase the amount of time he spends in his run. Because being outdoors is new and potentially scary, stay close by and visit with him until he is relaxed and comfortable in his new surroundings. Although it's never a good idea to leave your pet unsupervised, you must be certain that he is safe from any other pets you have and from any neighborhood animals who can gain access to your yard if you must leave him unattended in a run.

No commercial manufacturers of grazing runs exist, so you must construct one yourself. Sometimes called a grazing ark, the run consists of a lightweight wood frame covered with a heavy wire mesh with spaces no larger than 1/2 inch x 2 inches (1.3 cm x 5.1 cm). You can make the run with four sides and a top or with four sides, a top, a bottom, and a large door with a latch. The first type is not as secure because it must be pegged down so that a rabbit cannot tip it over, and without a wire mesh bottom, a rabbit can burrow and potentially escape. It's also not compatible with a perfect lawn, as a rabbit may dig a shallow scrape in which to stay cool and rest. A wire mesh floor can prevent these potential problems.

Placing the Indoor Cage

A rabbit's cage is relatively large, so deciding where to keep it takes some thought. To begin with, do not place it near a heating or air-conditioning vent, fireplace, wood stove, drafty window, or door that is constantly opened and closed. Also, don't put it in direct sunlight. Remember that the sun shifts position throughout the year. Rabbits are very sensitive to high heat, and temperatures above the upper 80s°F (30° to 32°C) can lead to heatstroke. Comfortable temperatures for a rabbit correspond to those found in most homes, between 59° and 72°F (15° and 22.2°C).

The floor is not an ideal location for the cage because it can be too drafty in winter. You can place it on a small table or on cinder blocks (sold at lumber stores) covered with an attractive fabric. Use the space underneath them for storing supplies. Keeping the cage somewhat low to the ground will enable your rabbit to easily exit and enter the cage via the door, which acts as a ramp, when he is allowed outside play. Until your rabbit has been safely introduced to other family pets (see Chapter 8), his cage should be placed out of their eye-level view. He will not enjoy a salivating dog or a staring cat outside or on top of his refuge.

Do not keep your rabbit in the basement or garage. Not only is the garage unhealthy from any automobile exhaust, but both locations are likely to have more extreme and variable temperatures, as well as less suitable lighting. Most importantly, your bunny is likely to be neglected.

Your rabbit should be part of your family, and his cage should be placed in a location where everyone can enjoy him. Even if he belongs to a child, a family room is often the best location. A bedroom is often not suitable because nighttime feeding noises and hind foot thumping can disturb sleep. Children thrive on attention, and sharing discoveries of their pet's antics with other family members will encourage their long-

Be sure that outdoor housing is secure and that it provides adequate protection from weather extremes.

term interest. Rabbits are also social creatures and can adapt to a family's activities. However, find a balance between your rabbit languishing in a quiet room and being subjected to too much boisterous activity.

OUTDOOR HOUSING

People who live in temperate climates sometimes prefer to keep their rabbits outdoors. If your rabbit is not going to be kept in your home, he must be housed in a safe and appropriate enclosure such as a hutch.

Hutches

Hutches cost considerably more than indoor cages. Commercially made hutches constructed of either wood and wire mesh or metal and wire mesh are commonly sold at pet and feed stores. No matter what materials they are constructed with, from functional metal to fancy wood that resembles a log cabin, high-quality hutches should share certain necessary design features.

All types should have wire mesh floors that allow droppings to fall out of the enclosure. However, the mesh must not be so large that a rabbit's foot can fall through or so large that a nimble-handed predator such as a raccoon can reach inside. A common mesh size is 1/2 inch x 1 inch (1.3 cm x 2.5 cm). As with an indoor cage, a rabbit housed on a wire floor must be provided with a section of solid floor.

Both wood and metal hutches each have advantages and disadvantages. Those constructed of wood can be difficult to keep clean because they tend to absorb urine and other odors. If washed with water, the wood can swell and split. Plenty of time must be allowed for it to dry before returning your rabbit to his home. The interior should be covered with a wire mesh to prevent gnawing. On the other hand, metal hutches can be lightweight and easy to clean. However, the metal retains heat during hot weather and cold during cold weather.

The minimum-size hutch to buy is based on the animal's size as follows: 1 square foot per 1 pound (0.3 sq m per 0.5 kg) of rabbit. Thus, for example, a 5-pound (2.3-kg) rabbit will require a minimum of 5 square feet (1.5 square m) of space. However, providing the largest-size hutch you can afford is always best. Remember, it must have room for food dishes, water bottles, toys, and a nest box and still allow your rabbit to move around. If you have two rabbits, double the minimum cage size.

Weatherproofing

A reliable hutch should be weatherproof, with three solid walls and a wire mesh front. It should have a waterproof sloping roof that sheds water and overhangs sufficiently to protect the sides of the structure. Besides a front door, it should also have a top door, which greatly eases access for cleaning and other needs. A hutch should sit above the ground, which will help it stay warmer in the winter and cooler in the summer. Tall hutches are thought to provide the best protection from potential predators and animals who could harass your rabbit; however, it should still be low enough that you can easily access it through the top opening.

A nest box is essential in an outdoor enclosure. It provides your rabbit with protection from uncomfortable weather and security when threatened. Most hutches have a nest box built onto one end. However, if the model you buy doesn't have one, you must provide it. In summer, it must be well ventilated to protect your rabbit from heat stress.

Outdoor enclosures must protect your animal from wind, rain, snow, sun, heat, and high humidity. A well-designed hutch can only perform these functions if it is properly located. It helps to know the pattern of sun, shade, and wind in your yard so that you can select a good site. Although a hutch can be moved at a later time, this can be a cumbersome process. Most importantly, it should be shaded and protected from direct sunlight, although an hour of morning or late afternoon sun is not harmful in temperate climates.

Rabbits tolerate cold better than heat and can acclimate to colder weather over time. However, in climates with days of freezing temperatures, the hutch might need to be moved inside a shed or building. If this is not possible, you must provide a heater. This is especially necessary with dwarf and small breeds less than 5 pounds (2.3 kg) because they are not hardy enough to be housed outdoors during cold weather without heat.

A heat source is also necessary so that drinking water remains unfrozen. Because most heat sources require an electrical outlet, the hutch must be situated accordingly.

Conversely, temperatures above 85°F (29.4°C), especially in conjunction with high humidity, can lead to heat stress. In such climates, you might need to modify a hutch to increase airflow. For example, a small battery-operated fan can circulate air inside the enclosure. You can also place a frozen bottle of water inside the hutch each day until the weather cools.

Additional hutch modifications for temperature control include heavy canvas tarps in winter and cooling shade cloths in summer.

Location

An additional consideration is that the hutch should be located where it will be easy for you to regularly interact with your rabbit. Ideally, you should be able to see your pet from your house. Do not place the hutch in an out-of-the-way part of the yard where your rabbit will be more isolated and the chances for neglect are increased. At the same time, it should not be situated in a location that is excessively noisy.

Outdoor Rabbits

The best time of year to purchase an outside rabbit is when you have the most time to play with him and the weather encourages outdoor activity. Because rabbits kept outside have less social interaction, strongly consider purchasing two at the same time to keep each other company. Remember, a rabbit who is neglected and lonely will become shy and fearful. Also, regardless of how fancy the hutch or cage may be, take every precaution to be sure that it is predator- and escape-proof.

An outdoor hutch should be located where it will be easy for you to regularly interact with your rabbits.

Safety

Purchasing a large, well-constructed hutch is of the utmost importance. Do not buy one constructed with chicken wire because it is too flimsy to keep your rabbit secure from potential predators. Many outdoor pet rabbits are killed by other family pets, such as a dog with a high prey drive who shares the backyard with a rabbit during the day and has plenty of time to figure out how to get him.

It is important to remember that rabbits are prey animals, so they must be protected from urban-adapted wildlife such as coyotes and raccoons. If you live in an area commonly visited by these animals, buy a tall hutch. This will help keep predators from staring into the enclosure, an action that can literally kill a rabbit over time. To prevent stalking animals from jumping onto the hutch, don't place it next to a fence or under a tree. Even if he can't directly see predators, a rabbit can usually tell if one is nearby using his keen sense of hearing and smell. A frightened rabbit can panic and hurt himself while frantically leaping about, so don't keep him outside where this situation is common.

CAGE/HUTCH MAINTENANCE

No matter how much a rabbit grooms, he cannot keep himself clean if his cage or hutch is dirty. Rabbits themselves have no offensive odors; however, their enclosure will smell if it is not cleaned often enough. Although most droppings do not smell bad, urine can develop a pungent odor. Bedding products designed to control or eliminate odor can be used to minimize this. However, no odor-control product will keep the cage from smelling if it is not cleaned often enough.

The ammonia vapors that develop in your pet's cage from accumulating urine can make owning a rabbit less pleasant. This harsh smell is also uncomfortable for your rabbit because ammonia is a severe irritant that can be detrimental to his health. It affects the mucous membranes of the eyes and respiratory tract. High levels can lead to a respiratory infection and may make your rabbit more susceptible to other opportunistic infections.

A rabbit housed on dirty, moist bedding, even for a day, is vulnerable to a number of problems. If you can smell your rabbit's cage, it is an unhealthy environment. You can prevent the cleaning task from becoming overwhelming by maintaining a consistent cleaning schedule. Always have fresh bedding available so that you do not postpone cleaning and expose your rabbit to improper conditions.

No matter how much a rabbit grooms, he cannot keep himself clean if his cage or hutch is dirty.

Cage Maintenance Schedule

Daily or Alternate Days

Empty the litter box daily or every other day. Using a kitty litter scoop, remove any droppings or urine-soaked bedding. Wash the dishes every few days; most can be safely cleaned in a dishwasher. Dishes that hold moist foods should be frequently washed to prevent the growth of mold and bacteria. Replace any that are cracked or chipped. Purchasing a second set can make cleaning easier because you can provide food in clean receptacles while others are being washed.

Weekly

Completely change the bedding on the cage floor and in the litter box. If the cage has a solid floor, you might need to change the bedding more frequently if your rabbit does not consistently use his litter box. Wash and dry the litter box. For hutches, use a shovel or dog pooper-scooper to remove droppings. At least once a week, use a narrow flexible brush to clean the slimy film that develops inside water bottles. Check that sipper tubes are not clogged with bedding or food.

Monthly

Once a month, do a thorough cleaning. Use a vacuum to remove any hairs that are stuck to the cage wires. If necessary, disinfect the cage and the surrounding area. Pet stores sell mild cleansers that are safe for animals. Wash inside the cage with warm, soapy water. Be sure to rinse and dry it thoroughly. Wash the water bottle, food dish, and any plastic toys. Wood toys can eventually splinter if washed in water; scraping grime off of them with a file is effective. Scrape or file off any grime that might have accumulated on the bars of a wire cage. Replace the nest box if needed.

Chapter 5

Diet and Nutrition

With your rabbit's basic housing needs taken care of, it's time to discuss his diet. As his caretaker, you are responsible for providing him with a balanced diet of good-quality food. This means making sure that he eats the best food possible and receives all the vitamins and minerals necessary to live a long and healthy life.

Rabbits need a balanced, varied diet to stay healthy.

DIET EVOLUTION

Pelleted rabbit food was first invented in the 1930s. Prior to that time, rabbit keepers fed loose hay supplemented with grain as well as seasonal greens that they picked. The pellets were made with alfalfa and a combination of grains in various formulas that varied in protein and fat content. It took a while for feed manufacturers to find a pellet size that rabbits preferred and one that could be consumed and result in the least amount of waste. The pellets needed to be hard and smooth with very little flaking and dust because rabbits would not eat the small "fines" if the pellets crumbled.

This original diet of alfalfa pellets was designed to safely and conveniently put weight on rabbits raised for meat and fur. The longevity of these rabbits was not a concern for commercial rabbit ranchers, but a long and healthy life is of course something pet owners desire for their animals. Because of potential health problems tied to diet, many authorities concluded that alfalfa pellets were not the best food for pet rabbits. However, manufacturers responded by developing different pellet formulas made specifically for them. Consequently, there are now a variety of packaged foods with different amounts of nutrients available. These reformulated pellets are made from different grasses that are lower in protein and fat compared to alfalfa pellets.

Although there are now more choices, no unanimous agreement exists among veterinarians, breeders, hobbyists, and rescue groups as to the best diet for pet rabbits. Nonetheless, with some caveats, you can typically purchase a bag of nutritionally dense rabbit pellets, feed them according to the directions, and your rabbit should be fine. It is also important to include hay and fresh vegetables to provide a fully balanced diet, which is discussed later in more detail.

BASIC NUTRITION

Good nutrition is a key factor in promoting a long and healthy life for your rabbit. A balanced diet includes the appropriate amounts of protein, carbohydrates, fat, vitamins, and minerals. All these nutrients interact in the growth, maintenance, and functioning of an animal's body.

Protein

Protein is needed for functions such as the growth and maintenance of muscle and the production of antibodies, hormones, and enzymes. The amount of protein that your pet requires is influenced by a number of physiological factors, mainly age and reproductive status. For example, rabbits older than six months need less protein than when they are in their most active growth period as newborns, and pregnant or nursing rabbits require increased protein.

Carbohydrates

Carbohydrates perform numerous functions, such as providing energy. Concentrated sources of carbohydrates include grains like oats and corn.

Fat

Fat is also a concentrated source of energy that provides twice as many calories per serving as protein or carbohydrates. It makes up part of the structure of every cell and is necessary for the absorption of fat-soluble vitamins, such as vitamins A and D. As a source of essential fatty acids, it helps provide your rabbit with a healthy coat and skin. A deficiency of fat can show up as scaly skin or rough, thin hair.

Vitamins

Vitamins are necessary as catalysts for chemical reactions in the body. They are important in preventing diseases and in regulating functions such as growth and blood clotting. They are classified as water soluble or as fat soluble.

Minerals

Minerals, which include calcium, phosphorous, sodium, and other chemical elements, are important in many body functions, such as the development of bones and teeth, muscle and nerve function, and proper water balance. A deficiency or excess can lead to serious medical problems. Trace elements, which include cobalt, copper, iodine, iron, manganese, selenium, and zinc, are also necessary nutrients but only in very small amounts. Trace elements perform many functions, such as the role of iron bringing oxygen to the body.

FIBER AND DIGESTION

Fiber is an important part of a rabbit's daily diet and is essential for normal digestion. Also called roughage, it is the indigestible part of plants. Fiber is needed to stimulate the gastrointestinal tract and to promote the movement of food so that digestion can occur. Without sufficient fiber, the movement of food through the digestive tract can slow or stop. This can lead to potentially life-threatening intestinal disease.

Rabbits are hindgut fermenters. They digest much of their food in the cecum, which is a sac about ten times larger than their stomach. The cecum is located at the juncture of the

Supplements not Necessary

A diet containing pellets, unlimited amounts of hay, and a variety of fresh vegetables provides all the vitamins and minerals your rabbit needs. He will also obtain vitamins from ingestion of cecal pellets. Unless your veterinarian recommends a vitamin and mineral supplement for a specific condition, most pet rabbits do not require supplements.

small intestine and large intestine, which is the same location as a person's appendix. At this juncture, most of the semi-digested food passes into the cecum, while the indigestible fiber moves into the large intestine, also called the colon. Water is absorbed from the material in the colon, and then the remaining matter is expelled about four to five hours later as round, hard droppings.

Meanwhile, in the cecum, bacteria and protozoa ferment digestible fiber and other parts of the food into proteins, essential fatty acids, B-complex vitamins, and vitamin K. The contents of the cecum are then excreted about eight to nine hours later in the form of nutrient-rich cecotropes, which look like tiny clusters of peas. Sometimes called night feces, rabbits eat the soft cecotropes directly from the anus, so normally you will never see them. Although this seems gross, digesting the food a second time allows the rabbit to obtain the most nutrition from it. Fiber is necessary for beneficial bacteria and protozoa, called microflora, to function properly.

Fiber is also abrasive, and a rabbit must grind it into small pieces before swallowing it. Because the fiber is rough, it helps maintain normal wear in his constantly growing teeth.

WHAT TO FEED

Feed your rabbit a combination of dry and moist foods. Dry foods include pellets, hay, and grains such as barley and oats. Pet and feed stores sell various types of dry packaged food for rabbits. Moist foods include fresh vegetables, fruits, and any plants your pet eats when you allow him outside in a grazing run. You can buy moist food while shopping in grocery stores.

DRY FOOD

Dry foods are a necessary element of your rabbit's daily diet. Commercial pellets should be a staple food, and a daily supply of loose, fresh hay is also needed.

Pellets

Pellets are convenient to feed and nutritionally balanced, and their hardness helps keep teeth trim. Currently, pellets are based on either alfalfa or timothy hay. Those made mostly with alfalfa are typically higher in protein than pellets made with timothy hay. Other ingredients, such as grains, can increase the protein level.

Some pellet mixes are sold as gourmet blends that include other ingredients, such as whole grains, kibble, and dried fruits and vegetables. The ingredients are balanced so that a rabbit cannot eat an excess of any item, such as oats or dried bananas. However, if he picks

Feed your rabbit a combination of moist and dry foods, including large amounts of hay.

out the tasty tidbits, leaves the hay pellets, and waits for you to refill his bowl, he is likely to end up with a poorly balanced diet and serious health problems. For this reason, some veterinarians and breeders recommend against feeding gourmet mixes. If you choose to feed a fancy food, you must exercise prudence and restraint.

Adult pet rabbits can be fed a pellet that ranges from 13 to 16 percent crude protein. Growing rabbits and pregnant and lactating does can be fed higher-protein pellets, up to 18 percent. However, once a young rabbit is grown, between 5 and 12 months and depending on the breed, he should be switched to a lower-protein pellet. Likewise, a doe should also be switched to lower-protein pellets after her young are weaned. When changing to a different type of pellet, gradually mix the new food in with the old. A complete change in food can usually be made over one week.

Don't buy pellet foods that are higher than 18 percent protein. Such pellets, sometimes labeled performance foods, are more appropriate for achieving maximum growth and weight gain in rabbits who are raised for meat and fur. Whatever brand you select, a good general rule is that the fiber level should always be higher than the protein level. Depending on the ingredients and how finely the hay in the food source is ground, different brands of pellets have different amounts of fiber. Your rabbit's pellet food should have a fiber level of at least 15 percent or be between 15 and 17 percent. Pellets with a higher fiber content (18 and 22 percent) can help prevent obesity. Do not choose a pellet diet that has a fat content higher than 5 percent. Ideally, fat levels should be 3 percent or less. Nuts, grains, and seeds can contribute to the fat content. A high fat content can contribute to unhealthy weight gain.

All these percentages can seem overwhelming. However, there are specific times you should pay attention to these percentages: when feeding a growing rabbit, when switching a rabbit to an adult diet, and when your veterinarian suggests a specific diet.

Reading Packaged Food Labels

Reading the nutritional analysis for pelleted foods can seem unnecessarily complex compared to simply purchasing a bag of pellets from a convenient source and feeding them to your pet. However, providing the appropriate food can help prevent and manage some health problems that afflict pet rabbits. For example, the incidence of obesity, diarrhea, and hairballs can be reduced in pet rabbits who are fed a high-fiber (at least 17 percent) and low-protein diet (12 to 14 percent).

Most commercial foods such as pellets are formulated to be nutritionally complete. Packaged rabbit foods may consist solely of hay, such as alfalfa or timothy, or they can be a pellet mix made with hay, grains, and added vitamins and minerals. The items that compose a food are stated in the ingredient list and are listed in descending order by weight. The first three to five items on an ingredient list make up most of the food.

On every bag of rabbit food is a guaranteed analysis that gives the percentage of nutrients, such as protein, fat, fiber, and calcium, as well as fiber and moisture. The protein and fat contents are usually listed as minimums, while the amounts of fiber and calcium are typically given as both minimums and maximums. The word "crude," which precedes each measure, refers to laboratory analysis rather than digestibility. Even commercial treats sold at pet stores provide basic nutritional information on protein, fat, fiber, and moisture content. Reading labels can help you ensure that your rabbit receives optimal nutrition.

Hay

The fiber found in pellets is often not sufficient, so you must supplement them with loose hay. Hay provides essential fiber, which helps prevent potentially life-threatening

Water Guzzlers

Rabbits drink a lot of water, between 1½ to 4½ ounces (44.4 to 133.1 ml) of water per 2½ pounds (1.1 kg) of body weight each day. A rabbit who weighs 4½ pounds (2 kg) drinks as much water as a dog who weighs 22 pounds (10 kg)! You don't want your pet to run out of water. A rabbit can survive several weeks without food, but a day without water can cause dehydration. Within four to eight days, a rabbit will lose 20 to 30 percent of his body weight and will die. Many water bottles are sold with milliliter or ounce markings on them. (There are approximately 29.5 milliliters in 1 ounce.) You can use these marks to monitor your rabbit's water consumption.

The amount of water a rabbit drinks each day depends on the type of food he eats. For example, a rabbit fed a diet high in fiber or protein needs more water than one fed a low-fiber or protein diet. A rabbit primarily fed a diet of fresh vegetables, which naturally have a high water content, will drink less water than one fed a diet of pellets.

gastrointestinal problems. It also provides your rabbit with something to do. Some rabbits kept for long periods in their cage become so bored that they develop the bad habit of chewing their own fur.

Most large pet stores sell a variety of types in convenient packages. If loose hay is unavailable, cubed hay is better than none at all. Feed stores also sell it, but you will need to buy it by the bale. Although it is cheaper, you need a dry place to store it. A bale of hay is quite large, usually 4 feet (1.2 m) long by almost 2 feet (0.6 m) high and 2 feet (0.6 m) wide. The bale must be placed on a wooden pallet to allow air circulation and to prevent mold from growing on the bottom portion. Do not feed hay that is wet or moldy.

There are two types of hay: grass and legume. Grass hay includes orchard grass, oat hay, timothy, and mixed grass. Legume hay includes alfalfa and clover. Young, growing rabbits, pregnant and nursing does, and outdoor rabbits can be fed alfalfa hay. But adult house rabbits kept inside do not need the higher amounts of protein, calories, and calcium found in alfalfa and should be fed a grass hay. Rabbits much prefer the tastier leaves and stems of alfalfa hay compared to grass hay, so slightly reducing the amount of pellets can encourage a rabbit to eat grass hay, as can offering different types of grass hay.

MOIST FOODS

Fresh vegetables and fruits make up most of the moist foods that house rabbits eat.

Vegetables

Rabbits love vegetables, and fresh foods provide important variety and nutrients in their diet. Eating is their favorite pastime, and munching on veggies is good for them; it can relieve boredom while providing something healthy to do while they are in their cage. Because of the risk of digestive problems, however, don't feed a growing rabbit vegetables until he is an adult.

In general, choose dark leafy vegetables, root vegetables, and dark yellow vegetables. Healthy vegetables for your rabbit include the following:

- alfalfa, radish, and clover sprouts
- beet greens
- bell peppers
- bok choy
- broccoli, including leaves and stems
- brussels sprouts
- carrots and carrot tops
- celery, including the leaves
- chard
- collard
- fennel
- kale
- radish greens
- watercress

Rabbits also enjoy salad greens, including endive, escarole, radicchio, spinach, and romaine lettuce. But skip the iceberg lettuce because it is mostly water and provides little nutrition or fiber. Fresh herbs such as basil, cilantro, mint, parsley, and peppermint are also relished by rabbits. Herbs can be expensive to buy in a grocery store, but they are relatively easy to grow in small pots that you can place in or near their cage.

Ideally, you should provide fresh vegetables every day,

Pellets provide basic nutrition but must be supplemented with other healthy foods, such as fruits and vegetables.

Certain vegetables, such as cabbage, can cause digestive upset in some rabbits. To prevent problems, offer only one type of vegetable at a time and wait several days before adding other kinds.

but offering them several times a week is better than not at all. You can feed up to 1 cup (16 oz/454 g) of vegetables for each 4 pounds (1.8 kg) of your rabbit's weight. For example, a 2-pound (0.9-kg) rabbit can be fed 1/2 cup (8 oz/227 g) of vegetables, while an 8-pound (4-kg) rabbit can be fed 2 cups (32 oz/908 kg). A container of prewashed, cut vegetables stored in the refrigerator can make feeding your rabbit veggies easier when life gets hectic. Bags of precut veggies are sold at most grocery stores, or you can make your own mix.

Some pet owners are diligent about feeding their rabbits vegetables every day, but more typically, owners feed vegetables intermittently. If you are reintroducing vegetables after a hiatus or feeding a new type of vegetable, always start with a small amount. Feed no more than 1 tablespoon (15 ml), which is a safe portion for an adult. Feeding a large amount can cause acute diarrhea. You can gradually increase the amount over a period of a week as long as your rabbit does not develop intestinal distress.

To prevent problems, offer only one type of vegetable at a time and wait several days before adding other kinds. This way, you will know if a particular vegetable causes digestive issues. If a vegetable causes soft stools or diarrhea, do not feed it to your rabbit again. Certain vegetables, such as cabbage, spinach, cauliflower, and broccoli, can cause digestive upset in some rabbits, while other rabbits will be perfectly fine.

Most rabbits quickly eat offered vegetables. However, it is important to remove any uneaten moist foods after a few hours. Moist food left in the cage can become putrid, and bacteria and mold can grow on it, which could make your pet sick.

Vegetables to Avoid

There are some vegetables you should not feed your rabbit. Even if he seems to eat these vegetables without noticeable problems, it is still best not to include them in his diet because they are known to cause gastrointestinal upset or intestinal stasis, and it is possible that he may react to them at another time. Any kind of bean, green beans, corn, peas, and potatoes are too high in sugar and starch for rabbits. Other vegetables that should not be fed include cucumbers, eggplant, red beets, rhubarb, tomatoes, and zucchini.

Fruit

Rabbits love fresh fruits even more than they love vegetables. They can safely eat just about any kind, including kiwis, peaches, and watermelon. High-fiber fruits are best. These include:

- apples
- blackberries
- blueberries
- melons
- papayas
- peaches
- pears
- pineapples
- plums
- raspberries
- strawberries

Unhealthy Foods

Some of the pet rabbit's biggest potential health problems have to do with digestive disorders caused by an improper diet. Although it can be fun to offer new types of food and see if your pet enjoys them, many are highly unsuitable. Even though they're herbivorous, rabbits won't eat just apples and carrots but will happily munch pizza crusts, crackers, and other human foods. They also have a powerful sweet tooth and will gladly eat chocolate, cookies, and other items that are downright bad for them. All these foods are very unhealthy, and your rabbit should not be allowed to eat them. Other unhealthy foods include the kibble in a dog or cat's dish, both of which are too high in protein for rabbits.

Keep in mind that fruits can be expensive, especially when they are not in season. Relatively inexpensive fruits, such as bananas, grapes, and oranges, are other suitable options. Small amounts of dried fruits, including banana chips and raisins, can also be offered.

To maintain your pet's trim figure, don't overfeed sugary fruits because they can contribute to excess weight. For rabbits weighing less than 5 pounds (2.3 kg), feed no more than 1 tablespoon (15 ml) a day. Larger rabbits can be fed up to 2 tablespoons (30 ml) a day. One tablespoon (15 ml) is not very much. It is worth taking out your measuring spoons every so often to remind yourself of the appropriate portion size. Too much fruit can lead to digestive upset and gastrointestinal stasis.

Preparation

All fresh fruit should be washed before it is fed to your rabbit. Remove the seeds and stems and any large seed pits.

Some pet owners find it convenient to prepare a container of prewashed and sliced fruit rather than cutting it up every day. Your rabbit's fruit salad can consist of several fruits. However, as with vegetables, always offer new types of fruit in very small portions to make sure that your rabbit does not experience digestive upset. Rather than feeding fruits as part of his regular meal, you can use tiny pieces to bond with him during playtime and training.

HOW MUCH TO FEED

The amount of food your rabbit eats will change throughout his lifetime. Factors that affect calorie intake will vary depending not only on his age and reproductive status but also on his activity level. A rabbit who is allowed to run and play outside his cage will require more food than one who sits neglected in his cage day after day.

Young, growing rabbits should have unlimited access to pellets, called free-feeding. Once they are adults, generally between four to eight months depending on the breed, the general rule is to feed 1/4 cup (4 oz/113 g) of pellets per 5 pounds (2.3 kg) of body weight divided into two meals per day. Reducing your rabbit's ration of pellets is important; feeding too many is a major cause of obesity, soft stools,

Feeding Schedule

Rabbits do best with regularly scheduled mealtimes. Feed your pet twice a day: once in the morning and once in the evening. Many owners find it convenient to feed their pets before they leave for school or work and shortly before or after their own evening meal. If you know that you will return home later than usual in the evening, provide your rabbit with extra hay in the morning.

Rabbits will greet any treats that you give them with delight. Occasionally offering your pet small tidbits of something yummy is also a great way to win his trust, although it is always best to stick to healthy foods.

The best treats are a favorite piece of vegetable or fruit. Another option includes sprouted wheat grass, which is available at pet stores. You can also sprout wild birdseed for your rabbit to snack on when the plants are several inches (cm) high. Green plants from your backyard, such as a handful of fresh grass or some dandelion leaves and flowers, will be relished by your bunny. If you collect plants from your neighborhood or a local countryside, be sure that no pesticides or herbicides were sprayed on them. Do not collect from roadsides with a lot of traffic due to pollution or from locations where wild rabbits live because disease transmission may be a problem. Make sure that any wild plants or herbs you feed are not toxic to rabbits, and always wash them before feeding them to your bunny.

Many owners enjoy buying the various commercial rabbit treats sold in pet stores, such as honey-coated seed and nut sticks, dehydrated fruit and vegetable puffs, and nut cakes. Although the packaging might claim that the product is healthful and nutritious, read the list of ingredients. Many are too high in fat, carbohydrates, and sugar, just like human junk foods. Starchy foods are notorious for causing digestive problems in rabbits due to their adverse effect on gut microbes. They should only be offered on special occasions and in moderation. If you feed a "gourmet mix" pellet food, it is best not to feed treats other than fresh vegetables because these mixes already contain treat foods. If you want to feed your rabbit commercial treats sold in pet stores, switch his main diet to a plain pellet.

All this being said, both moderation and doing your homework are important. Why should you be concerned about feeding too many treats, the wrong kind of treats, or allowing your rabbit to eat treat foods that are high in protein and carbohydrates and low in fiber? Because a simple gut ache is not the likely result; rather, junk food treats can cause gastrointestinal diseases that can be deadly to your rabbit.

and gastrointestinal health problems.

Packaged foods come with feeding instructions, and you can use these as a starting point. They are general recommendations, usually based on a rabbit's adult weight—your pet might need to eat slightly more or less. The proper portion to feed is whatever amount is necessary to maintain his optimum weight and condition.

No matter how old your rabbit is, he should always have loose hay in his cage. Each morning, remove any uneaten hay and replace it with fresh hay. Likewise, remove any uneaten pellets. Do not just put new food on top of the old food.

Freshness

The food you feed your rabbit should be fresh. Food that is old can lose its nutritional value. Pellets should have a smooth, hard surface and smell pleasant. Soft, crumbly pellets are old and stale and should not be fed. Packaged food mixes should be sweet smelling, not rancid or dusty.

Buy no more than one month's supply of food at a time. Although it can be cheaper to purchase large quantities of manufactured food, it will take too long to use up before becoming stale. Check to see whether there is an expiration date on the package. Some manufacturers stamp a date on food bags and recommend that the food be used within one year of this date. Typically, the freshest, best-quality packaged food is found at busy pet and feed stores that constantly turn over their stock.

Store your rabbit's food in a cool, dry environment. Sunlight, heat, and time degrade the vitamins in food. Keep the food in an airtight container, such as a glass jar with a lid, or be sure to completely close a container or bag that is self-sealing. This will keep the food fresh and prevent it from spoiling.

THE OVERWEIGHT RABBIT

Just as with humans, obesity can be a serious problem affecting the health and longevity of your pet. Overweight rabbits suffer from a variety of health problems. They also cannot groom themselves adequately, and if they are too fat to reach their rear end, they will not be able to consume their cecotrophes.

Keeping a monthly record of your rabbit's weight will help you monitor his well-being. Some scales are sensitive enough to give the weight of small rabbits. If your scale is not, you can weigh yourself and then weigh yourself again while holding your rabbit. Subtracting the difference between the two weights will provide your rabbit's weight. If your rabbit is purebred, the breed standard will let you know the weight he should be when fully grown.

(See the weight table in Chapter 2.) If your rabbit is a mixed breed, your veterinarian can help you determine his ideal weight.

In between monthly weigh-ins, you can still tell if your rabbit is receiving the right amount of food by examining his body. If his backbone and hip bones are covered by a thick layer of fat and difficult to feel, he is probably overweight.

It can sometimes be difficult to control how much food a rabbit eats if there is more than one rabbit in a cage. The dominant individual can sometimes eat food meant for the subordinate one. If this occurs with your pets, you might need to separate them into two cages. They can still visit if you place the cages side by side.

Rabbits have a hard time losing weight, and rapid weight loss, such as a pet owner feeding drastically less food, can cause liver damage. The best way to help your rabbit shed excess pounds (kg) safely is to gradually decrease the amount of pellets you provide, increase the amount of loose hay, and eliminate treats such as nuts, seeds, and fruits. If your vet diagnoses your rabbit as overweight, she will provide more detailed information on how to achieve weight loss, which will also include additional exercise outside the cage.

Just as with humans, obesity can be a serious problem affecting the health and longevity of your pet. Keeping a monthly record of your rabbit's weight will help you monitor his well-being.

Chapter 6

Grooming Your Rabbit

Despite some misconceptions, rabbits are naturally clean creatures. Much like cats, they spend some portion of their day grooming themselves, washing their faces, delicately cleaning each ear with their hind foot, using their tongue to clean their paws, and even scrubbing their bodies. However, all furry animals shed hair. House rabbits shed throughout the year, but some shed more in fall and spring.

Brushing your rabbit will help keep him from swallowing this excess hair and will also reduce the amount of fur drifting about your house and clinging to his cage. Moreover, brushing can be a quiet bonding time you spend with your pet.

BRUSHING

All rabbits benefit from regular brushing. It distributes the natural oils in their fur, providing protection from the elements and giving the coat a healthy sheen. It also gives you an opportunity to get to know your pet's body and learn if there are any changes that may indicate health concerns.

Shorthaired Rabbits

The amount of time required to brush your rabbit will depend on his breed. If you've chosen a rabbit with a normal shorter coat, grooming will be fairly easy. Shorthaired rabbits should be brushed at least once a week.

You can brush your rabbit while he sits on your lap or while he is on the floor. (Be careful

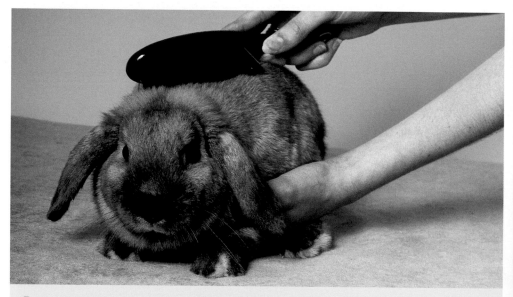

Regularly brushing a rabbit's fur helps keep it healthy and shiny.

not to place him on a table or other high surface because he may decide to jump off unexpectedly.) Gently brush the fur in the direction it grows. Do not brush too hard because your rabbit has sensitive skin, and he may become fearful of being brushed if it is a painful experience. When he is not shedding much, use a soft brush, such as a rubber brush, a soft-bristle brush, or a grooming glove. When your rabbit is molting, you can use a wire slicker brush as long as you use gentle strokes.

While you brush, observe the condition of your rabbit's coat and skin and check for scabs, lumps, or evidence of external parasites, such as flea droppings.

Longhaired Rabbits

Longhaired rabbits, including Angoras (French, English, Satin, and Giant), Jersey Woolys, or any mixed breed with long hair, require grooming once or twice a week, and some individuals may require daily grooming with a wire slicker brush and wide-toothed comb.

A grooming session for these animals takes time and dedication. Yet regular brushing is a must because the long hairs on many of these breeds are so fine that they quickly form knots, or mats. It's easier to prevent mats than it is to remove them, but if you must deal with them, learn to do so properly. Your vet or breeder can give you instructions.

Mats typically form behind and under the legs, behind the ears, and near the rabbit's rear end. Some people use grooming shears with a ball tip (made for cutting hair around a dog's face) to cut them. Because rabbit skin is delicate and easily cut, removing the mats requires great care; therefore, this is not the preferred method of removal for inexperienced pet owners. A safer alternative is to use mat splitters or mat rakes, which can take the knot apart. In a worst-case scenario, your veterinarian can help you shear your rabbit if you don't have your own clippers or you are nervous about grooming him yourself.

Many owners of longhaired rabbits also use a hair dryer set on low or cool as a standard grooming tool. In conjunction with a slicker brush, blowing will force the coat apart and help get rid of loose hair before it mats. It blows out dust and dander as well. Your rabbit's coat should be blown from the rear going forward, up the back, and on the belly. Do not use the blower on his head or ears, though. In general, most rabbits seem to be comfortable with this procedure.

Special Fur

A rabbit's fur is tantalizingly soft to pet. This is because the cuticle scales on the outside of each hair lie mostly flat and smooth. A rabbit with a normal shorthaired coat has two types of hair, guard hairs and down hairs. Guard hairs have rough points and lie on the coat to seal it. Down hairs are short and fine with rounded points. Although they are the most numerous type of hair (depending on the breed, there can be 60 down hairs to one guard hair), down hairs are usually covered by guard hairs and are not very visible. Down hairs form the rabbit's insulating undercoat.

MOLTING

You may need to do some additional grooming when your rabbit goes through a molting cycle. You'll often know that he is about to molt because you will find more tangles when you brush him, or you'll notice more shed fur around his cage.

Adult house rabbits shed hair throughout the year, but some shed more in fall and spring. Usually, at least once a year, a rabbit will molt heavily for several weeks. Rabbits kept outdoors will molt their summer coats in fall and then grow long, dense coats for winter, which they will then molt in spring. The spring molts of some rabbits can be quite impressive, with lots of shed hair. The summer coat is less dense with short hair, hence the molt is less dramatic. Growing juvenile rabbits molt several times before they attain their adult coat. For some breeds, such as the Sable and Silver, the color changes with each molt as well.

Molting Patterns

Every rabbit has a different pattern of molting. A rabbit will usually shed most of his coat over two to three weeks, but some will molt more slowly and irregularly over a longer period. Some rabbits will molt their guard hairs first, followed by their undercoat. Others will molt in patches with bald areas, and still others will molt almost completely at one time. Besides molting in response to changes in season and temperature, a rabbit can lose hair due to stress and changes in diet.

At first, some pet owners are surprised that their longhaired rabbits don't seem to shed. What happens is that the shed hairs become tangled with the attached hairs and form dense

Hairballs

Like cats, rabbits spend up to 20 percent of their waking hours grooming themselves. They also swallow a lot of fur when they are grooming. However, unlike cats, rabbits cannot vomit the hair back up in "hairballs"; the hair must be passed with their droppings. Sometimes the hair forms a mat inside the rabbit's stomach. If it blocks the stomach contents from emptying, the hairball becomes a veterinary emergency. You can help reduce the likelihood of such an event by brushing your rabbit, especially when he is molting.

mats. Longhaired rabbits typically shed heavily once every three months; in between, they will shed more lightly.

Hand-Plucking

During heavy molts, a longhaired rabbit should be sheared with clippers or hand-plucked. This removes the dead wool and keeps the fur in better condition.

To pluck, hold the skin flat with one hand, then take hold of a small section of fur with the forefinger and thumb of your other hand and give a gentle tug. You can usually see the new coat coming in underneath the removed fur.

Plucking is not painful if done correctly. You do not need to pull very hard; the wool should easily come loose when plucked. Some rabbits don't enjoy this, so only do a little portion of your pet's body per day. You can reward him for his patience with some gentle strokes on his head or cheeks.

NAIL CARE

Many owners find that the hardest part of rabbit grooming is trimming their nails. Just like his teeth, a rabbit's nails grow continuously. You will find that those long nails can make handling him unpleasant at times—they've been compared to sabers in their ability to inflict painful scratches! Besides being sharp on human skin, long nails present a hazard to a rabbit who is allowed to roam loose in the house. They can get caught in carpeting, and a rabbit's unnoticed struggles can cause a nail to rip or tear out by the root. If you can hear your bunny's nails clicking on hard floors, it is time for trimming.

Pet stores sell a variety of clippers that can be used to trim your rabbit's nails. Those designed for birds, cats, or dogs are suitable. Several styles are available, including guillotine clippers, scissors-style clippers with O-ring handles, and spring-loaded clippers. Some rabbit owners have difficulty using the guillotine style because the nail has to be partially inserted into the opening. In doing so, the nail can be more difficult to see, and an inexperienced pet owner might insert too much of the nail and cut it too short. If you choose the style with O-ring handles, be certain that the openings are large enough for your fingers to fit in and use comfortably. Some pet owners try to use nail clippers made for people. Although these might work with the dwarf breeds, they are not strong enough to use on the nails of larger rabbits. Make sure that the clippers you use are always sharp because it will make the task much easier. Over time, they often become dull and need to be replaced.

Nail Trimming

If you begin nail trimming when your rabbit is young, he will more readily accept new

Clipping your rabbit's nails regularly will not only help reduce the likelihood of getting scratched but will also protect him from mishaps that can cause him injury.

procedures later. You can prepare for this by getting him used to having his feet handled while he is still a baby. By doing so, you will also learn what they feel like and how to examine them. When your rabbit is comfortable, you will be able to thoroughly check each foot, hock, and between the toes to see whether there are hair mats, bare spots, cuts, or scabs.

Before attempting to trim your rabbit's nails, be certain that you know where the quick is. This is the living portion of the nail that contains nerves and blood vessels. You will need to push back the fur around your rabbit's foot to expose the nail. White-colored nails are easy to trim because you can see the pink quick and avoid cutting the nail too short. The quick can sometimes be hard to detect in dark-colored nails, but if you look underneath the nail, you can usually see where it ends. Determine from the underside of the nail where the flesh ends; you will only want to trim the part of the nail that is hollow.

The nail should only be cut above the quick. If there is not much nail in front of the quick, it does not need to be trimmed. If the nail is trimmed too short, it can cause bleeding, and your rabbit might bite if he is in pain. A small, single cut is usually adequate and just enough to remove the sharp, pointed tip. If your rabbit has really long nails, you might need to make several successive thin slices to trim the nail enough.

Pet stores sell styptic powder, which can be used to stop any bleeding if you accidentally cut the nail too short. Prior to nail cutting, place some styptic powder on a paper towel or in the lid of the container. If you accidentally draw blood, you can dip your rabbit's nail into the styptic powder or pat some on the nail to stop the bleeding. Doing so might be slightly painful, and your rabbit might jerk his foot away. You can also use flour or corn starch if you don't have any styptic powder handy.

The best time to trim your rabbit's nails is when he is tired, not when he is wide awake and playful. If you aren't very experienced, it's a good idea to enlist the help of another person who can hold your pet to ensure his safety as well as yours. The person holding the rabbit should place him on his back so that he is resting securely on her lap. It is often best to sit on or close to the ground so that your rabbit will not get hurt if he struggles and gets away. If he begins to squirm, try gently stroking his forehead while talking softly to calm him. The person with the nail cutters can then begin to trim the nails. Keep the wound powder and some damp cotton swabs handy. Until you and your rabbit handler are comfortable and competent with the process, you might only get one foot done per session. The less nervous you are about the procedure, the easier it will be on your pet. Eventually, you will likely be able to cut your rabbit's nails without a helper.

Because nail trimming can sometimes be difficult, and if done improperly, painful and traumatic for your rabbit, it is often best to have a veterinarian show you how to do it. If you don't have someone who is willing to help you cut your pet's nails, you can also have her show you how to wrap your rabbit in a towel so that you can pull one leg out at a time to do the trimming.

EAR CARE

Examine the inside of your rabbit's ears every few weeks. If needed, you can gently clean the outer ears with a cotton swab and a veterinary ear cleanser. The wax in the external ear should be carefully removed without going into the ear canal—do not push the wax farther into the ear canal or allow the cotton swab to enter the ear canal.

The skin on your rabbit's ears is fragile because it is thin and also because the inside of the ears is usually not covered with much, if any, fur. You might notice an occasional scratch or scab there. This is usually due to vigorous scratching with nails that are too long or even from a sharp piece of hay. These wounds

Grooming Tools

Before grooming your rabbit, be sure that you have the right tools on hand:
- cotton swabs
- flea comb
- grooming glove
- nail trimmers
- rubber brush
- soft-bristle brush
- styptic powder
- wide-toothed comb (for longhaired rabbits)
- wire slicker brush

Grooming Show Rabbits

If you're planning on showing your rabbit, be aware that grooming takes on a whole new dimension. Just brushing and combing him won't be enough if you want your bunny to compete with other show-quality rabbits. Showing, especially at large-scale exhibitions, is extremely competitive, and breeders and exhibitors take participating in these events very seriously.

The longer your rabbit's hair is, the more time you will obviously have to invest in a regular grooming routine. And don't think you can neglect this chore for weeks at a time and then make up for it the week of the show. A savvy judge will easily recognize the difference between the coat of a well-maintained rabbit owned by a serious competitor and the coat of one who lives with a casual exhibitor.

Dedication is a key word when showing rabbits. You must be committed to good grooming practices as well as to optimal feeding and training. Also, be aware that you cannot create a show coat on a pet-quality rabbit; good coats are bred, not made. Unless you start with a good-quality coat that you treat with optimum care, you will never be competitive in a professional arena.

will normally heal fine by themselves. However, persistent inflammation or a scab that never heals requires veterinary attention.

Ear Mites

Rabbits can get ear mites. If left untreated, mite infestations can cause serious problems. Take your rabbit to a veterinarian if you notice excessive scratching, heavy wax buildup, discharge, redness, swelling, or odor. The most effective treatment and advice on remedying the problem is available from a veterinarian. Do not automatically assume that any discharge is from ear mites and treat it with an ear mite medication sold at pet stores. Accurate diagnosis of the condition will speed your rabbit's recovery and save him from unnecessary discomfort and pain.

EYE AND NOSE CARE

Rabbits sometimes have small dried "sleepers" in the corner of each eye. This is nothing to be concerned about, and if necessary, can easily be removed with a damp tissue. Constantly weeping eyes or eyes with abundant exudate require a veterinary examination. A rabbit with visible mucus around his nose is likely sick. If the mucus is present for more than a day, especially if other symptoms such as frequent sneezing are present, contact your veterinarian.

SCENT GLANDS

The scent glands next to a rabbit's genitals can sometimes become clogged with a waxy, smelly substance. The glands, which are present in males and females, are located in folds of skin on both sides of the genitals. These glands might need to be cleaned occasionally if their secretions become dried and clumped. You can use a damp cotton swab to gently clean and remove the buildup. The musky odor you might notice during the cleaning will disappear after a short while. If you don't want to perform this chore, your rabbit's veterinarian can do so.

BATH TIME

You might wonder if you should bathe your rabbit. If he is dirty and smelly, it is usually because he has been lying on dirty bedding. Cleaning his cage, providing fresh, sweet-smelling bedding, and allowing your rabbit to groom himself is usually better than a bath. However, if he was sick or had loose droppings, you might need to clean the area around his hind end. This can be done by spot cleaning him using a warm cloth followed by a dry cloth to absorb the moisture.

As part of your grooming routine, examine your pet's ears, eyes, and teeth weekly.

Grooming time offers an opportunity to build the bond of trust with your pet.

GROOMING AS BONDING TIME

In addition to helping you maintain your rabbit's appearance and good health, grooming is a wonderful opportunity to build the bond of trust between you and your pet. It's ideal one-on-one time. With your pet sitting on your lap, being gently brushed, what could be better for him? Spending as much time with you as possible fulfills your pet's need for social interaction, which is an equally important aspect of his contentment and well-being.

Grooming for Good Health

A regular grooming routine can help you maintain your pet's health as well as his appearance. When you groom your rabbit, take time to inspect his body and overall condition:

- Monitor his weight: Does he feel too thin, too fat, or just right?

- Examine your pet's coat and body: Are there any bald spots or any unusual lumps or bumps since you last groomed him?

- Check his teeth: Are they in good condition or are they overgrown?

- Check his eyes, ears, and nose: Does he have discharge from any or all of them?

Knowing what's normal for your pet and noticing changes in his appearance and routine are the first steps in maintaining good health. If you find something unusual, contact your veterinarian. It's much easier to treat minor problems before they become serious health issues.

Chapter 7

Health Care

Rabbits tend to remain healthy and resistant to disease when they are purchased from a reliable source and given good care. Even when the best precautionary measures are taken, though, rabbits, like all animals, can still become ill. Understanding how to reduce the chance of illness and knowing what to do if your rabbit becomes sick are critical parts of rabbit ownership.

Many factors can contribute to the ill health of rabbits. Animals kept in unsanitary conditions, for example, will be more susceptible to disease. A poorly ventilated cage can create a noxious-smelling environment with high levels of ammonia that can cause an outbreak of a latent respiratory ailment. Similarly, other physical and environmental factors have an important influence on how sick an animal becomes from a particular infection or condition. These factors include the rabbit's age, dietary deficiencies, and whether he is already sick with another illness.

FINDING A VETERINARIAN

As for all animals, a veterinarian is often very important to maintaining the health of your rabbit. Those who routinely treat rabbits and have a special interest in their care are best qualified and will most likely have the smaller-sized equipment needed. Such individuals are also more likely to be aware of advances and changes in treatment protocol.

Veterinarians who specialize in rabbits can be easier to find in some areas of the country than in others (such as in urban areas compared to rural areas). To locate a qualified veterinarian, check with the American Veterinary Medical Association (AVMA) at www.avma.org. You can also inquire at local veterinarians' offices, breeders, critter clubs, rescue groups such as the House Rabbit Society (HRS) (www.rabbit.org), and pet stores.

Cost of Veterinary Care

Even when you recognize that your rabbit may not be well, you might hesitate to take him to a veterinarian due to the potential expense. Such a visit can be costly, and many owners, or the parents of a child who has a rabbit, may find it difficult to spend large sums of money on a pet who is relatively inexpensive. This is why it's important to consider the cost of caring for him throughout the course of his lifetime before deciding to bring him home. If you cannot take on this commitment to your pet's well-being and good health, which is part of being a responsible owner, it's best not to get one in the first place.

At some point, it may become necessary to provide medical intervention and treatment to help a sick or injured pet. If you are concerned about costs, discuss them with your veterinarian beforehand. She may offer

Your rabbit is dependent on you for his good health and well-being.

options such as payment plans or may be able to guide you to some pet insurance programs that are available.

Be cautious about seeking aid from pet store employees or rescue groups. Although they might be helpful and able to give an educated guess, the expertise, diagnostic skills, and medication needed to treat your rabbit are only available from a professional. Keep in mind that the sicker a rabbit is, the more likely he is to be traumatized from the procedures that may be required if a condition has reached an advanced stage. Prompt medical attention is the best guarantee of a successful outcome.

ANNUAL HEALTH MAINTENANCE EXAMINATIONS

Rabbits do not require annual vaccinations. Nonetheless, annual veterinary examinations are a good idea even if your rabbit isn't sick. During these exams, diseases can be detected early, when they are more likely to be cured. The treatment of disease in its early stages is also likely to be less expensive than later on, when the animal becomes very ill. By listening to your rabbit's heart, checking for swellings, examining the teeth, and so forth, your veterinarian can detect a disease early. The cost of the annual examination is less than the treatment cost of difficult diseases that are well established in the animal.

A little bit of preparation on your part can help your veterinarian in her examination. She will be interested in how you feed and house your rabbit. You may be asked to bring your rabbit to the office with his cage or to have a photograph of the cage setup so that his

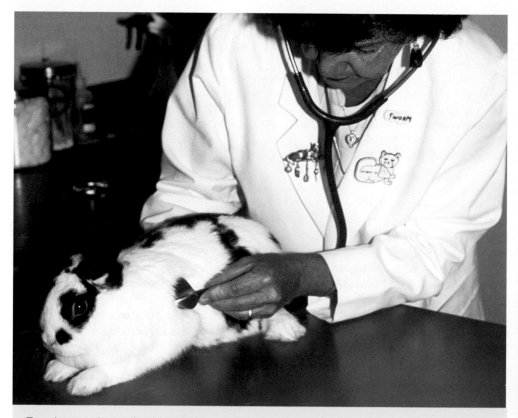

Regular veterinary checkups help prevent potential health problems.

Signs of Emergency

The following symptoms indicate that your rabbit needs immediate care—delays in treatment may have serious consequences.

- bleeding
- bloated abdomen
- broken bones
- constant grinding of the teeth
- constant tilting of the head
- constipation
- hunched sitting posture, reluctance to move
- labored breathing
- loss of appetite, refusal to eat
- lying on side, refusal to stand
- noticeable salivation
- paralysis
- rapid breathing
- seizures
- sudden weakness
- watery diarrhea

environment can be assessed. (Otherwise, plan to use a transport or carrier cage, available wherever you buy your pet supplies.) Don't be afraid to ask questions about caring for your pet. Your veterinarian cares for rabbits every day and is an excellent source of information. She is also likely to know about the latest health and maintenance information available on rabbits.

Once your rabbit is a senior, at about five to six years of age, it is usually recommended that he get checkups once every six months. By analyzing urine and blood samples, your vet can establish a baseline function for your pet's health. The results can be compared with information obtained during future visits. Any changes could indicate illness, which can then be dealt with in a timely fashion.

GENERAL SIGNS OF ILLNESS

Take note of any changes in your rabbit's appearance or behavior because they can sometimes be indicators of a health problem. Many physical signs of illness in rabbits are similar to those in other animals and are fairly obvious. These include runny nose, watery eyes, labored breathing, diarrhea, and constipation.

Quarantine your pet from other animals if he is diagnosed with an infectious disease.

More subtle changes in behavior can also be symptoms of illness. For example, rabbits tend to be fastidious about cleanliness, so a dirty, matted coat means that something is wrong. Sudden changes in behavior such as huddling in a corner, lethargy, reduced appetite, or not eating may indicate that a serious problem exists or could be looming.

Some signs of disease can be difficult to detect in rabbits, but the more you are alert to them, the sooner you can provide appropriate care. Watch for changes in coat condition, such as rough hair, hunched posture, constipation, and weight loss. Pay particular attention if your rabbit is sensitive when touched on a certain part of his body. Any of these symptoms suggests that something might be wrong and a visit to the veterinarian is necessary.

Initial indications that your rabbit may be sick are often subtle, and unfortunately, he is not capable of effectively communicating his discomfort to you. The ability to hide an illness is believed to be a self-protective behavior because in the wild, a weak or ill animal is easy prey for predators. By the time you realize that your rabbit is not well, he will likely have been sick for quite some time. In many cases, treatment is difficult because the condition is more advanced at the time of detection. Although some diseases progress rapidly and an affected rabbit can die in 24 hours, early recognition may mean the difference between life and death for your pet. By familiarizing yourself with the symptoms of various ailments, you may be better prepared to recognize and better communicate his symptoms to your veterinarian.

INFECTIOUS DISEASES

Infectious diseases are caused by microorganisms such as bacteria, viruses, or protozoa. When a veterinarian has determined that your rabbit has an infectious disease or when you suspect that he has been infected, he should be isolated from other rabbits to prevent the disease from spreading.

Diseases that are infectious can be spread between rabbits in a number of ways. Some infectious organisms can be transmitted through the air, some are spread through water, and many are found in rabbit stools. They are also often spread from rabbit to rabbit by their human handlers on clothing, the handlers' hands, or on feeding dishes. Be sure to wash your hands, and do not share supplies and accessories between an infected rabbit and any others without first thoroughly disinfecting each item. Professional breeders are extra cautious and often use disposable surgical gloves when tending to sick rabbits.

At times it may be difficult to determine when a rabbit is infected. Sometimes an infectious disease is subclinical, meaning that symptoms are not apparent. This is because individuals differ in their resistance to infectious organisms. Some exposed rabbits never display any symptoms at all but may still be actively shedding the infectious organism and spreading the infection. Because of these considerations, vigilance and prompt action on your part (in the form of an accurate diagnosis by a qualified veterinarian) are necessary to prevent the spread of disease, whether you have just one rabbit or many.

All this being said, exposure to infectious agents does not necessarily mean that your rabbit will become sick. Healthy rabbits have a competent immune system capable of warding off many disease organisms. However, numerous environmental factors can make infectious disease more likely or more severe. These include stressing factors such as overcrowding, poor sanitation, malnutrition, or concurrent infections. Obviously, single rabbits kept alone are less at risk for disease, both because they are less likely to encounter the disease agent and because their living conditions are less likely to be stressful. Generally, infectious diseases are often preventable through good husbandry.

Pasteurellosis

The most common infectious disease of rabbits is caused by infection with *Pasteurella* bacteria, which are found widely in the environment. Although many rabbits carry them without ever becoming sick, the bacteria can get out of control, causing an illness called pasteurellosis. The bacteria typically infect the upper respiratory tract but can affect any part of the rabbit's body, causing ear infections, abscesses, and pneumonia. Pasteurellosis is often called snuffles because the most common symptoms are runny eyes, sneezing, coughing, and a thick discharge from the nose. The inside of the rabbit's front legs will usually be dirty from nose wiping.

A rabbit showing these symptoms must be seen by a veterinarian; pasteurellosis can only be diagnosed from cultures and blood tests. Although *Pasteurella* infection cannot be entirely eradicated by treatment, the symptoms are easy to manage and the prognosis for treated animals is good. Antibiotics are used to treat mild cases of snuffles and can relieve a rabbit's symptoms. Injections are often preferred, however, because oral antibiotics cause additional problems. Many rabbits are chronically infected but only show signs of infection when stressed and will require long-term management of the disease.

Pasteurellosis is a good example of a disease that can be effectively managed with good husbandry. Because *Pasteurella* bacteria are so ubiquitous, it is difficult, if not impossible, to isolate rabbits from the disease, especially if you have a large flock. The bacteria are easily transmitted among rabbits by sneezing or close contact. Pasteurellosis

Pasteurellosis is often called snuffles because the most common symptoms are runny eyes, sneezing, coughing, and a thick discharge from the nose.

Preventing Common Health Problems

Prevention of disease is far better than treatment, and it is relatively simple to prevent most common health problems. Rabbits who are properly cared for are less stressed and have better natural resistance to diseases. What is the proper care for a rabbit? To a great degree, proper care is merely maintaining common-sense husbandry practices.

A plethora of problems can affect rabbits due to poor husbandry. Husbandry, or how a pet is taken care of, includes aspects of care such as housing, food, water, and medical attention when indicated. Your rabbit cannot modify the size, temperature, air circulation, and cleanliness of his home. He is completely dependent upon you to provide him with a proper environment that will ensure his well-being and comfort.

A clean cage is one of the most important ways you can help your rabbit stay healthy. Spoiled food and soiled bedding are invitations to illness. Routine hygiene is the most effective way to prevent disease organisms from becoming established in his home and overpowering his natural resistance to disease. Your rabbit is most likely to get sick when you become forgetful about cleaning his enclosure.

Paying daily attention to your rabbit's physical condition and behavior can also prevent him from becoming seriously ill. Note any weight changes, check teeth alignment, and feel for lumps and bumps. Significant changes in the amount of food or water consumed and unusual changes in behavior or level of activity may also signal illness. Knowing your rabbit's regular routine is helpful when trying to detect if he is not feeling well.

Changes in your rabbit's appearance or behavior may signal that he is ill.

often develops when rabbits are stressed due to environmental conditions, such as dirty cages or poor air circulation. Good living conditions can therefore significantly reduce the incidence of an outbreak or relapse.

NONINFECTIOUS AILMENTS

Many rabbit aliments are noninfectious; they are not typically transmitted from one rabbit to another. Noninfectious ailments can be caused by a number of factors, including poor diet, trauma, or noninfectious microorganisms. The following are descriptions of some of the most common noninfectious ailments in rabbits.

Parasites

Parasites are organisms that survive by living and feeding on other organisms. When pet rabbits are obtained from a reputable source and kept in a clean environment, parasites are not a common problem for them. Two of the most common types that may affect them are fleas and ear mites.

Fleas

If the family dog or cat has fleas, then it is possible for your rabbit to become infested with them as well. Scratching is the most obvious symptom. You might also see the fleas or their dark droppings. A treatment approved for use on kittens is usually safe to use on your rabbit. However, your veterinarian might recommend one of the spot-on flea control products, which are more convenient. Besides treating your rabbit, you must also treat his cage and surroundings. Use a flea comb to help control and remove them in between treatments. Don't forget to also treat your dog and cat.

Ear Mites

Ear mites live in a rabbit's ear canals and cause a dark, crusty discharge. They also make his ears very itchy, causing him to scratch at them and shake his head constantly. The scratching can lead to infected wounds on or inside his ears. Your veterinarian must diagnose ear mites using a microscope because they are not visible to the naked eye. Medication will eliminate the condition but must be continued for several weeks to kill all stages of the mite's life cycle.

Fur Mites

Loss of hair can be caused by a variety of factors, including some parasites. Bald patches between the shoulder blades and down the back are often due to fur mites. Loss of hair on the feet, legs, and head can sometimes be due to ringworm, a fungus that usually causes hair loss in round patches. The skin without hair is often red and may be covered with a dry crust. Because ringworm is contagious to people, any rabbit with hair loss should be examined by a veterinarian, who will provide an accurate diagnosis and treatment.

Care of a Sick Rabbit

Taking proper care of a sick rabbit can help his recovery. Keep your pet in a warm, quiet area and monitor his water and food intake, as well as his urine and fecal output. After any kind of surgery, make sure that your rabbit's cage remains clean to prevent secondary bacterial infections of the surgery site. Check the incision site each day for swelling or discharge. Also monitor whether your rabbit is chewing the stitches. Try to control all potential sources of stress, and consult with your veterinarian if your rabbit has not eaten within 24 hours after returning home.

Hairballs and Resulting Gastric Stasis

Rabbits regularly shed their hair, some of which is swallowed when they groom themselves. Hair is therefore common in the stomachs of healthy rabbits and is normally passed in the stools. This is the only way they can pass hair because, unlike cats, they cannot vomit and expel the hairballs. Problems develop when the swallowed hair is not passed out of the stomach but instead accumulates into a blockage that leads to the development of gastric stasis, or a blockage in normal gastric and intestinal flow. Symptoms of gastric stasis resulting from hairballs include loss of appetite and reduced or no droppings. Affected rabbits might not eat for two to seven days. Any droppings the rabbit passes are smaller and fewer in number and may or may not contain hair.

Gastric stasis is an emergency that requires immediate veterinary care. If left untreated,

To ensure the best recovery, seek treatment at the first sign of illness.

the rabbit will die. A veterinarian can usually palpate the stomach and locate a large, doughy mass. However, even a small hairball, which might not be readily detected, can be serious if it blocks the passage of the stomach's contents into the small intestine. Hairballs can be diagnosed with X-rays, but doing so is not always definitive. The X-rays might show a large mass in the rabbit's stomach, or they may show the presence of gas in the stomach and intestines, which suggests gastric stasis. Usually, clear symptoms of the condition should be treated, even if the hairball cannot be positively identified.

Hydration of the stomach contents, which loosens them and stimulates motility of the gastric system, is the preferred method of treatment. Most rabbits respond to this treatment. Surgical removal of hairballs is sometimes required if the mass in the stomach is excessively large or dry. Because a rabbit who needs surgery is likely to be sicker, the chances of success are greatly reduced. This is why hairballs should be treated promptly.

Hair is not the only cause of gastric stasis. It can also occur when a rabbit is fed the wrong diet—one that is too high in carbohydrates and too low in fiber. Prevention includes feeding the right diet and regular brushing to reduce the amount of loose hair a rabbit might swallow. Some veterinarians suggest the preventive use of petroleum laxatives and offering juices that contain protein-digesting enzymes, such as fresh pineapple or papaya juice, in addition to feeding loose hay.

Bladder Stones/Sludge

A diet too high in calcium can cause bladder stones or sludge in rabbits. Unlike people, who get rid of extra calcium in their stools, rabbits excrete extra calcium in their urine. The extra calcium makes the rabbit's urine thick and pasty with whitish-tan calcium carbonate sediment, which can stick to the cage. It can also form sludge or stones in the rabbit's bladder. In addition, stones can affect the kidneys and other parts of the urinary tract. Calcium deposits in any of these areas can make urination difficult and painful and can cause general abdominal pain. If you see your rabbit straining to urinate or hunched in pain, take him to a veterinarian promptly.

If caught early enough, this condition can often be treated without surgery. Symptoms of pain or distress are the most reliable indicators of problems; interestingly, many rabbits produce thick urine but do not develop problems with bladder sludge or stones. Rabbits who have had sludge or a stone removed should be permanently placed on diets lower in calcium. If they are eating alfalfa-based pellets, for example, they should be switched to timothy-based pellets. Some veterinarians also recommend that water be provided in a bowl to encourage drinking enough water, along with the usual sipper bottle method.

Red Urine

Normally, rabbit urine is cloudy and ranges in color from light yellow to rusty red. Red color in urine is often mistakenly believed to be caused by blood, but this is not the case. The source of the color is not definitively known, but it is not necessarily abnormal—even wild rabbits make dark red urine. Microscopic analysis is necessary to determine whether there is blood in the urine, but in general, this is only required on the basis of symptoms such as urinary distress or abdominal pain.

Pudding Stools

Pudding stools are very soft, sticky droppings. They might stick to the cage or even to your rabbit's fur. Normal hard droppings do not smell, but pudding stools can stink. This condition is caused by a disruption in the normal microflora in the gastrointestinal tract. The ultimate cause can be a diet too high in protein, too high in carbohydrates (such as treats with grains as the main ingredient), or too low in fiber. The bacteria and protozoa in a rabbit's gut are sensitive and easily thrown out of balance by the wrong foods or sudden changes in diet.

Although pudding stools are not a serious condition, they do indicate that your rabbit is eating the wrong foods. If you don't change his diet, a more serious gastrointestinal disease, such as gastric stasis, could result. Pudding stools can be cured by feeding more hay, less pellets, and eliminating any treats other than small amounts of vegetables.

Look, Don't Touch

Although it is only natural that you would want to nurture and comfort an ailing pet, do not handle your rabbit more than usual while he is ill. Normally skittish, he is usually better off left in peace to recuperate. This does not mean leaving him alone, but rather reassuring him by talking softly to him, caressing him gently with some petting, or offering him treats if he's allowed to eat. Senior rabbits, especially, need to be handled more carefully as they will develop aches and pains from conditions due to aging, like arthritis.

Malocclusion

A rabbit's teeth have a difficult job to do: They have to clip and shred roughage in the form of plant materials every day. For reasons due to heredity, trauma, infection, or an improper diet that does not include enough hard foods to wear them down, a rabbit's teeth can fail to wear down properly and will become overgrown. Teeth can also become overgrown if they become misaligned, a condition called malocclusion. This is a problem that typically requires veterinary care.

Maloccluded teeth can prevent a rabbit from eating. He will lose weight and can starve to death. He might show a symptom referred to as "slobbers," which are threads of saliva

Rabbits need to chew on hard objects to keep their teeth trimmed down.

around the mouth that are sometimes wiped on the front paws. Another sign is droppings that contain large pieces of undigested food because the rabbit cannot chew properly.

Although a rabbit with malocclusion will show interest in food, he will not eat or food may drop from his mouth as he tries to chew because he is in pain. If you notice that your rabbit is not eating, check his incisors by pulling back his lips. If they appear normal but his symptoms persist for more than a day, you must take him to your veterinarian for an examination. Malocclusion can affect either the front teeth, incisors, or the broader teeth in the back of the mouth called molars. Only a vet can diagnose malocclusion of the molars. Left untreated, misaligned molars can cut the rabbit's tongue and soft cheeks, resulting in an abscess.

A veterinarian can easily treat overgrown incisors. While the rabbit is still conscious, the vet can clip overgrown teeth. However, this procedure sometimes does not produce good long-term results and can cause other problems to develop. An incisor can split, fracture, or have jagged edges. If it splinters all the way to the gum, it not only will cause the rabbit pain, but bacteria may also enter and form an abscess in the root. When clipped teeth are left with jagged edges, the inside of the rabbit's mouth and his tongue might be cut by the rough edges, causing further discomfort and possible sites for infection. To prevent such problems, many veterinarians prefer to use a high-speed drill, which leaves a smooth surface while cutting through the overgrown incisors without splitting or fracturing them. The only potential drawback is that your rabbit must be sedated for this procedure. As an alternative to constantly trimming overgrown incisors, your veterinarian might discuss the possibility of extracting these teeth. However, because of their long roots, this process is sometimes difficult to successfully perform. It is important to note that if you choose not to extract them, maloccluded incisors, particularly when they result from a genetic basis, may have to be trimmed every four to eight weeks for the life of your pet.

Maloccluded molars always require veterinary treatment. The rabbit must be sedated for this procedure as well so that specially designed cheek dilators and mouth specula can be used.

Lumps and Bumps

A lump under your rabbit's skin could be a tumor or an abscess. If you notice a swelling or bump, your pet needs to be seen by a veterinarian, who can determine what it is. If it is a tumor that's diagnosed to be cancerous, surgery might be necessary to remove the growth.

An abscess typically also forms a lump, but it is caused by a bacterial infection. The bacteria that cause an abscess are often opportunistic and can infect other organs besides the skin, so they should be checked. If

Rabbits are very sensitive to heat. If you take your bunny outdoors, shade and cool water are necessary to prevent dehydration and heatstroke.

the lump is suspected to be an abscess, your veterinarian will use a needle to biopsy it, then drain and clean the site. Usually, a topical antibiotic is applied to the area. To choose the proper medication, your veterinarian might need to culture a sample of the fluid to identify the type of bacteria present. An antibiotic selected on the basis of the culture and sensitivity test results is likely to be highly effective. It is important that your rabbit be properly treated.

Because an infection from bacteria is always possible when a rabbit is bitten in a fight, immediately clean any injuries with warm water and an antiseptic. Monitor the wound, and if you detect any prolonged swelling, take your rabbit to your veterinarian. Facial swelling is often an abscess in the rabbit's cheek caused by malocclusion of the molar teeth.

Heatstroke

Rabbits are very sensitive to heat. When exposed to high temperatures (above 85°F [29.4°C]) for prolonged periods, they can experience heatstroke. A rabbit who is stressed from heat will stretch out and breathe heavily. Heavy panting, similar to a dog, indicates a very serious situation. When dehydration is advanced, the rabbit will stop panting.

Therefore, long before he reaches this state, you must cool him down. Do not put him into cold water or use ice cubes because he could go into shock. Instead, wet his ears with a cool cloth, place a wet towel on him, and immediately get him to a veterinarian.

It is important to understand that rabbits are not capable of efficiently losing heat by sweating or panting. They also do not necessarily drink more water when temperatures rise and in fact may even drink less. As with many ailments, proper husbandry can eliminate most problems related to heatstroke. Shade and cool air temperatures are necessary to prevent dangerous overheating. Cages and holding areas should be set up to avoid direct sunlight and to allow the rabbit to remain cool when it gets hot out.

Handling Injuries

A rabbit's skeleton is delicate and lightweight, but his muscles, which are developed for running, are extremely strong. If not securely held when picked up, he can kick violently with his powerful hind legs. Not only can the kicking result in fractures to the leg bones, but the vertebrae can fracture and damage the spinal cord. Also, because owners might be scratched by a struggling rabbit, they may sometimes drop him, causing further harm.

Properly holding your rabbit can prevent such injuries from occurring. Be extra cautious when placing him into his cage or onto the floor—this is when you are most likely to be scratched because he will feel least secure and often begin to struggle. Returning your rabbit to his cage hind end first can prevent him from kicking.

Stress

Stress is any condition that disturbs or interferes with an animal's normal physiological equilibrium. It weakens him, making him more prone to illness, and can be a major factor in the development of what might otherwise remain a dormant disease. Therefore, it is wise to recognize and minimize the stress in your pet's life. Conditions that cause fear, anxiety, or abnormal exertions are examples of stressors.

Other than health problems, many common environmental or care issues can also cause stress. These include a change in diet, exposure to temperature fluctuations, loud noises, overcrowding, and fighting. For example, the trip from a pet store or breeder to a new home is frightening and stressful for many rabbits.

Rabbits exhibit variable tolerance to stressful situations. Once in their new home, some settle down right away, while others take longer to adjust.

A rabbit who is stressed may be irritable, perform repetitive movements, show lack

Over time, stress can cause a number of problems for your pet, so working to eliminate his fear and discomfort is well worth the effort.

Saying Goodbye

At some point, you may have to consider whether to euthanize an old or very sick rabbit. Saying goodbye to a cherished pet is painful, but your veterinarian can help you with this decision. You will know that it may be time to discuss this option when your rabbit is terminally ill or when he can no longer leave his nest box or must be force-fed. In some cases, it might be better for a rabbit to be painlessly put to sleep rather than be subjected to treatment, such as surgery, for a condition that has a poor prognosis. Always consider what's best for your pet, even if the decision may be a difficult one for you.

of appetite, have loose droppings, or suffer from hair loss. He will also be skittish and avoid contact.

Over time, stress can cause a number of problems for your pet, so working to eliminate his fear and discomfort is well worth the effort. A relaxed bunny will be friendlier and easier to tame, and he will also be more easily handled by people, including your veterinarian.

SENIOR RABBITS

As your rabbit gets older, you might begin to notice changes in his behavior and body condition. Middle-aged and older rabbits are more prone to illnesses than they were when younger. They can suffer from a whole host of problems, most manageable, once they reach six or seven years of age. Most commonly, your rabbit might experience stiffness and arthritis in his joints. In particular, he can have problems with his back legs. In turn, joint pain can cause him to become inactive, and as a result, overweight. Overweight seniors have a harder time grooming themselves and can be more susceptible to skin problems. For a variety of reasons, they can also have more problems with overgrown teeth, which can lead to difficulties in maintaining a healthy weight.

Your veterinarian can help manage all these conditions for your senior pet. Providing the appropriate care and medical treatment can prolong your rabbit's life. Seniors should have veterinary checkups, including blood tests and urinalysis, once every six months to catch an illness or disease early. Doing so will provide him with a better quality of life and spare him unnecessary suffering.

Chapter 8

Rabbit Behaviors

Your rabbit displays a variety of behaviors in response to different stimuli. Recognizing and understanding his body language and vocalizations will help you tame and train him. It is also the best way to develop a strong relationship, build trust, and form a lifelong bond. Some owners instinctively know what their pet is thinking or feeling based on the flick of an ear or the sound of a particular grunt. Learning to properly interpret what he communicates through these physical cues is a great way to get inside your rabbit's mind and understand his thoughts and moods. More importantly, it will help you to better care for him.

Here are examples of rabbit behaviors and what they mean:
- biting: dominant, angry, fearful, get away now
- charging: pay attention to me, get away
- chewing: keeping the teeth trim
- chin rubbing: territorial scent marking
- circling feet: courtship, sexual behavior
- digging: natural behavior
- ears back: leave me alone, might bite
- ears forward: alert, curious
- flop suddenly onto side : content, eyes shut, clean paws
- freezing low to ground: frightened, trying to hide
- grunts, growls: angry, might bite
- happy dance: kick up heels, jumping, twisting in midair, racing around, leaping on and off furniture
- head shake: annoyed
- hissing: aggressive sound to another rabbit
- loud continual teeth grinding: pain
- lunging: go away, scared, angry
- lying on ground, legs sprawled behind: very relaxed
- mounting another rabbit: breeding, dominance
- nipping: leave me alone
- nudging: pet me, feed me
- rolling: content
- scattered droppings: marking territory
- scream: badly hurt
- sitting up: curious
- spraying urine: marking territory
- teeth grinding: contented
- thumping hind legs: scared, angry
- tongue kisses: rabbit shows affection by grooming you
- tossing objects: playing

Along with understanding these behaviors, it's important to also realize that rabbits will be rabbits. What we may perceive as a bad behavior on the part of an animal may just be a normal instinctive behavior. Contrary to what many

Medical Issues and Problem Behaviors

Before beginning any kind of behavior modification, the first thing you should do is take your rabbit to the vet to rule out any medical factors that may be causing him to display aggressive behaviors. Rabbits who are in pain will be extremely aggressive to avoid more pain. Once health problems are ruled out, you can begin trying other methods to break unwanted behavior patterns.

people may think, animals do not misbehave out of spite. They simply do what makes sense to them. To correct any problem behavior, an owner must first figure out what the animal is trying to communicate and then redirect that unwanted behavior toward an acceptable, positive behavior. Of course, some instinctive behaviors can never be changed, but with knowledge, patience, and good management, you can make the situation better for both you and your pet rabbit.

PROBLEM BEHAVIORS AND SOLUTIONS

Docile and friendly creatures, rabbits usually adapt well to living with a loving human companion. But just as with people, adjusting to new situations or coping with conditions that cause stress can result in your rabbit resorting to unwanted behaviors to protect himself. More than likely, your rabbit is reacting to environmental or health issues that are causing him pain or discomfort. Knowing the possible root causes of problem behaviors will help you be one step ahead of them and ready to offer gentle corrections and positive reinforcement so that you can live happily together.

Raging Hormones

Young rabbits are playful, curious, and energetic. When they reach sexual maturity, they can become ornery due to their raging hormones. Your rabbit will probably be more independent and less cuddly. Spaying or neutering can help reduce some of the more obnoxious behaviors. However, just as young dogs have lots of energy, so too will your young bunny. He will calm down after a year or so. Unfortunately, due to an unwillingness to deal with their rabbits' high energy, many people get rid of their pets right before this stage ends. Senior rabbits are mellow—they slow down, sleep more, and are less likely to be destructive.

Nipping and Biting

Some pet owners have problems with their rabbits nipping or biting. There are several potential reasons for these behaviors. A rabbit in pain from an injury to his back will not cry like a dog might. He will huddle quietly and not move. However, if you reach to take him out of his cage, he might bite.

Rabbits who bite out of fear will usually stop when whatever has scared them is stopped. If your rabbit seems to be scared whenever you try to pet him, especially when he is in his cage, pay attention to the position of your hand. Some sensitive rabbits don't like a hand placed below their eyes or in front of their nose. Other rabbits react defensively to being pulled out a small side cage door, so use the top door. The scent of another rabbit on your hand can sometimes cause intact bucks (males) to bite. Washing your hands in between handling each of your rabbits can prevent this problem.

However, the more common reason for biting is that the rabbit has become territorial

Training and proper handling can strengthen the bond between you and your rabbit.

and protective of his cage. Usually, the behavior change will occur after a baby rabbit becomes sexually mature. He might growl, lunge, strike with the sharp nails on his front feet, and/or nip whenever you put your hand inside the cage, even when you are giving him food. Both does (females) and bucks will exhibit this behavior.

Squawking in pain when your rabbit nips or bites might help signal to him that this is inappropriate behavior. You might also try gently holding his head to the cage floor for a few seconds to assert your dominance. You must do this quickly so that you don't get bitten. Your rabbit might struggle during the first few seconds, but persevere. However, be careful if you choose to use this method; you are not trying to hurt your rabbit. This approach can be effective with many extremely aggressive rabbits but will need to be repeated until the behavior ceases.

What you don't want to do is let your rabbit know that you are intimidated by his aggressive behavior. For example, if you quickly grab the food bowl when removing it from the cage because you are afraid of being bitten, you are reinforcing his behavior. Continually changing where you place the food dish within his cage can sometimes mute this behavior. Hand-feeding your rabbit some tasty treats outside his cage will help him associate your hand with the arrival of food. Try placing the food on your flat open hand, and make your rabbit come toward you to get it. Once he routinely eats from your hand, you can then offer him the food while your hand is next to his cage and finally while your hand is inside his cage. As a last resort, you can fill the food dish when your rabbit is exercising outside his cage.

You may become flabbergasted and indignant when your rabbit is aggressive and even nasty, but resist the urge to hit him, throw things at him, or do anything else that could scare him. He is just being a rabbit, and any of these actions could make him feel that he can never trust people. You must instead do what seems counterintuitive: Be calm and predictable. Kind words, nice petting, and small food treats can often work wonders.

Chewing

One of the most common problems owners have with their pet rabbits is their incessant chewing. However, chewing is just a natural part of being a rabbit. Because he doesn't have hands, a rabbit uses his teeth to explore the world around him through taste and texture. Chewing also promotes good health because it keeps his teeth worn down and helps him maintain strong jaw muscles.

Unfortunately, there is no way to train a rabbit not to chew. It's a behavior necessary to his survival. The best you can do is to provide your rabbit with good-quality chew toys to take care of his chewing needs and to rabbit-proof your home so that he cannot get to your valuable personal items. If you catch your rabbit chewing something he shouldn't, you can

make a firm verbal correction, but it's far better to just keep things out of his reach and to supervise him during out-of-cage time.

Chewing problems are much worse during adolescence as a young rabbit discovers and tests everything in his environment. The desire to sink his teeth into everything he comes into contact with will dissipate as he gets older.

Digging

In the wild, a rabbit makes his home beneath the surface of the earth by digging burrows. A house rabbit doesn't know the difference between his outdoor home and his indoor home—all he knows is that nature tells him to burrow. Some owners are extremely frustrated by this digging behavior because it is often destructive. And knowing that rabbits instinctively dig will likely do nothing to pacify you after you find that big hole in the living room carpet. So what can you do?

The obvious solution is to provide your rabbit with a place he can dig or scratch. If you have a house rabbit, give him materials that are acceptable for him to burrow in, such as old T-shirts, blankets, and towels, which are great burrowing materials. You can even create a playhouse with a carpet-covered floor and tunnel beneath it to give him the illusion that he has created a burrow himself.

WHY SPAY OR NEUTER?

Spaying or neutering can help tame some instinctive behaviors quite a bit, so it is an alternative you may want to consider if you find that behavior modification hasn't quite done enough to make life with your house rabbit as manageable as you'd like.

Just as kittens and puppies grow up, so too will an adorable baby bunny. Once rabbits reach sexual maturity, their behavior often changes. They will develop behaviors aimed at finding a mate and breeding. When pet rabbits were primarily kept outside in hutches, these changes were not as obvious or as objectionable. But many of the behaviors are undesirable for a pet kept inside a house.

Intact, or unneutered, male rabbits spray pungent urine to mark their territory, a behavior that is most unwelcome in a house. Adult males can sometimes become aggressive,

Digging is an instinctive behavior. A house rabbit doesn't know the difference between his outdoor home and his indoor home—all he knows is that nature tells him to burrow.

display excessive mounting behavior, and be more difficult to handle. Female rabbits may undergo false pregnancy and may even pull hair and make a nest in the expectation of pregnancy. They may also spray urine and be aggressive, not to mention the possibility that they may become pregnant if a male is around. Rabbits of either sex may stop using their litter box. Both genders may begin to dig in the carpet and other areas when out exploring.

These reproductive behaviors lead many pet owners to give up their rabbits. In some cases, the rabbit is neglected and left in his cage because his owner doesn't want to deal with an unfriendly pet. Surgically altering a rabbit so that he or she can no longer breed is highly recommended because doing so typically eliminates or reduces undesirable behaviors.

As the popularity of pet rabbits has increased, a better appreciation and understanding of their potential as house pets has led to an increased awareness of the benefits of spaying and neutering. Also called altering, these procedures used to be uncommon but are now fairly routine for pet rabbits. Along with the behavioral benefits, spaying female rabbits is recommended as a means of preventing disease, specifically uterine cancer, which is relatively common in female rabbits older than two years of age. Because altered rabbits are less prone to reproductive diseases, they tend to live longer than those who are not spayed or neutered.

In general, altered rabbits make better pets because they are calmer and more people-oriented. They are less territorial, so their instinct to spray urine is eliminated. Odors from a rabbit's droppings and urine are reduced due to less hormone production. Litter box "accidents" tend to be less frequent. Finally, altered rabbits are more likely to get along with other rabbits and less likely to fight. Although not all undesirable behaviors will disappear, they are likely to be greatly diminished.

Female rabbits mature earlier than male rabbits—males do not reach maturity until more than one to two months after puberty. The best age to alter a rabbit is shortly after sexual maturity, which varies according to the breed. Small rabbit breeds develop rapidly and are mature at four to five months of age. Breeds of medium size reach maturity at four to six months. Large breeds are mature when they are between five and eight months.

INTRODUCING TWO RABBITS

Rabbits also display aggressive behaviors toward each other, so pet owners must be aware of their territorial issues. Rabbits are social animals with dominance hierarchies, and these behaviors can lead to some impressive fights should you decide to get a second rabbit. If you do not properly introduce a newcomer to your original rabbit, you could be in for some trouble on the hoppy home front. Even littermates or two different rabbits who grew up together might fight once they reach sexual maturity. Two females are just as likely to fight as two males. Again, spaying or neutering can reduce the likelihood of fights occurring. A female and male will get along but should be altered so that they will not constantly have young. Sometimes your original rabbit might start marking his territory during the initial introduction period.

Proper introductions can make all the difference. You must introduce a new rabbit to your original rabbit in neutral territory, a place neither rabbit has ever visited. Using a small room such as the bathroom can work. If the two rabbits ignore each other or rest quietly, you are likely to have a positive outcome—they will probably get along as cagemates. Aggressive rabbits will put their ears back, growl, and box each other with their front feet. If their interaction escalates to chasing and biting with fur flying, you must separate them. Use a towel or squirt gun so that you don't get bitten or scratched.

If you would rather use a method that won't provide an opportunity to send fur flying, or if you tried the previous method with less than favorable results, try placing each rabbit in his own cage and setting the cages side by side. Keep this arrangement over time and see if

Introduce your new rabbit to established pets gradually to prevent territorial disputes.

the aggression fades. It can take patience and persistence to get two rabbits to like each other. Once they do, though, you will enjoy watching them groom, play, and sleep together.

Keep in mind that not all rabbits will bond. It is best to acquire the second rabbit on a trial basis so that he can be returned if the situation does not work.

INTRODUCING OTHER HOUSE PETS

It is possible for some dogs and cats to make friends with a pet rabbit, which can certainly make your house run more smoothly. However, it is not necessary for them to become bosom buddies. At the least, you want your other pets to be trained to tolerate your rabbit without chasing or harassing him. If you constantly have to worry about the safety of your rabbit, both of you will be quite stressed.

It's generally not a good idea to allow your rabbit to interact with natural predators such as dogs and cats. At the least, other pets must be trained to tolerate your rabbit without chasing or harassing him.

Meeting the Family Dog

Certain dogs are not good candidates for becoming friends with a house rabbit. For example, a young, rambunctious dog or one with a high prey drive should not meet your pet. The ideal canine candidate should know basic obedience commands such as sit, stay, and lie down, and you must be able to control him.

Let your dog first meet your rabbit while he is still in his cage. Correct your dog if he barks, paws at the cage, jumps around, or otherwise scares your rabbit. Pay attention to your rabbit—if he panics, take the dog away. Lower the level of introduction so that your dog is just walking by the cage. When your rabbit no longer reacts to that, you can increase the level of interaction.

Once your dog behaves appropriately near the cage, he is ready to meet your rabbit out of his cage. Have your dog on a leash, and make him lie down while your rabbit is exploring.

Shy Behavior

If your rabbit is timid, you will have to spend a lot of time with him to build up his trust so that he can be confident that his human caretakers will not allow any harm to come to him and that they will provide him with everything he needs, including comfort and security. The easiest way to do this is to spend as much time as possible with him every day on his terms. Don't force him to sit in your lap or do the things you want him to do; instead, provide him with a safe area in which he can comfortably explore and find his way to you. If you don't have a small bunny-proofed room available for out-of-cage time, a small collapsible exercise pen is a safe option.

Simply sit inside the pen with your rabbit and do the things you normally do—read a book, talk on the telephone, and watch television—while your rabbit does whatever he pleases. Place some of his favorite toys, a litter box, and a safe house (a small crate) for him to escape to if he becomes frightened in the pen. Don't do anything that may appear threatening to him; don't attempt to pet him or force him to do anything—just allow him to feel comfortable in your presence. Soon his curiosity will get the better of him, and he will begin to come closer.

Once your rabbit has come to you on his own terms, it is time to slowly and gently reach out and touch him. If he flinches or backs away, simply remove your hand and go back to what you were doing (reading, talking, etc.). Before long, he'll make another attempt, and you can repeat the exercise until he is comfortable being handled—and hugged.

As your rabbit becomes tamer, you can allow him to play in larger areas as long as they are rabbit-proofed and he is constantly supervised.

Do not let him lunge or bark at the rabbit. Reward your dog with praise or a food treat for good behavior. Eventually, your rabbit's curiosity will cause him to approach and investigate your dog. If you can keep your dog under control, you are on your way to encouraging their friendship. It is often best to perform out-of-cage introductions after your dog has burned off energy on a long run.

Meeting the Family Cat

Cats and rabbits can become friends, but there are always exceptions. Cats are predators, so you should be cautious, especially with dwarf and small-breed rabbits, because some cats are capable of hurting them. Medium and large breeds are usually able to discourage cats and might even bound after them, scaring them away. Yet friendly cats may accept a rabbit and may even groom him. Some cats enjoy wrestling with a rabbit, which some rabbits don't seem to mind. However, other rabbits might vigorously kick when scared or pushed too much by the cat. In doing so, they can become injured.

For proper introductions, either have your cat on a harness and leash or have a squirt gun handy. Correct

As a good pet parent, you need to understand your rabbit's natural instincts and work to find a balance between unwanted behaviors and those you can successfully change through training.

undesirable behaviors, such as your cat whacking at your rabbit with his paw. Encourage suitable interactions with praise and a food treat. Always keep in mind that even if your cat (or dog) becomes friendly with your rabbit, all interactions must be supervised to ensure everyone's safety.

Meeting Small Pets

What about any other pets you might have? With the exception of guinea pigs, who can successfully cohabitate with rabbits, no other small pets are suitable companions for rabbits. Ferrets are predators who historically have hunted rabbits. Other small pets, such as hamsters, mice, and rats, are likely to be attacked by your rabbit. Parrots will squawk, and if their wings are unclipped, even dive-bomb a loose rabbit. Regardless of either pet's size, always supervise any interactions between them—they will thank you for it.

RABBITS WILL BE RABBITS

No matter how much you may want to change certain behaviors, rabbits will still be rabbits. They cannot be trained in the same way as other pets, nor can you expect the same level of responsiveness from them. When your rabbit is doing something good, reward him. When he is doing something bad, correct him or remove him from the area so he cannot continue his bad behavior. While training your rabbit, don't try to rush or expect instant success. As a good pet parent, you need to understand your rabbit's natural instincts and work to find a balance between unwanted behaviors and those you can successfully change through training. If you make your rabbit feel as comfortable and secure as possible by providing him with a safe and secure home, a good diet, enough proper chew toys to soothe his cravings, and lots of attention, the love, trust, and better behavior will just come naturally in time.

Chapter 9

Taming and Training

Taming and proper handling can strengthen the bond between you and your rabbit. However, this cannot occur until he is confident that he can trust you to be consistent and patient while he settles into his new home. Once he feels more comfortable being around you, the routine that training provides will make him feel secure and let him know what's expected of him.

Although you can't train a rabbit to follow complex commands as a dog would, you can hand-tame him, teach him some simple tricks, and share many fun activities together. This can be one of the most enjoyable parts of owning a rabbit, so make the process fun for both of you. And don't forget to choose a name for your pet— rabbits can learn their name, which will help with the taming process as well.

Along with handling your rabbit properly, you must know how to pick up and carry him correctly. To do so, place one hand under his chest just behind his front legs, and then scoop your other hand under his rump.

PROPER HANDLING

Your rabbit depends on you to handle him appropriately so that he can feel secure. Proper handling is also necessary to ensure that neither you nor your pet is unnecessarily hurt. Aside from teaching him that humans are friendly, it helps him become accustomed to being held and petted. In time, he may come to you on his own looking for some attention and snuggling.

Along with handling your rabbit properly, you must know how to pick up and carry him correctly. To do so, place one hand under his chest just behind his front legs and then scoop your other hand under his rump. With your rabbit supported by both hands, snuggle him against your stomach for extra security. Medium and large rabbits should rest on your forearm, and your other hand should always remain on his shoulders to provide extra security.

Until they become more familiar with handling, some rabbits might fuss a bit. Some may even become quite acrobatic, twisting and squirming to get away. Your rabbit is more likely to remain quiet and relaxed while carried if his head and eyes are covered. To do so, smooth back his ears and tuck his head under your arm. Be aware that once you start walking, your rabbit might begin to struggle. Talk gently to him and let him calm down before continuing. Take only short walks while carrying your rabbit until you are both comfortable with the routine.

It shouldn't need to be said, but rabbit ears aren't handles, so never pick up your bunny by his ears! Also, always support his hindquarters—never let his hind legs dangle while you are carrying him. Without the support, a rabbit will flail and kick. If the kicking is vigorous enough, he can fracture or dislocate his spine. You may sometimes see experienced breeders and veterinarians pick up a rabbit by the loose skin on the nape of the neck, but their other hand immediately supports his rear end. However, do not attempt this yourself because you could injure your rabbit if you do it incorrectly.

It can take patience and practice for your rabbit to get used to being picked up and carried. Over time, you will also gain confidence handling him. You might want to wear long sleeves to protect your arms from possible scratches until your rabbit is accustomed to you. Keeping his nails trimmed can prevent you from getting scratched as well.

HAND-TAMING YOUR RABBIT

A tame rabbit will let you pick him up without becoming frightened or frantically struggling. The more time you spend visiting with him, the more quickly he will learn to trust you and become tame. Once your rabbit is familiar with you and daily life in your home, household noises and events are unlikely to frighten him. If he is sleeping when you want to visit with him, call his name and allow him a few minutes to wake up before you expect to interact with him. Establishing a routine, such as visiting with your rabbit at approximately the same time every day, can help with the taming process.

You can begin hand-taming your rabbit by placing your hand in his cage and letting him get used to your smell, the sound of your voice, and being gently stroked along the cheeks or top of the head. Visit with him in the late afternoon or early morning; this is the time he is most awake. Next, offer him a food treat from your hand—place your hand with the treat inside the cage. Your rabbit's curiosity will prompt him to investigate and eat the treat. Do not startle him by making sudden movements or loud noises. Whenever you pass your rabbit's cage, call his name and say hi. Once he knows you, he will hop to the cage door to greet you, asking for attention.

Trust Before Training

The first thing that any rabbit should learn is that he can trust you, his owner and caretaker, implicitly; he needs to know you have his best interests at heart. Once your rabbit feels secure, you can hand tame him very easily and give him the opportunity to safely go outdoors on a leash. You can even teach him to do simple tricks and participate in some fun activities together such as rabbit hopping or agility.

Be sure that you are always consistent and patient in your training because any variations in routine can confuse your pet, undoing any progress you may have made. Never punish your rabbit or yell at him—only use positive training methods, and remember to offer him treats or praise to reward him when he performs correctly.

Rabbits Are not Toys

Parents must expect to help a child properly handle and care for a pet rabbit. The child's age and maturity determine how much parental involvement is necessary. Generally, children younger than eight must be taught how to treat an animal with care and respect. They must learn that he is not a toy and that he has needs separate from their own desires. For example, a pet rabbit may sometimes need to sleep, even when a child would rather take him out to play.

The loud, rambunctious behavior of young children can scare a rabbit. Hitting, shouting, poking, pulling ears, and running around screaming are all behaviors that can traumatize a pet. Parents must help their child learn to treat the rabbit with compassion, how to play gently, and what hurting means. This assistance and supervision must extend to the child's friends as well. Children should be shown how to sit quietly in the rabbit's playroom or exercise pen, speak softly, move slowly, and gently pet the rabbit when he comes to visit.

Parents should also know that if a child's interactions with the rabbit are unpleasant, she will quickly lose interest once the novelty has worn off. Children, young ones in particular, sometimes unknowingly hurt small animals when trying to pick them up. Rough handling can frighten a rabbit and cause him to scratch or bite, which can cause a child to become frightened and drop the pet. Parents should reduce this risk by showing their child how to properly hold him. However, whether the child is strong enough to pick up and hold the animal should be taken into consideration. It's probably best to encourage small children to open the cage and let the rabbit come outside on his own rather than rudely pulling him from his home. In general, children need to be supervised when they are playing with pets.

Eventually, you will also want to visit with him outside of his cage. Never drag him out of his cage because he will become frightened. Let him hop out the door on his own, or carefully lift him out of the door.

If you consistently work with your rabbit, he will soon trust you and want to spend time with you. Depending on the rabbit, expect the taming process to take a few days to a week. Some timid individuals may require more time and patience. Your rabbit is likely to become tame more quickly if you visit with him more than once a day. Use his response to you to judge how fast to proceed. If he becomes skittish, go slower. You will know that he trusts you if he approaches you to be petted and is soft and relaxed when you visit with him.

LITTER BOX TRAINING

Both adult and baby rabbits can be trained to use a litter box inside their cage or while they are out of their cage spending time in a playroom or exercise pen. However, rabbits can never be as thoroughly housetrained as can dogs or cats. Expect accidents to occur because rabbits are not consistent users of litter boxes. There are numerous reasons for this. For example, rabbits leave single droppings to mark their territory, and they also urinate or defecate when they are nervous or excited. Healthy rabbit droppings are fairly dry, odorless, and easily swept up.

Start litter box training by watching where your rabbit goes to the bathroom in his cage. He will probably establish an area in one corner, away from his nest box. After a few days, place a litter box containing some soiled bedding in this corner. Putting some hay in it will also encourage him to use the litter box. It is perfectly fine for him to sit there eating hay

Rabbits can never be completely housetrained. This is because they leave single droppings to mark their territory, and they also urinate or defecate when they are nervous or excited.

because he will not consume the dirty portions.

While your rabbit is in his playroom or exercise pen, provide several litter boxes in various locations to housetrain him while he is out of his cage. He is likely to have fewer accidents if he has more options available to him. Each litter box should have sufficient litter, soiled bedding, and hay to attract him. Pay attention to your rabbit while he is wandering. When he crouches, extending his rear and tail, he is about to urinate. If he is in a litter box, praise him and give him a treat after he is done. If he is not, tell him no and place him in his litter box. Do not scare or punish him, and do not make him frightened of you or the litter box. If he does urinate on the carpet, clean the spot with a product designed to completely remove pet odors or he is likely to use this spot again. (Keep in mind that spayed and neutered rabbits are more likely to consistently use a litter box and not mark with their urine.) Remember, it will take time and patience for your rabbit to become housetrained.

PLAYTIME FOR INDOOR RABBITS

Every house rabbit needs time to play and exercise outside of his cage to remain physically and mentally fit. You may decide to let your pet have the run of one room, but letting him exercise in a playpen made for small pets or puppies is fine, too. Ideally, the room you select should be at least partially carpeted because rabbits can slip on tile and hardwood floors when they jump and run. To keep your pet in his playroom, install temporary gates or close the doors.

Any area in which your rabbit is allowed to play must be rabbit-proofed. Place telephone and computer wires and exposed electrical cords out of reach. Some people place them in hard plastic piping to protect their pets from chewing on them, and in some cases, from electrocuting themselves or possibly starting a fire. Rabbits will also chew any items lying about, such as shoes, plants, or books on a low shelf; all such items should be placed out of your pet's reach. Unless you are watching your rabbit every moment, you should protect your furniture as well. Although unattractive, you can put bubble wrap, sold at shipping stores, around furniture legs. Bitter sprays sold in pet stores to discourage chewing are not usually effective.

Also, keep in mind that rabbits don't just stay on the floor. Your pet can hop onto a couch, a chair, or a table. From there, he can access parts of the room that you thought were off-limits. Always curious, he will stand on his hind legs to reach places above his head. To prevent accidents, supervise your rabbit whenever he is out of the cage; even though you may think that he is safe because you have pet-proofed the area, he can still get into trouble.

Many people let their rabbits exercise while they are busy doing other things. However, remember that rabbits can be very destructive. (Many pet owners are surprised and horrified at just how much damage one cute little bunny can do!) Rabbits are natural gnawers and burrowers. They may dig at and chew the edges of a carpet, urinate on rugs and furniture, scratch wood floors, and chew floorboards, wood doors, wallpaper, or even sheetrock. They can squeeze into small spaces and get behind an area you did not want them to access. A rabbit can crawl under a couch or recliner, chew the furniture's underside, become stuck, or become injured if someone sits on him. And that's not all. Eating carpet or blanket fibers can cause an expensive, potentially life-threatening digestive blockage that must be treated by your veterinarian.

Knowing about these potential hazards should not dissuade you from letting your rabbit exercise out of his cage. Rather, it means that you must supervise him during playtime. You cannot change his natural behaviors, but you can plan for them, redirect them, monitor them, and keep both your pet and home safe.

If you don't think that you can closely monitor your rabbit while he is out of his cage, the

Poisonous Plants

Many houseplants are poisonous to rabbits, so it is safest to completely remove them from the areas in which your rabbit plays. Some of the plants in your yard may also be toxic to him. If your rabbit is confined while outside, limit him to safe grassy areas that have not been treated with chemicals. However, if he has the run of the yard, consult the American Rabbit Breeders Association (ARBA) for information about plants that may be dangerous for him before allowing him to do so. You can visit its website at www.arba.net, or call (309) 664-7500.

The American Society for the Prevention of Cruelty to Animals (ASPCA) also provides a listing of both safe and unsafe plants on its website at www.aspca.org. Click on the site's animal poison control center page and select the appropriate link.

If you think that your rabbit has ingested something toxic, you can reach the ASPCA Animal Poison Control Center hotline at (888) 426-4435. This center is open 24 hours a day, 7 days a week, 365 days a year, and it is staffed with the best experts in animal poison control. A consultation fee may be charged to your credit card, but this is on a per-incident basis (not a per-call basis), and you can call as many times as you need to obtain advice about your particular crisis.

best alternative is to use a portable exercise pen set up in a given area. When not in use, the pen folds up and can be easily stored away. Whether you use a pen or a pet-proofed room, provide your rabbit with toys so that he has something to do.

Supervising Playtime and Building Trust

Supervising your pet shouldn't be work but a fun time when you get to play and visit with him. You should begin by letting your rabbit explore from his cage. Place it on the floor or build a ramp so that he can easily get in and out of it. He will use the cage as a familiar home base. Open the door and invite him to come out by calling his name. It might take a while, but his curiosity will eventually cause him to come out to investigate.

You can assist your rabbit when he is first learning about his playroom or pen. Your objective is to build his confidence and keep him from becoming frightened. Sit quietly, don't make any sudden movements, and talk sweetly to him. Encourage him to return to his home base frequently by restricting his first explorations to a small area. Block off other parts of the room using furniture or cardboard boxes. You don't want him to be able to dart away, become frightened, or make it difficult for him to return to his cage. Gradually increase the size of the area your rabbit can explore.

Eventually, he will know the entire room and will be confident when out exploring. You'll discover that he has favorite areas in which he likes to play. Be careful that he does not chew anything when he is roaming. He might find an item he wants, grab it, and run away with it to chew in peace. If you hear or see him do something you don't want him to do, gently correct him.

Once your rabbit knows his playroom well, you will find that he seeks you out for attention. Try calling him to you and rewarding him with a small treat. You can also toss a small ball for him to chase in a game of catch or train him to do a few simple tricks. For a different, more quiet kind of bonding time, you can brush him.

Don't forget to provide one or more litter boxes in exercise areas. Be prepared to move the location of the boxes to wherever your rabbit seems to prefer.

OUTDOOR EXERCISE

During nice weather, you can let your indoor house rabbit or your outdoor rabbit exercise in a protected area within your backyard. Use a grazing ark or exercise pen, or construct a rabbit run with a permanent fence that extends more than 1 foot (0.3 m) below the soil to prevent him from tunneling out. The fence should also be high enough to keep out dogs, cats, and other animals. Whatever enclosure you use, it must include a sheltered area and fresh water.

Teaching Commands and Tricks

Rabbits can be taught a few simple commands and tricks. However, they are not enthusiastic about learning new things and don't respond reliably like a well-trained dog will. Not all rabbits will learn, but some can be taught simple commands such as to come when called, sit up on their hind legs, or go into their cage when commanded. Some rabbits learn slower than others, and some trainers aren't as good as others. You must be consistent and not give up.

To train your rabbit, you will use a type of training called the method of approximation, or shaping. This technique helps you shape your rabbit's behavior by rewarding those behaviors that are close to the one you want. As you train, you build on a behavior by asking your rabbit do a little more until he is eventually doing exactly what you want. By using a reward, such as a small piece of tasty food, you can change and reinforce the desired behavior.

For instance, suppose you want to train your rabbit to come when called, whether he is nearby or farther away lounging behind the couch. You can't train him effectively if he is far away, so you will have to start working with him during opportunities in which he is very close to you. Sit on the floor next to your rabbit's cage. When he leaves his cage and is a few feet (0.5 to1 m) from you, call his name and say "Come." Let him see and hopefully smell the treat so that he is tempted to come and get it. You will need to do this until your rabbit consistently comes to you. Once he performs the command from a short distance, which can take days or weeks, you can increase the distance. If your rabbit does not respond from a greater distance, you will know that you have moved too fast and should decrease the distance.

Most of what you can teach a rabbit isn't clever, but it can be useful. Not all will respond to training, but some can be taught simple commands. At the least, the time spent together can be fun, and it will strengthen the bond you share.

For more information about this method of training, go to www.clickertraining.com or www.clickerbunny.com.

Your rabbit won't walk on a leash like a dog, but you can follow around behind him and guide his exploration.

It is always best to be around to make sure that your rabbit is safe while he is outside. In other words, don't leave to go shopping for several hours unless you are absolutely positive he is safe and secure and protected from hot or cold weather.

Leash Training

Although it is grand to imagine walking a rabbit through your neighborhood, especially an imposing breed like the Flemish Giant, the reality of it is very different. Your rabbit won't walk on a leash like a dog, but you can follow around behind him and guide his exploration. Be careful not to walk in front of or to the side of your rabbit because he will probably jump in the opposite direction. Essentially, your rabbit will take *you* for a walk while you keep him away from any hazards. He may feel safer under bushes, so be aware that he may suddenly dart under shrubs or toward other shelter.

For walking a rabbit, use a figure-H or figure-8 harness, along with a lightweight leash no longer than 6 feet (1.8 m). Longer ones can get tangled and allow your rabbit to get beyond a safe distance. Large- and giant-breed rabbits are typically more secure in a sturdy harness designed for small dogs.

To begin getting your rabbit used to being on a leash, put a harness on him while he is exercising outside his cage. Let him get used to wearing it for a few days. Some rabbits won't like it and will bite at it, trying to remove it. If your rabbit reacts this way and continues to be upset by the harness, it may be best not to try this again for a while or perhaps to accept that he may never adjust to it. Never leave your rabbit in the harness without watching him. Once he is used to the harness, you can add the leash, which should attach to the girth portion of the harness, not to the collar. Do not pull or yank your pet at any time.

Walking your rabbit in locations other than your house or backyard is not recommended because you may not be able to ensure his safety or sense of security. Many potential hazards could frighten him, including loose animals and backfiring cars. Also, make sure that none of the plants in the area have been sprayed with pesticides or herbicides. Happy trails!

Chapter 10

To Breed or
Not to Breed

In an effort to discourage overpopulation, many pet care books no longer include information on breeding. However, not providing the information has obviously done nothing to diminish the number of unwanted rabbits. Moreover, knowing about responsible breeding is an important component of animal husbandry.

WHY NOT BREED?

Why does a chapter on breeding rabbits start out with the subheading "Why not Breed?" Because there are more reasons *not* to breed than to breed your pet rabbit. Although many people are aware of the overpopulation problem with dogs and cats, far fewer know that the same problem affects rabbits. Thousands and thousands of rabbits are surrendered at animal shelters and rescue groups every year, and breeding your pet rabbit is likely to add to the growing problem of homeless rabbits.

Things to Consider

Although the expression "breeds like a rabbit" suggests that rabbit breeding is simple and easy, breeding purebred domestic rabbits actually takes a great degree of skill and knowledge. Why breed purebred rabbits and not mixed breeds? Purebred rabbits are more likely to find homes, especially if they are a popular breed or if the baby rabbits have particularly attractive colors or markings. You are more likely to get such combinations from known parentage than you are from mixed breeds. Also of importance is that if you breed mixed-breed rabbits, you cannot tell potential owners how large the babies will grow.

Another important factor to consider, regardless of breed, is whether you will be able to find homes for all your rabbit's babies (kits). Depending on the breed, a rabbit can have between 1 and 12 babies, although the average is around 3 to 7 per litter. Until you find homes for all the kits, you must be able to house them. Because female rabbits can generally become pregnant for the first time around four to six months of age, you will need to house the males separately from the females. Besides two more cages, you will need additional water bottles and food dishes and extra bedding and food. Taking care of all the baby rabbits will also require more of your time until they find new homes.

If you line up prospective owners before breeding your rabbit, they will have to wait at least 12 weeks before they can get their new pet. Some people might not have the patience to wait that long.

You can advertise your baby rabbits in a variety of sources, including the newspaper, Internet sites, and some feed stores and veterinary hospitals, but be prepared to refuse to sell a baby to someone whom you don't think will provide a good home. Ideally, you should also be knowledgeable enough to discuss spaying and neutering with any potential purchasers. Consider also that many new pet owners might want to be able to call you to ask questions about their new pet.

Medical costs are also possible. The unexpected can happen, and your rabbit might need veterinary care while pregnant or after the babies are born. Although not common, emergencies can occur. The female can have difficulties delivering, or she could develop an

Breeding purebred domestic rabbits takes a great degree of skill and knowledge.

infection. Both situations require veterinary care. In the worst-case scenario, your rabbit could die during delivery. If the babies are alive, you will need to feed them, a situation that is a lot of work with no guarantee of success. Other potential problems include a doe who produces too much milk, not enough milk, or no milk at all. Again, you will need to step in and help the babies with supplemental or exclusive feeding. You should also keep in mind that even when they are raised by their mother, some of the baby rabbits may die for no obvious reason. For all these reasons, make sure that you can afford medical care and that you have a knowledgeable rabbit vet on call should those veterinary services become necessary.

SO YOU STILL WANT TO BREED RABBITS...

If you still think that you want to breed rabbits, buy the best-quality animals you can afford. They will not be sold at pet stores; high-quality rabbits take time, effort, and money to find and will likely require that you be willing to travel and attend many rabbit shows.

Don't Breed Mixed-Breed and Pet Rabbits

If you have a mixed-breed rabbit, don't breed him or her. Although your pet is undoubtedly a wonderful rabbit, finding homes for the babies can be much harder than with purebred rabbits. You may think that you can give the babies to a pet store or to friends, but often what happens is that by the time the babies are weaned, the pet store no longer needs rabbits and your friends have changed their minds.

You should also not breed a pet-quality purebred rabbit, such as one purchased from a pet store. An experienced breeder has already determined that the rabbit does not have necessary qualities and "culled" it (selectively excluding animals to improve breeding stock) from her breeding program.

Even having a great temperament is not a good enough reason to breed your rabbit because there is no guarantee that the baby rabbits will have the same personality as the parents. Consider that you found a pet who has a wonderful personality, which means that there are plenty of other rabbits out there who also have similar potential. Moreover, if you can't find homes for your rabbit's babies, you will likely feel guilty if you need to turn them over to an animal shelter or if you find out later that some of the people who adopted your rabbit's babies gave them to a shelter when they no longer wanted to care for them.

The best choices for a beginner are rabbits with pedigrees whose ancestors have no known faults. Ideally, you should join the national breed club for your breed of interest before making your purchases. The club members can be mentors and help you choose the best rabbits. They can provide advice on what traits to avoid so that you know that you will obtain some babies with show qualities from your breeding stock. You must also consider that starting with good-quality rabbits is no guarantee of success; much will depend on your dedication and willingness to learn.

How will you decide which breed you would like to raise? Consult with local breeders, pet store personnel, and veterinarians to determine whether the breed you are interested in is one that other people where you live also find desirable. In general, large white rabbits with red eyes, such as the Californian and New Zealand, are not popular pets. Pet stores typically prefer small-breed rabbits. Some national livestock suppliers now provide pet stores with rabbits who are already spayed or neutered, and you might be competing with them for places to sell your baby rabbits.

The Rabbit Business

People don't make money raising rabbits unless they have large commercial meat operations with hundreds of rabbits continually being bred. You will not get rich raising rabbits, not even show-quality rabbits who win lots of blue ribbons and trophies. Properly raised rabbits take money to rear, including housing, food, bedding, veterinary care, money to advertise, and lots of your time. You might look at the prices rabbits sell for in pet stores and think that you can make money. However, pet stores typically pay breeders only one quarter to one half of the amount they sell the rabbits for in their shops.

Most people who breed rabbits do so because they love them and find them fascinating.

Improving the Breed

Rabbit fanciers are dedicated to the ongoing development and improvement of their rabbit breeds. Improving the breed refers to the process breeders use to produce better

Being prepared and well researched and choosing the right rabbits to breed are essential to a good breeding program.

rabbits over time. Better rabbits are individuals who most closely resemble the breed standard by which each breed is judged. No rabbit is perfect and can ever exactly match the breed standard. However, knowledgeable breeders learn all they can about the breed standard, set goals, and constantly work to improve their rabbits.

Knowledgeable breeders recognize the strengths and weaknesses of each rabbit, and they match a male and female to correct the weaknesses in future offspring. For example, consider a buck Dwarf Hotot with narrow shoulders who is otherwise a fine example of his breed. He would be bred to a doe with shoulders that are uniformly wide to the hips, as required in the breed standard. Such breeding is purposeful and not random. Thus, over time, a breeder improves the rabbits in his "herd."

Good breeders also understand the color genetics of their chosen breed. They will breed rabbits to produce desired colors and patterns, and they will also work to avoid producing rabbits with traits that are faults or disqualifications according to their breed standard. For example, if two broken marked rabbits are bred together, many of the kits will be "charlies,"

American Rabbit Breeders Association (ARBA)

Formed in 1910, the American Rabbit Breeders Association (ARBA) develops the standard for each breed, and it is in charge of the criteria judges use to evaluate rabbits in shows. Rabbit shows are as formal as dog and cat shows. The ARBA currently recognizes 47 rabbit breeds. Some breeds are old and have been recognized in Europe or the United States for more than 75 years. Others are new, such as the Mini Satin white variety, which the ARBA recognized in 2005. It is quite an accomplishment for an individual to develop a new breed, as it takes years of devoted hard work.

The ARBA is an excellent resource for rabbit owners. It has links to the breed standards for each of the recognized breeds and links to national breed clubs, as well as general care information. Here's how to contact the ARBA:

ARBA
8 Westport Court
Bloomington, IL 61704
Telephone: (309) 664-7500
Fax: (309) 664-0941
E-mail: info@arba.net
www.arba.net

who have extremely light markings and are a color fault. Because experienced breeders usually have pedigrees for their rabbits, they will know what colors and patterns to expect in a given pair's offspring. To "fix" desired traits, breeders will sometimes mate fathers to daughters, mothers to sons, and other related individuals.

Thus, reputable breeders work to improve the breed by investing time, skill, and an understanding of the breed standard. They are not just breeding rabbits to make more rabbits—they have a plan. They are also responsible for finding homes for rabbits who do not meet their objectives.

GENERAL PRINCIPLES OF BREEDING

Being prepared and well researched and choosing the right rabbits to breed are essential to a good breeding program. Although the following may be obvious to most breeders, to new breeders the basic rules may not be quite as obvious: Always breed rabbits of the same breed, only use healthy rabbits, and mate rabbits at the appropriate age and time.

The Doe and the Buck

The age at which a doe can first become pregnant depends on her breed. Small breeds develop fastest and are mature at four to five months of age. Medium breeds become mature between four and six months of age. Large breeds reach maturity in five to eight months, while giant breeds are usually not mature until they are between nine and ten months of age.

Females can continue to produce babies until they are about four to six years old. Does should normally be bred for the first time before they are one year old. It is not advisable to breed a doe for the first time if she is older than two years of age. Overweight does have a difficult time becoming pregnant and delivering babies. Although female rabbits can have between six and ten litters each year, most breeders limit them to no more than four. Does reared in hot climates are not as prolific as those living in cooler areas.

Males mature at almost the same chronological rate as females. However, their breeding life typically begins one month later and usually lasts longer than a female's. Factors that can adversely affect a buck's ability to breed include being overweight and high temperatures.

Natural light and temperature influence the breeding of both does and bucks. Breeding activity decreases during winter, when there is less daylight and temperatures are colder. (Commercial breeders keep their rabbits in light- and temperature-controlled sheds so that they continue to breed throughout the winter.)

The buck and doe must be in good health. They should not be molting, nor should they be underweight. Rabbits with obvious genetic defects, such as malocclusion, should not be bred.

The Mating

The female should always be taken to the male's cage for mating, or the two rabbits should meet in a clean cage that has not been previously occupied by other rabbits. If you put the male in the female's cage, she may attack him, and sometimes the buck will be more interested in marking the new territory than in mating with the doe, although he will eventually get down to business.

Sometimes the pair will mate fairly quickly, but usually some courtship occurs. The male will sniff the female's rear end, and she will also smell him. Using the scent glands on his chin, he will mark the cage and doe. He may also spray the female with his urine. The male will chase after the female, who will occasionally stop to let him sniff her before she hops away again. The two might stretch out and lie next to each other. When the doe is ready to mate, she will flatten herself close to the ground and lift her rear end. The buck will mount the female from behind and rapidly thrust until he ejaculates. After mating, he will fall to his side and will usually let out a grunt or squeal.

When your doe is pregnant, treat her accordingly. Keep her cage clean, make sure that she always has fresh water, feed an appropriate diet, and minimize stress.

Sometimes the doe will run away from the buck and refuse to mate with him. Try keeping her cage next to the male's cage. You can then return her to the male's cage over a series of days, and eventually they will mate.

Even if you see that the two have mated, you can still keep them together for 24 hours to ensure that with additional matings, the breeding is successful. You can then return the doe to her cage and mark your calendar for the litter's arrival in approximately 30 to 33 days.

Before you mate your doe, check your calendar. Make sure that her due date will occur at a good time for you; in other words, don't plan to be gone when your rabbit will have her babies. You need to be around in case something goes wrong.

Induced Ovulation

Most female animals have heat cycles and are only receptive to breeding and conception for a short period followed by a longer period when they cannot become pregnant. For example, dogs come into heat for several weeks once or twice a year. A dog can only become pregnant if she is bred during her heat cycle.

Rabbits, on the other hand, do not have a heat cycle. They are induced ovulators, which means that eggs are not released until after a female has mated. Cats and ferrets are also induced ovulators. Although rabbits do not have a heat cycle, does still vary in their receptiveness to breeding. Generally, a doe will be willing to breed for a period of 7 to 14 days, which is followed by a few days when she will not breed. A doe is most receptive when her vulva is enlarged and dark red. When a rabbit is unreceptive, she will run away from the male, may try to bite him, will often grunt, and will not allow the male to mount.

A doe can mate within 24 hours of giving birth and can produce another litter four weeks later. This is inadvisable because it is very stressful on a rabbit's body, so it's important that she not be housed with a male.

Gestation

Gestation is defined as the period from conception to birth. The length of gestation varies from 30 to 33 days, depending on the rabbit's breed. Larger breeds typically have longer gestation periods.

Once pregnant, some does eat more. However, this increase is usually not noticeable until about two weeks before they are due to deliver.

The belly of a doe with a large litter will grow in size, and it will be obvious that she is pregnant. However, you are unlikely to know if your doe is pregnant when she has a small litter of only a few babies.

Experienced breeders and veterinarians can safely palpate a doe's abdomen and feel the

grape-sized babies at approximately two weeks' gestation. They will do so by placing her on a solid surface with her head facing them. Using one hand to hold the rabbit over her ears and shoulders, they will place the other hand, palm up, under the rabbit's lower abdomen and gently press up with their fingers and in with their thumb. Palpating a doe correctly takes practice and experience. Don't do it yourself, or you could hurt your rabbit or damage her kits.

Assume that your doe is pregnant, and treat her accordingly. Keep her cage clean, make sure that she always has fresh water, and minimize stress. You do not necessarily need to increase the amount of food she is fed. You can monitor her weight by using your hands to ascertain her condition. If she seems bony, increase the amount you offer but do not add any novel foods or supplements that she has not previously eaten. It is normal for some does to lose their appetite a few days before they deliver.

You should also keep handling to a minimum to prevent any accidental harm to the mother and her developing babies. Some does become irritable once they are pregnant and growl when touched. Be careful if your rabbit reacts like this because she might progress to biting. After her kits are born, although sometimes not until after they are weaned, she will regain her regular temperament.

CARING FOR MOM AND HER BABIES

Does require particular care during pregnancy, and special preparations will be necessary for her as well as her kits once they are delivered. Also, after the babies are born, it is important that they receive proper care. As with human babies, they will have special needs, even when they are still being weaned by their mother.

Litter Size

The number of kits in a litter depends on the breed and whether the doe is a first-time mother. Generally, a doe has fewer kits in her first litter compared to her subsequent pregnancies. Small breeds, such as Netherland Dwarfs and Mini Lops, have small litters, typically three to five kits. Medium-sized rabbits average 7 to 8 kits, while large breeds, such as the New Zealand, have large litters of 8 to 12 kits. Commercial meat breeds, such as the New Zealand and the Californian, have been selected to have large litters and to produce sufficient milk.

Nest Box

You must provide your pregnant rabbit with a nest box. The nest box will provide a safe, secure place for her to have her babies. The baby rabbits will live the first few weeks of their life inside the box, which will help keep them from becoming separated and cold. Newborn rabbits will become chilled and die if they are not protected in a nest.

Nest boxes are constructed from a variety of materials and are available in different sizes. You can find manufactured nest boxes made from metal, metal and wire, and wood. The first two styles are usually used by commercial rabbit breeders. The boxes have disposable liners that make cleaning easier. A pet store can special order a nest box for you, or you can buy one from a rabbit supply site on the Internet.

Because some kits do not survive the first three weeks, many experts recommend that you continue to check them each day until they leave the nest.

Some nest boxes have a cover, which helps keep the babies warm and provides a place for the doe to perch and get away from her babies once they become more mobile. Several styles have one lower end to reduce the chance of the doe accidentally landing on a kit when she jumps into the box. You can also make a nest box out of 1/4-inch (0.64-cm) plywood. Make sure that the box you buy or build is the right size. It should be a few inches (cm) longer and wider than your rabbit, with just enough room for her to turn around in it. Suggested dimensions are:

- small breeds: 12 in (30.5 cm) long x 8 in (20.3 cm) wide x 8 in (20.3 cm) tall
- medium breeds: 15 in (38.1 cm) long x 10 in (25.4 cm) wide x 10 in (25.4 cm) tall
- large breeds: 18 in (45.7 cm) long x 12 in (30.5 cm) wide x 12 in (30.5 cm) tall
- giant breeds: 21 in (53.3 cm) long x 14 in (35.6 cm) wide x 14 in (35.6 cm) tall

Nesting Materials

Fill the box with nest-building material, such as a thin layer of kiln-dried shavings and lots of hay.

You can also place a pile of hay in the cage. The doe will collect the hay in her mouth and carry it into the nest box. Then she will arrange all the bedding into a cozy nest for her babies. If your rabbit starts to make a hay nest on the cage floor, try moving the nest box to her chosen location. If the babies are born outside the nest box, their chances of survival are reduced.

Unsuitable nesting materials include towels, old T-shirts, or a layer of shavings without hay. Your rabbit will also pull fur from her belly, sides, and dewlap (if present) to line her nest. Most rabbits pull fur shortly before kindling (giving birth), although some pull fur a few days before giving birth and some pull fur after kindling. Some does pull so much fur that they have bald patches and the skin looks red.

Place the nest box into your rabbit's cage on the 28th day after breeding. Don't put the box in the cage any earlier because your rabbit might decide to use it as a litter box.

Kindling

As mentioned earlier, "kindling" is the term used by rabbit breeders for giving birth. Rabbits usually kindle 31 days after mating, but babies can be born from 30 to 33 days after breeding. A doe can give birth at any time of day or night, although many tend to do so in the early morning. If you see your doe giving birth, leave her alone. She will bite through the umbilical cord, lick the babies clean, and eat the placenta. The whole process doesn't take long and is usually completed within 30 minutes.

Checking the Babies

The doe will usually cover the kits with fur and leave the nest box after she has finished giving birth. If you are present during this time, count and check them, and remove any dead kits or afterbirth. Breeders of dwarf rabbits also must remove any kits with obvious genetic defects. Referred to as "peanuts," up to a quarter of the babies in a litter of dwarf rabbits are much smaller than their littermates, having misshaped heads, ears set far back on their heads, and thin, pinched hips. These kits can be born dead or alive. The live ones might nurse, but they will not grow. Some breeders euthanize live "peanuts" because they usually die within a week, if not sooner. Other breeders leave them with the doe and remove them after they naturally die.

A pet rabbit who is used to being handled typically won't object to you examining her kits. However, the behavior and temperament of some does change during pregnancy and lactation. They become very protective and might even be aggressive when someone tries to touch their kits. Be careful not to get bitten in such a situation. Inviting the doe out of her cage for a special treat is a good way to distract her. She will usually become less protective as the kits grow older.

Because some kits who are born alive do not survive the first three weeks, many experts recommend that you continue to check them each day until the young leave the nest. Only one person should do so to minimize stress to the doe. It's important to make sure that the young are being fed and that any kits who have died have been removed.

Your doe should also clean herself. If you see evidence of excessive bleeding or other signs of trouble, such as a potentially stuck baby, bring your rabbit to the veterinarian immediately.

Handling Kits

You can examine recently born babies, but do so sparingly. As long as they are comfortably cuddled up in the nest and being fed, you shouldn't need to disturb them. In fact, avoid handling the babies as much as possible until they are ready to leave the nest box on their own.

If you do want to examine the babies by hand, pet the mother first. This will help hide the human scent of your hands. Also, don't wear heavy scents.

Healthy Kits

Kits who are being fed do not have wrinkled skin; they're warm and snuggled together. Those who have nursed will have a full, rounded belly. If their stomachs don't look full, check on them again in about eight hours. If they still don't look fed after checking them a second time, consider hand-feeding them. (See "Caring for Orphaned Kits.") Sometimes only one or two kits won't feed as well as the others and will benefit from a supplemental

Cannibalism and Other Mishaps

Female rabbits sometimes kill and eat their young. This occurs most often as a response to external stress, although an inadequate diet can also be a cause. The babies may be completely or partially consumed. When a stressed doe (or first-time mother) severs the umbilical cord and cleans her baby, she may be too vigorous, which causes their death. In other cases, the kits are maimed and have a missing ear or foot but are still alive.

Unusual sights and sounds that the rabbit is not used to can also stress her and cause the accidental death of her babies. If the doe is frightened, she will jump in the nest box to protect her kits. If she lands on a fragile newborn kit, she can kill him. If the doe is still scared, she might thump her foot to warn of danger and unintentionally stomp her babies to death.

To minimize the likelihood of such problems, it might be necessary to move your rabbit's cage to a less noisy part of your house before she has her kits. Children, their guests, and other visitors must be told to keep noise down and not disturb the mother and her newborns.

feeding. Professional breeders often do not have to contend with this possibility because they make sure that they have other does with similar-aged litters. They can then foster these babies onto another doe.

Stray Kits

Domestic does will not retrieve their young if they fall or crawl out of the nest box. It is thought that the behavior for kit retrieval never evolved because wild rabbit babies are born at the end of a private burrow, which the doe digs specifically for kindling. Any stragglers fall back into the nest due to gravity. Therefore, you must return any of your doe's babies to their nest. Very young kits might be found chilled and dead on the cage floor. This is usually because they hung onto a nipple too long and were accidentally dragged out of the nest by the doe. Even kits who are two weeks old and can move around should be returned because they usually cannot find their own way back into their nest. If you find a live but weak and cold kit outside the nest box, immediately try to warm him with a hot water bottle or heating pad. If neither is available, run your hands under hot water to warm them and use your hands. Then provide a supplemental feeding of warm kitten milk replacement (see "Caring for Orphaned Kits") before returning him to the nest.

Lactation

Unlike other small pets, such as hamsters and rats, a mother rabbit does not lie in her nest to keep her babies warm and does not nurse them throughout the day and night. Instead, the babies keep each other warm in their fur-lined nest. The doe nurses her kits once or twice in a 24-hour period and only for a short period, typically three to five minutes. Rabbits are crepuscular and will usually nurse early in the morning or evening, times when you might not be around to observe the process. A baby rabbit can drink 20 percent of his body weight during this brief period of nursing. Rabbit milk is very nutritious and comprises at least 12 percent fat and 10 percent protein.

You are unlikely to see your rabbit in the nest box with her babies, but this does not mean that she is neglecting them. She is still vigilant and knows where her babies are located. Her behavior is similar to that found in wild rabbits. By infrequently visiting the nest, the mother rabbit reduces the chances that a predator will find and eat her babies. The mother rabbit also does not check on her babies throughout the day and night.

A doe may not feed her kits for the first 24 to 48 hours after giving birth. Sometimes she might not even begin to nurse her young until three to four days after their birth. If the babies have not been fed in two days, you will need to provide supplemental feedings as described in "Caring for Orphaned Kits."

To nurse, the doe crouches over her kits, who lie on their backs beneath her stomach. After they finish, the mother rabbit licks them to stimulate defecation. She eats their droppings and urine, which helps keep the nest clean.

The mother will nurse her young for six weeks, sometimes up to eight weeks. Lactating does require quality food and fresh water to produce enough milk for their babies. Your doe should retain good condition while nursing. If she loses weight, increase the amount of food you offer.

Signs of Trouble

Baby rabbits can become dehydrated. You can tell if your rabbit's kits are dehydrated because their skin will appear wrinkled. You can also test whether a baby is dehydrated by gently pinching a small bit of skin between your fingers. If the skin remains tent shaped rather than snapping back, the baby is dehydrated. If one of the kits is dehydrated, you must

Many breeders prefer to keep kits with their mother for a full eight weeks because older kits are better able to withstand various stresses.

provide a supplemental feeding as described in "Caring for Orphaned Kits." Continue to provide the extra food if the kits don't appear to recover. However, if they aren't recovering, your doe is probably not producing enough milk or is sick. Be prepared to remove the doe and take on full-time care of the litter.

ALL ABOUT KITS

Kits are born blind, deaf, and without hair. A few days after birth, a sheen of fur covers their pink skin. By the end of the first week, you can tell the general color of the kits' coats. The babies weigh twice as much as they did at birth, and they begin to squirm around in the nest. Between four and six days of age, the young eat droppings left in the nest by the doe, which helps them acquire microbes needed for digestion.

When the kits are approximately ten days old, their eyes and ears open and they can see and hear. At this age, they will be almost three times as large as when they were born. At two weeks of age, their fur becomes denser. Some of the more adventurous kits may cautiously leave the nest box and begin exploring. Between 11 and 14 days, they begin to nibble solid food. They are still clumsy and often topple over when they attempt to groom themselves. By three weeks of age, the kits have teeth and are fully furred. At this stage, the babies may be gently handled inside the cage.

Three-week-old kits will readily sample their mother's hay and pellets, so be sure to increase the amount as needed. There should always be good-quality hay and pellets available. The hay's fiber will help prevent digestive upset in the kits. You should also observe the kits learning to drink water from the water bottle and make sure that the sipper tube is low enough for them to be able to reach it.

During this time, the kits are still nursing and will do so for another three to five weeks. You might notice that the doe tries to avoid them if they try to nurse. Eventually, the babies will stop harassing her and she will continue to allow them to nurse once in a 24-hour period. Besides occasionally sitting on their mother, the kits will also sit in the food dishes. The food could become dirty from their waste and need frequent replacement. Kits are quite adorable at this stage as they hop and bounce about.

Once the kits are active and feeding more on solid foods, the nest box should be cleaned every few days or at least by day ten. Replace any soiled hay with fresh hay, and return the doe's plucked hair if it is clean. Then place the kits together in the fur-lined depression you create. When all the kits have left the nest box, usually by 21 days of age, remove it. Clean the cage at least once a day after the babies have left the nest box. They may follow their mother's example and occasionally use her litter box when they are about four weeks old. It is also around this time that they will begin to eat their own cecotrophes (droppings).

Weaning

The kits should be weaned from their mother when they are between six and eight weeks of age. Small breeds are often weaned at six weeks of age and large breeds when they are older. Many breeders prefer to keep the kits with their mother for a full eight weeks because older kits are better able to withstand various stresses.

The kits can be weaned all at once or gradually. Under the gradual method, two babies a day are removed from the mother until they have all left her cage. This method can help the mother adjust to the decrease in demand for nursing. Be sure to also reduce the amount of food in her cage as the number of babies declines.

Baby rabbits can go to their new homes after they are weaned. Weaning is a stressful time for them because they leave their mother and are placed in an unfamiliar environment. When sending babies to their new homes, provide their new owners with some of the food they have been eating or the name of the brand you use. You can also give a new owner some slightly soiled bedding from the rabbits' cage to provide familiar smells for the baby rabbit.

Sometimes a doe will experience a false or pseudopregnancy. She will develop symptoms of pregnancy, even producing milk. The false pregnancy usually lasts about 17 to 19 days, at which time the female begins to pull fur and build a nest. You will know that your doe has a false pregnancy if she exhibits this behavior because a rabbit does not build a nest this early if she is really pregnant.

A false pregnancy can be caused by an intact female being kept in close proximity to an intact male or by mounting behavior among females.

If you don't have homes for all your babies, place them in a separate cage from their mother. Some breeders prefer to move the doe to a new cage because she is better able to adapt to a new environment. The weaned kits will need to be placed into separate "boy" and "girl" cages by the time they are 12 weeks old. Keeping brothers and sisters in the same cage can result in unplanned pregnancies. For the same reason, do not skimp on cage space by keeping the male kits with their mother.

It can be difficult to determine the sex of young rabbits, especially for inexperienced breeders. Comparing several babies at the same time, with the assistance of a second person, can often help in making the right call. To do so, both people should sit low to the ground and turn the babies on their backs. Use one hand to hold a baby's head. Use the thumb and finger from your other hand to gently press on either side of the rabbit's genitals. A male's penis will appear rounded, while the female's vulva will be shaped like a "V."

The longer you must keep your rabbit's babies before finding homes for them, the harder it will be. Make sure that their cages are appropriately sized for the number of growing kits whom you must house. Depending on the number of babies, small breeds can be kept in a 36-inch (91.4-cm) x 24-inch (61-cm) x 12-inch (30.5-cm) cage, while medium and large breeds will need more room. If you notice any fighting among the siblings, you will also need to provide those individuals with their own cage. By four months of age, each baby rabbit will require his own cage. The growing babies must be provided with a constant supply of hay as well as pellets. Don't give fresh greens at this age because they may be too difficult for the babies to digest.

CARING FOR ORPHANED KITS

Hand-rearing orphaned kits is time consuming and difficult, and there is no guarantee of success. If your doe dies, rejects the kits, or cannot produce sufficient milk, you must rear the "orphaned" babies. Be prepared to lose a few, especially very young kits, but once they are fully furred, their survival will become more assured. If you are committed to rearing the orphans, buy a postage or diet scale that can accurately provide weight in grams or ounces. The scale will ensure the best method of determining whether they are growing and healthy.

Keep Them Warm

The first step in caring for orphaned babies is to keep them warm and dry. Kits have few energy reserves and chill easily. If the kits are cold, warming them in your hands is often not sufficient because their body temperature is higher than a human's. A heating pad or hot water bottle filled with warm water is a convenient method of providing the necessary warmth.

Place a heating pad under the nest box, and make sure that it will produce sufficient heat for the kits when they are inside of it. If necessary, you may need to use a cardboard box so that the heat can adequately transfer. Be prepared to fiddle around with the heat source and its location (partial or full) under the nest box so that the temperature does not become too

If your doe dies, rejects the kits, or cannot produce sufficient milk, you will need to rear the orphaned babies. The first step is to keep them warm, dry, and fed.

hot or too cold. If using a hot water bottle, wrap it in a towel so that the kits are not in direct contact with it.

Once the kits are warm, they should be able to retain their heat without the extra heat source if they are kept in their insulating nest and in a warm room. However, when there are only one or two kits, an additional source of heat, such as the heating pad, is needed.

Feeding Supplies

You can use a small plastic bottle or a syringe to feed the kits. Pet stores sell small bottles designed to feed orphaned puppies and kittens. If you choose to use syringes (without the needle, of course), get them from your veterinarian. Syringes that are 1 to 3 cc are best.

Because you can create and thus control the size of the opening in a bottle's nipple, many people find them easier to use than syringes. Make a hole in the rubber nipple using a needle or fine scissors. The right-sized hole will produce a fine spray rather than big drops. Hand-feeding requires a lot of finesse because if you are not careful, a kit can accidentally suffocate if the milk is forced into his lungs.

In between each feeding, wash and dry the bottle or syringe. The nipples on the bottles should be replaced as needed. Some people use a separate nipple or syringe for each baby to minimize possible contamination between kits. However, when kits are sharing a nest, this is not really necessary.

The Formula

There are two readily available milk substitutes that you can use for formula: kitten milk replacement sold at pet stores, which is available in cans, and goat's milk, which is sold at health food stores. Do not dilute either formula—use them full strength. However, if the kits appear to be having difficulty staying full and hydrated, you can dilute the formula with water and offer an additional feeding. Although both solutions are lower in nutrient content than rabbit's milk, the kits will thrive on them. Feed either formula at room temperature or at a temperature that feels *slightly* warm on your wrist.

Experts vary in opinion about the addition of probiotics to the milk formula. The purpose of the probiotics is to provide important intestinal bacteria. However, many of the readily available commercial formulas are of questionable value because the species of bacteria in them are not part of a rabbit's normal gut flora. Nonetheless, there is no evidence they cause any harm, and anecdotal observations suggest that they are helpful. Some breeders prefer to mash up fresh cecotrophes from a healthy rabbit and add the mash to the formula. However, it can be difficult to obtain cecotrophes because most rabbits consume them.

Do not breed your rabbit unless you are prepared to care for the babies long-term in the event you are unable to find appropriate homes for them.

Ideally, the formula you provide should be freshly mixed for each feeding. Saving old formula that was already in a bottle or syringe, even if it was refrigerated, can create potential problems with bacterial contamination.

How Often and How Much to Feed

The babies should be fed twice a day, once in the morning and again in the evening. However, if they do not appear to be thriving, that is, they appear dehydrated and are not gaining weight, you should feed them more often. Some pet owners find that they need to feed their kits every four to six hours for the first week or two.

The following table shows the recommended feeding amounts of kitten milk replacement according to age. Keep in mind that this information should be used as a starting point. Larger-breed kits will consume more, smaller breeds less. Notice that the amount of formula per feeding increases as the kit gets older.

Milk Formula Requirements by Age

Age	Amount First Daily Feeding	Amount Second Daily Feeding
Newborn to 1 week	2.5 ml	2.5 ml
1 week	6 to 7.5 ml	6 to 7.5 ml
2 weeks	12.5 to 13.5 ml	12.5 to 13.5 ml
3 weeks	15 ml	15 ml
3 to 6 weeks	15+ ml	15+ ml

How to Feed

Do not feed kits upside down. In this position, they are more likely to accidentally breathe in the formula, which could lead to aspiration pneumonia and death. Instead, hold

Baby rabbits should be fed twice a day, once in the morning and again in the evening.

a kit in your hand on his belly or feet. Offer the formula in a small amount until he begins to more eagerly consume the milk. Touching his lips with a few drops from the nipple or syringe will usually cause him to lick his lips and begin to drink. It can take up to 30 minutes for a kit to consume the necessary amount of formula. When his belly is round and firm, he is usually full.

Keep a paper towel handy to absorb any formula that runs into the baby's nostrils or onto his skin. Don't expect the babies to always be agreeable when you feed them. Be ready for them to jump and squirm, especially older individuals. If they cry or have wrinkled skin, they are probably not getting enough to eat. Don't hesitate to contact your veterinarian for help if you are having trouble.

Cleaning Orphaned Babies

When a doe nurses her babies, she stimulates them to defecate and urinate by licking their rear ends. For newborn babies up to two weeks old, you will need to help them eliminate. After each feeding, gently wipe a kit's genitals with a warm, damp cloth or a cotton ball dipped in warm water—usually this will encourage him to urinate and defecate.

When the kits get older, they can often urinate and defecate on their own. This is especially true if they are sharing a nest with more than three littermates. The kits are stimulated to eliminate as they push and burrow amongst themselves. Do pay attention to each baby, though—it may still be necessary for you to provide some help. You will need to keep their nest clean, so part of your daily chores will involve removing droppings and replacing soiled nesting material. If at all possible, try to reuse the plucked rabbit fur in the nest.

When the kits are furry, you may find that they wiggle more during feeding. Should some formula get spilled on them, their coat can become a sticky mess. Use a warm, damp cloth to clean their fur, then gently rub them dry with a towel or use a hair dryer on a very low setting. The latter can frighten some babies, so be prepared in case a kit jumps.

Hand-rearing orphaned kits is time consuming and difficult, and there is no guarantee of success.

Older Orphaned Kits

Be sure to provide hay and pellets in a location the kits can easily reach once they start crawling around, usually after their eyes have opened. Don't provide any fresh foods at this age, as such items are likely to cause digestive upset and could lead to death. Although the babies will begin to nibble solid food, you will still need to provide them with formula until they are about six weeks of age. The kits can be weaned from the formula when they are six weeks or older.

Once they are eating solid food and beginning to crawl, put a few droppings from a healthy doe in their nest. The babies will nibble the droppings, and in so doing, begin to acquire the proper gut flora. Although more difficult to obtain, one or two cecotrophes should also be provided. You can also offer diluted formula in a water bottle at this stage. The diluted formula must be changed several times a day to prevent it from becoming fouled. The sipper tube must be at a level where the kits will readily encounter and investigate it.

A Veterinarian's Help

For various reasons, it might be impossible for you to hand-rear the babies. In such a case, a veterinarian can humanely euthanize them for you. Alternatively, you can see if a vet hospital has a technician or two who can be enlisted to help you feed them. For a young kit who won't nurse but who is otherwise viable, a veterinarian can provide an alternative feeding method. The vet will temporarily insert a feeding tube into the kit's esophagus, which will make the initial feedings easier. The goal is to revive the kit so that he can nurse on his own.

ACCEPTING RESPONSIBILITY

Raising rabbits can be a challenging hobby. They live a long time—between seven and ten years—compared with other small pets, such as hamsters and rats, who live only two to three years. Although many people find long-term care of a rabbit rewarding, others are unable to maintain their interest. If you have any doubts regarding your ability to commit to care for this amount of time, do not choose a rabbit for a pet, and certainly do not breed your rabbit without being prepared to care for the babies if you are unable to find appropriate homes for them.

Chapter 11

Things to Do With Your Rabbit

There are many activities you may enjoy participating in with your rabbit, including showing, agility competition, and pet therapy programs. Whatever you choose to do, any time spent having fun with your pet is quality time that will strengthen the bond you share.

SHOWING

What's the appeal of showing rabbits? Some people find the competition appealing, and both adults and children can participate. Raising a rabbit who is judged better than the others in his class is very rewarding. Winning first place is great, too, but winning "Best of Breed" is even better. Using your skills to selectively breed your rabbits so that each generation is better than the last is gratifying and can win you admiration for your skills. But more than winning—because no one wins all the time—showing is a lot fun. You will share your love of rabbits with others who feel the same way. Plus, you will learn more about your chosen breed and have the opportunity to learn from others and share with them what you know.

Winning at a rabbit show is not as easy as it looks. Much depends on the quality of the rabbits and the knowledge of the exhibitors. There are many challenges, and it's

There are many activities you may enjoy participating in with your rabbit, including showing, competitive sports, and pet therapy programs.

harder for some breeds to win "Best in Show" (BIS) than others. However, you may find yourself hooked on the idea and wanting to breed your own show rabbits. Doing so will take knowledge of genetics and the ability to understand and know the pedigree and background of your rabbit's ancestors. Within a breed, pairings of certain colors can result in the unintentional introduction of genes that modify an offspring's color into one that is undesirable. Some breeds, such as the Sable, require patience to show because they go through many coat color changes before the exhibitor knows what the rabbit will look like as both a junior and adult.

Registering

Some shows require that a rabbit be registered with the American Rabbit Breeders Association (ARBA), while others do not. You need to be a member of the ARBA to register a rabbit, and a registration fee is required. You will also need your rabbit's pedigree. Unlike other animals, such as dogs, rabbits are registered on their own merit. They are examined by an official ARBA registrar to determine whether they are eligible for registration.

Each rabbit must have a three-generation pedigree that shows ancestors of the same breed, and he must look like the breed. However, the parents need not be registered for a rabbit to be registered. The registrant must be six months or older and must meet his breed's senior requirements, such as being within the correct range of weight. If the rabbit has any of the disqualifying traits defined in his breed standard, he cannot be registered.

Once a rabbit has passed inspection, he will receive an ARBA Registration Certificate and number. Besides your name and address, the information on the certificate includes his three-generation pedigree, breed, sex, variety, date of birth, and even his name. If the rabbit has any winnings, these will also be recorded.

The Ear Tattoo

Most show rabbits have a tattoo in their ear. Like registering, some shows, such as those recognized by the ARBA,

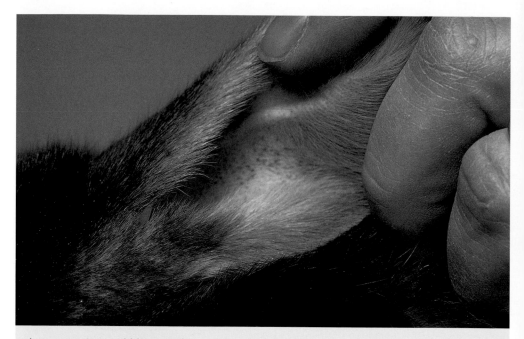

In some cases, rabbits must be registered and permanently tattooed in order to be eligible to compete in shows.

require that a rabbit be permanently tattooed.

Breeders tattoo their rabbits in the animal's left ear using their own system of numbers and letters. Because some breeds can look very similar, the tattoo is an important method breeders use to distinguish amongst their rabbits. Breeders with lots of rabbits often do their own tattooing. A tattoo in the right ear is the rabbit's ARBA registration number.

If your rabbit is not tattooed, you can usually have an experienced person such as the show registrar tattoo him prior to a show's start. Various methods can be used to tattoo a rabbit, including an ear clamp or an electric tattoo needle. Any method is painful, but the pain can be minimized in the hands of a skilled person.

Show Organization

Rabbit shows are organized by breed. Each breed class is divided into either bucks or does and then into age classes and weights. For small breeds, junior rabbits are six months of age and younger, while senior rabbits are six months of age and older. The larger breeds (greater than 9 pounds [4.1 kg] when an adult) also have an intermediate age class comprising rabbits six to eight months of age; hence the senior rabbits are eight months of age and older. A breed standard also sets a weight associated with each gender and age class. Based on these class divisions, a breed is sometimes referred to as 4- or 6-Class.

Many ARBA shows also have other types of classes in which rabbits can compete. The Commercial Fur Class is for breeds with a standard that conforms closely to the requirements of fur normally used in the manufacture of fur clothes or trim. The second group of classes is for meat rabbits. The Meat Pen Class consists of a trio of rabbits who are the same breed and variety. The rabbits are judged on meat type, condition, fur, and uniformity. The Single Fryer Class and Roasters and Stewers Class are judged on meat type, condition, and fur.

What's a Show Rabbit?

To improve your chances of doing well at an ARBA-sanctioned show, you must have a rabbit with good breeding or good genetics. Your show rabbit's ancestors need to have been bred with the tendency toward good muscle tone and fur condition. You won't be able to make a rabbit with a poor background into a winner, no matter what you feed him or how well you groom him.

A good show rabbit, or one with strong potential, will cost several times more than a pet-quality rabbit. If you think that you will be serious about showing rabbits, purchasing a few good-quality rabbits of your chosen breed is a good investment. You won't be able to find a show rabbit at a pet store but will instead need to find a breeder through the national breed club. Ideally, you will visit the breeder's "rabbit barn" in person. Be sure to have them review the breed standard with you and demonstrate why they think that the particular rabbits you are buying have good show potential.

Breeders will only sell a rabbit as a show or breeding prospect. They cannot guarantee his success in either endeavor. Some people get around this by purchasing rabbits who have already proven their worth by winning in shows. However, this approach does not gain an exhibitor the same respect and admiration as someone who wins with rabbits she breeds herself.

Rabbit shows are also divided into age classes for the people who are showing their rabbits. Youth classes are for exhibitors aged 19 and younger. All ages can enter open classes.

For some shows, you can register the same day as the show. However, other events require preregistration.

Show Judging

Every rabbit in a class is carefully examined by a judge. The judges in ARBA shows have rigorous training and are tested before they become licensed. By observing the rabbit while he is picture-perfectly posed, the judge evaluates his body type for characteristics such as the width of the shoulders compared with the width of the hindquarters, as well as the profile of the rabbit's shoulders, back, and hindquarters when viewed from the side (called the topline). To further evaluate a rabbit's condition, the judge also runs her hands over the rabbit's body. For example, if the breed standard calls for short, heavily boned legs, the easiest way for the judge to determine whether the rabbit meets this standard is by touch.

One of the ways a judge assesses the length, density, and texture of a rabbit's fur and determines whether the coat conforms to the breed standard is to stroke the fur from the hindquarters to the shoulders. If the rabbit is supposed to have rollback fur, the hair will gradually return to its normal position. If the hair is too short, it will snap back into place too quickly, called flyback fur. If the fur is too long, it might have to be petted back down to its normal position.

Every breed has a different schedule of points assigned for categories such as body type, condition, fur, and color. Depending on the breed, certain categories have more weight than others. For example, more than half the points for Angoras are for their wool, and half the points for Dutch are for their markings. Each category can be broken down into

Judge Worthy

Before someone can become an ARBA judge, they have to have knowledge of all the rabbit breeds, have experience in breeding and owning rabbits, and pass a written test provided by ARBA regarding every rabbit breed they will be approved to judge. Then they have to apprentice under licensed judges for several shows before they will be allowed to apply for their own license. The ARBA has final say as to who can and cannot become a licensed and approved rabbit judge.

individual traits. The wool of the Satin Angora has points assigned for density, texture, length, and sheen.

Interestingly, a rabbit is not judged on behavior, although one who bites can be disqualified. When a judge has two rabbits who are tied in points, the one who is more tractable is usually the one who wins the class.

The Winners

For every breed, a judge will rank the rabbits within each age group or variety. The first-place winner from each class remains at the judging table. After all the classes for that breed have been evaluated, it is time for the judge to decide on "Best of Breed" (BOB). The winners of each class are compared with one another, and the rabbit who most closely meets the Standard of Perfection is named "Best of Breed." The rabbit can be either a buck or a doe from any age group. The "Best of Opposite Sex" winner is chosen from the age group winners who are the opposite sex of the rabbit named BOB.

Prizes are also awarded to the winners of other classes, such as "Best of Variety" and "Best of Group." In most cases, a "Best of Opposite Sex" winner is chosen for each class. The winner of each class receives a ribbon, and the winner of "Best of

If you show rabbits, you will hear the word "condition" quite often. It refers to a rabbit's overall appearance and health, or "flesh and fur."

Meeting Other Rabbit Enthusiasts

Organized events such as rabbit shows and rabbit hopping are great places for you to meet other people who have similar interests, and they are also great places to have fun. And if you are so inclined, these events always need volunteers. But don't expect your rabbit to frolic with newfound buddies. Although rabbits are social animals, they are also territorial, so fights can easily break out. You'll also want to minimize the chances of your rabbit coming into direct contact with another rabbit who might have an undetected illness.

Breed" often receives a trophy. There can be only one "Best in Show" (BIS) winner—this is the rabbit judged the best amongst all the other winning rabbits at the show. The BIS is chosen by comparing all the BOB winners. The rabbit who most closely meets the standard for his breed is the winner of the coveted title. Besides the pride of winning such an accomplishment, the owner of the "Best in Show" rabbit receives a large trophy.

Rabbits who compete and win first place in ARBA-sanctioned shows can earn "legs" toward their Grand Championship. A leg is granted only if there were at least five rabbits competing for that particular win owned by at least three different breeders. Three legs are required for the title. Rabbits who are Grand Champions are very valuable, and their offspring are also valuable.

GOOD SHOWMANSHIP

Showing rabbits is about more than winning—it is also about showmanship. This means graciously winning and losing. It means that you don't speak poorly of a judge or another exhibitor's rabbits just because you didn't win. Use a loss as an opportunity to learn from the judge's comments. Constructive criticism will help you know what needs improvement. Don't cheat with your rabbit. Believe it or not, some exhibitors paint mismatched nails and pluck or dye stray white hairs. If discovered, the exhibitor will be disqualified for such activities.

Condition

If you show rabbits, you will hear the word "condition" quite often. This term refers to a rabbit's overall appearance and health, or "flesh and fur." A rabbit in good condition is healthy, and his body will feel solid and firm. He will never feel doughy, which means that he is fat, nor should he feel bony, which means that he is too skinny. The fur must be in top condition, so a show rabbit will not be molting, and the fur will not be stained or bleached from the sun.

Keeping a rabbit in condition and having him in top flesh and fur for show day is not as simple as it might seem. A rabbit can inexplicably lose weight, or his fur won't hold its finish for the entire length of his body. Competitors each have their own secret formula for conditioning their rabbits. Some breeders might share some tips, but you will usually have to learn what works best for your particular rabbit.

There are a number of feed supplements you can try to enhance your rabbit's condition. Giving supplements can be tricky, though, because you can have too much of a good thing if the richer food causes your rabbit to molt or develop digestive problems. However, special foods won't help a rabbit who isn't endowed with good genes.

Posing

To be judged, your rabbit must be posed according to his body type profile, which is listed in the ARBA's Standard of Perfection. Compact, commercial, and cylindrical types of rabbits are posed in specific fixed positions. Breeds that belong to the semi-arch type are also posed, but some are allowed to move after an initial pose. With one exception, all breeds that belong to the full-arch type move, or "run the table."

Getting a rabbit to pose isn't always easy. Although some will naturally pose or run, most must be taught. Otherwise you will have to contend with a poorly prepared show rabbit who might flatten himself out, stand up on his hind legs, squirm, or jump. You will need patience and practice to teach your rabbit. It's best to start training him when he is still young.

Once or twice a day, take your rabbit out of his cage and work with him. Put him into the correct pose, and help him learn to hold the pose for brief periods and then gradually for longer periods. You should also get him used to having you run your hand over his body. Rewarding him with a favorite treat, gentle words, and a scratch on the head will help your rabbit gain confidence and learn the routine.

Before the Show

In many ways, a rabbit show is a beauty contest. As such, appearance is all that matters. Besides grooming your rabbit, it is important to know and control factors that can affect the condition of his coat, including climate and stress. For rabbits kept outside, sudden changes in temperature can cause the coat to begin to molt. A rabbit who basks in the sun can end up with a faded coat. Not much can be done with a rabbit whose coat is bleached by the sun—you must wait until he molts before he can be shown.

Stress can also cause a rabbit to molt. Going to shows every weekend can be stressful for him and can make it difficult to keep him in prime condition. Many serious competitors will not go to smaller shows if a major show date is approaching. Feeding supplemental foods that are rich, such as sunflower seeds and oats, can cause some rabbits to begin to molt. If you choose to feed your rabbit such items, don't suddenly do so a few weeks before a show.

Several weeks prior to a show, make sure that your rabbit is looking good. His fur should not be dirty, stained, or damaged from the sun. A dirty, stained coat will make it more difficult for the judge to evaluate his fur. Some judges will deduct points for a coat that is presented in this manner. You can avoid this penalty by cleaning your rabbit several days before the show.

Other similar conditions can result in penalty deductions. Urine stains are not acceptable, and they can be difficult to remove. The best approach is to keep the cage clean so that they can never develop. Yellowish stains on the bottom of a rabbit's feet are not usually penalized because they are fairly typical. Don't forget to make sure that your rabbit's nails are trimmed. You should also weigh him and determine how old he will be on the day of the show to know which show category he will qualify for and enter.

At the Show

When you arrive at the show, the animal coops will usually be set up with bedding and food and water cups. Food and water are usually provided, but many exhibitors prefer to use their own sources to prevent potential digestive upset in their rabbits.

If you have been properly caring for your rabbit, you should not have much grooming to do on the day of the show. For shorthaired breeds, a quick rub will remove any loose fur. Longhaired breeds might need another going-over with a brush.

Some rabbits become stressed at shows. Covering their carrier with a towel can help keep them calm by reducing strange sights and sounds. However, be sure that your rabbit won't overheat if the cage is covered.

If you forgot something, big shows sometimes have vendors selling various supplies, including food supplements, grooming supplies, and cages.

After the Show

Shows can be stressful for rabbits. Most will not become stressed, but some don't tolerate the showing process well. Although rabbits at a show are disqualified if they look sick (and competitors aren't likely to knowingly bring a sick rabbit to a show), it is still important to carefully observe your pet for several weeks following a show. Be alert for any signs of illness or a problem caused by stress, such as lack of appetite, lethargy, diarrhea, or runny nose. If

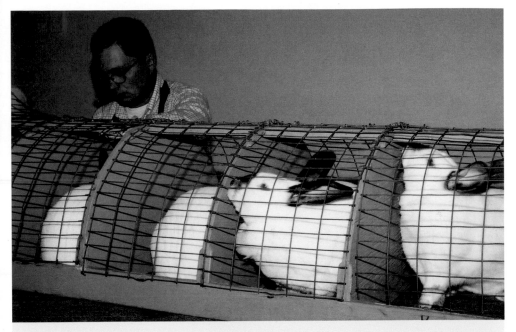

Rabbit shows are organized by breed. Each breed class is then divided into either bucks or does and then into age classes and weights.

symptoms persist, a trip to the veterinarian is warranted. If a your rabbit seems to become stressed from showing, consider no longer doing so because this could actually cause him to die.

Consider quarantining any rabbits who were at a show to protect any other rabbits you own. Isolating them for a few weeks is usually sufficient to ensure that they were not infected with a disease picked up at a show or other event.

Managing a Herd of Show Rabbits

Rabbits who participate in ARBA shows must be intact, that is, not neutered or spayed. Although rabbits are naturally clean and frequently groom themselves, intact males can be messy animals. As part of their natural behavior, they will spray their cage and surroundings with urine. Their urine can also get on them. If intact males are housed next to one another or next to does, they will also spray their neighbors. Cage dividers can prevent them from getting the spray on another rabbit or his cage.

Because urine can stain the coat, it is important to keep your buck's cage clean. A rabbit with a urine-stained coat is usually not worth showing until he has molted into a clean coat.

Separate your juniors into their own cages as soon as you can to prevent coat chewing brought on by boredom, crowding, or hormones. A chewed coat ruins the rabbit for showing until an entirely new one grows in.

4-H PROGRAMS

The 4-H Program began in the early 1900s. The program's name is an abbreviation for "head, heart, hands, and health" and is represented by the four-leaf clover. 4-H has its roots in agriculture; it was originally created to help children learn how to care for and exhibit livestock. However, the program has now been expanded to include a variety of projects, including rocket building. There are 4-H programs at the local, state, and national level. 4-H is administered by the county extension services in each state. Each club is run by volunteers who are usually parents or interested members of the community who pass a federal background check.

The youth members play an important part in running and planning club meetings and deciding upon personal goals and goals for the clubs. 4-H is open to children ages 9 to 19, although some clubs permit younger members. If you have children interested in the 4-H rabbit program or if you are interested in volunteering, contact your local extension office, which is listed under county government in the telephone book, or you can look the organization up online.

4-H Rabbit Projects

Rabbit projects are often run by fanciers who actively breed and show their rabbits. Children can learn about proper rabbit care, handling, feeding, grooming, and how to exhibit their rabbit in a show. Most youngsters find showing their rabbits exciting and enjoyable.

Rabbits can be entered in shows run solely for 4-H members. The shows follow the same rules and breed standards established by the ARBA. One of the most exciting places to show rabbits is at the county fair, where a child has the opportunity to share her love and knowledge of rabbits with a wide audience. A county fair is also a great place to see a large variety of different rabbit breeds all in one place.

There is even a place at shows for pet rabbits who are not purebred. The rabbit can be entered in showmanship classes or specific pet rabbit classes. Children in these classes are evaluated on their knowledge about rabbits, including anatomy, grooming, conditioning, proper handling, and showmanship techniques. Rabbits in these classes must not exhibit fear or aggression. Children who successfully exhibit a rabbit can earn medals, ribbons, and certificates. But of equal importance are the confidence and personal growth they will gain through hands-on experience.

RABBIT HOPPING AND AGILITY

Activities with pet rabbits, such as rabbit hopping and agility, are becoming more and more popular in the United States.

Activities with pet rabbits, such as rabbit hopping and agility, are becoming more and more popular in the United States.

Rabbit Hopping

Rabbit hopping began in Sweden in the 1970s and then became popular in Scandinavia, England, and Germany. As many as 200 rabbits might compete in a major competition.

In rabbit hopping, a rabbit must hop over barriers in a course that is similar to horse show jumping. The competition involves jumps on a straight or curved course. The course can have one or a series of jumps set up for each rabbit to hop over. The rabbit is kept on a harness and leash and is encouraged to jump far and high. The event is timed, and the rabbit with the least course errors and the fastest time wins. Prizes are also given for the rabbit who jumps the highest and the farthest.

Although rabbits are natural jumpers, they must be trained to jump barriers around a course surrounded by spectators. If you want to enter your rabbit in competition, he must first get used to wearing a harness and walking on a variety of surfaces. When he is able to ignore the harness, attach a leash. Eventually, you can introduce the jumps.

Encourage your rabbit to go over a jump by placing one hand under his front legs and the other hand beneath his rump to help him over an initially low barrier. He will likely then learn to hop on his own. Let your rabbit take the lead—if you get in front of him, he probably won't go over the jump. Plan to train him for 10 to 20 minutes, at least once a day, prior to a competition.

You will need to transport your rabbit to the event in his carrying cage. Be sure that you have plenty of water and food once you arrive. Many rabbits seem to enjoy competing; they readily and speedily jump through the course. However, if your rabbit dashes about, he is not ready and may need more training. It may also be possible that rabbit hopping isn't suitable for his particular temperament.

Candidates for Rabbit Hopping

If you are interested in participating in rabbit hopping, your best choice of rabbit is one who is curious and outgoing. In terms of size, many people think small- and medium-sized breeds are best. Experienced participants recommend not using rabbits with short backs, long wool, or those who are overweight. Intact adult male rabbits often do not make good hoppers because they are usually more interested in the scent of female rabbits than in jumping over the course.

Rabbit hopping has some restrictions. Rabbits less than four months old are not allowed to compete. This rule is to discourage people from training their pets before they have finished growing, which could damage their bone structure or otherwise hurt them. Although some folks are serious competitors and have talented rabbits, others enjoy rabbit hopping as just another fun way to spend time with their pet.

In the United States, the sport of rabbit hopping is not yet as organized or as popular as it is in Europe. You are more likely to see a demonstration of hopping at a 4-H rabbit show or perhaps at a county fair. Some rabbit fanciers have mixed feelings about the sport, believing that it is too unnatural for rabbits. However, hopping enthusiasts point out that their rabbits enjoy the experience, often showing their pleasure by hopping straight up in the air after going over the jumps.

Rabbit Agility

Rabbit agility is another fun activity that you may be able to compete in with your pet. In agility, a rabbit is trained to go over, under, around, and through different obstacles. If the course is fenced, he can perform off leash, which is truly amazing to see. The rabbit who completes the course with the fewest errors and fastest time wins.

A rabbit learns to run an agility course through patient training. It can be difficult to

In agility, a rabbit is trained to go over, under, around, and through different obstacles.

Pet Sitters

If you're going on vacation for a week or longer, you may want to hire a professional pet sitter to watch your rabbit. To locate someone reputable, contact the National Association of Professional Pet Sitters (NAPPS) at www.petsitters.org. This organization can recommend an animal-loving trained professional in your area. Your veterinarian may also be able to recommend several pet sitters whom clients have used before. Never hire anyone for whom you're unable to get references or recommendations, and make sure that the business is bonded and/or insured.

The pet sitter whom you choose should like and understand rabbits. (If at all possible, she should be someone whom your rabbit knows and trusts.) Leave specific written instructions about feeding times, the amount of food to feed, the general schedule, and any medications he may need. Give the pet sitter the name, address, and telephone number of the vet's office, as well as directions there and a contact number where you can be reached in case of an emergency. Stock up on enough rabbit supplies to last until you return.

find an organized event, though, so consider organizing your own agility course with some rabbit-loving friends.

THERAPY RABBITS

If you enjoy meeting people and your rabbit is confident and potentially comfortable in different settings, consider joining an animal-assisted therapy program. As a trained volunteer, you and your rabbit can visit a variety of facilities, including nursing homes, hospitals, and hospices, or you can work with home health-care services or physical therapists.

Participating in these programs is very rewarding. Stories of magical moments are plentiful, such as when an elderly person who hasn't spoken in quite some time pets a soft rabbit and then suddenly says "Goodbye" or "Thanks" afterward. Somehow animals are able to reach people in ways that humans sometimes cannot. People of all ages, including youngsters in 4-H, participate in animal-assisted therapy with a variety of pets, including dogs, cats, and rabbits.

The Delta Society has trained evaluators who can certify you and your rabbit as a therapy team. You will have to pass a written test, and you will also have to learn how to conduct a therapy visit. Your rabbit will be tested on his ability to be held and how he responds to the different sights and sounds he might encounter on a visit, such as the commotion of crowds, machines, wheelchairs, medical carts rolling down corridors, etc. The evaluator must be certain that both you and your rabbit interact well with each other, with strangers, and with unfamiliar surroundings. She will also review any concerns you may have about how your rabbit should interact with visitors (for example, lying quietly on a bed next to someone rather than being held), Some of your responsibilities will include keeping your rabbit well groomed and his toenails trimmed.

Although you may be interested in doing this kind of volunteer work, your rabbit may not be right for the activity. The best type of rabbit for therapy work is one who is bold with little to no fear of the unknown. A trusting, confident rabbit has the right personality, but you should also make sure that he can adapt to this type of work before scheduling a test with the Delta Society. Begin by taking your rabbit with you when you visit friends and family. If he gets scared, return him to his travel kennel and try letting him out again later.

If you enjoy meeting people and your rabbit is confident and potentially comfortable in different settings, consider joining an animal-assisted therapy program.

Taking your pet rabbit with you when you go on vacation is not recommended.

Offering a small tasty treat can encourage him to enjoy himself. Once your rabbit is used to different surroundings and people, make sure that he also enjoys being stroked. A therapy rabbit must accept attention and tolerate having his ears, face, and feet petted by a variety of people. Again, treats can help. You can bring your rabbit into different rooms holding him in your arms, or if he is properly trained, you can use a leash and harness.

If you find that your rabbit is a good candidate, you will both offer a valuable service while enjoying a rewarding and pleasant time together.

VACATIONING WITH RABBITS?

Taking your pet rabbit with you when you go on vacation is not recommended. Just as cats do not have much flexibility in adapting to new environments, neither do rabbits. Furthermore, a rabbit's status as a prey species makes him much less likely to appreciate the hullabaloo and changes associated with traveling.

You have several options when it comes to your pet's care while you are gone. If you are going away for the weekend (two nights, two days), you can double-stock your pet's cage with an extra water bottle and extra dry food, such as hay and pellets. If you routinely feed your rabbit fresh foods as a major part of his diet, though, this method will not work because the disruption in his feeding plan can cause digestive problems. It is then best to have a trusted friend or neighbor check in on your rabbit to make sure that everything is okay. Problems can occur, such as a leaking water bottle, that will leave your pet without water to drink.

For longer vacations, you will need to arrange for your rabbit's care with a trusted friend, neighbor, or a professional pet sitter. Provide the caretaker with a list of everything that needs to be done for your rabbit each day, and include information about special needs or anything she should not do. Be sure to leave a sufficient supply of food.

Provide your veterinarian's phone number in case there is a health problem or emergency. (Contact your vet's office and find out what kind of payment arrangement it will accept in your absence.) Review any symptoms of possible ill health that your rabbit's caretaker should be alerted to, such as lack of eating or diarrhea. Finally, leave a contact number for the caretaker so that if she has questions or problems, she can contact you to get information or advice.

Travel Checklist

· · · · · · · · · · · ·

When traveling with your rabbit, bring everything he will need while he is away from home, both to provide for his comfort and to prevent problems caused by travel issues.

Proper Paperwork: It's a good idea to carry a current health certificate for your rabbit, especially if you are traveling across any state or country borders. Some localities/countries will not allow you to transport your rabbit without first presenting necessary documentation.

Identification: Be sure your pet is wearing an ID tag at all times. Although unlikely, he may manage to escape his carrier or your travel accommodations. This tag should show your name and a phone number at which you can be reached. Because you will not be at home, a cell phone number, your vet's number, or someone who will forward any messages are all good choices. Always keep your rabbit closely confined when you're away from home. Having a lost rabbit is bad enough when you're on your own home turf, but in strange surroundings it can create overwhelming problems. Carry a photograph of your pet with you in case he is lost so you can create "lost pet" posters. Photos can also be used as identification and proof of ownership if your rabbit is turned into a shelter.

Food and Water: Always carry a generous supply of rabbit food when you travel. Don't count on being able to find your normal brand in other parts of the country. Be sure it's kept in a well-sealed container and that you have enough to last the duration of your stay away from home, plus extra in the event your trip is extended. It's a good idea to feed your rabbit a little less while traveling to lessen the possibility of stomach upsets. Plenty of water is also very important because stress can easily cause a rabbit to become overheated when riding in a car; the stress of the unfamiliar can also cause him to crave extra fluids.

Litter Pan: Purchase a small litter pan that will fit in the travel cage.

Toys and Bedding: Take along some of your rabbit's favorite toys and the bedding that he's had in his cage at home. Both will make him feel more secure and help him to realize that you are a common denominator in all situations in his life. Wherever *you* are is home.

Lightweight Collar: Keep a lightweight collar on your rabbit at all times during travel, complete with an identification tag and a bell. The bell might help you find him, and the ID tag will help his finder contact you. (Again, don't include your home phone; instead, use your cell phone, vet's, or a friend's or relative's phone number.)

Resources

CLUBS & SOCIETIES

American Rabbit Breeders Association, Inc. (ARBA)
P.O. Box 426
Bloomington, IL 61702
Phone: (309) 664-7500
Website: www.arba.net

American Beveren Rabbit Club
Website: www.beverens.8m.com

American Cavy Breeders Association
Website: www.acbaonline.com

American Checkered Giant Rabbit Club, Inc.
Website: www.americancheckeredgiantrabbit.com

American Dutch Rabbit Club
Website: www.dutchrabbit.com

American English Spot Rabbit Club
Website: www.englishspots.8m.com

American Federation of New Zealand Rabbit Breeders, Inc.
Website: www.geocities.com

American Harlequin Rabbit Club
Website: www.americanharlequinrabbitclub.com/index.html

American Himalayan Rabbit Association
Website: www.ahra.homestead.com

American Netherland Dwarf Rabbit Club
Website: www.andrc.com

American Satin Rabbit Breeders Association
Website: www.asrba.com

American Tan Rabbit Specialty Club
Website: www.atrsc.net

The British Rabbit Council
Purefoy House, 7 Kirkgate
Newark, Notts, NG24 1AD
UK
Phone: 44 01636-676042
Website: www.thebrc.org

Creme D'Argent Rabbit Federation
Website: www.hometown.aol.com

Havana Rabbit Breeders Association
Website: www.havanarba.com

Holland Lop Rabbit Specialty Club (HLRSC)
Website: www.hlrsc.com

Hotot Rabbit Breeders International
Website: www.blancdehotot.com

Lop Rabbit Club of America
Website: www.lrca.net

Mini Lop Rabbit Club of America
Website: www.miniloprabbit.com

National Californian Rabbit Specialty Club
Website: www.nationalcalclub.com

National Federation of Flemish Giant Rabbit Breeders
Website: www.nffgrb.com

National Jersey Wooly Rabbit Club
Website: www.njwrc.bizland.com

National Lilac Rabbit Club of America
Website: www.geocities.com/nlrca2002

National Mini Rex Rabbit Club
Website: www.nmrrc.com

National Rex Rabbit Club
Website: www.nationalrexrc.com

National Silver Fox Rabbit Club
Website: www.nationalsilverfoxrabbitclub.org

Palomino Rabbit Co-Breeders Association
Website: www.geocities.com/showpalominos

Rhinelander Rabbit Club of America
Website: www.angelfire.com

Silver Marten Rabbit Club
Website: www.silvermarten.com

VETERINARY & HEALTH RESOURCES

Academy of Veterinary Homeopathy (AVH)
P.O. Box 9280
Wilmington, DE 19809
Website: www.theavh.org

American Academy of Veterinary Acupuncture (AAVA)
66 Morris Avenue, Suite 2A
Springfield, NJ 07081
Website: www.aava.org

American Animal Hospital Association (AAHA)
P.O. Box 150899
Denver, CO 80215-0899
Website: www.aahanet.org

American College of Veterinary Internal Medicine (ACVIM)
1997 Wadsworth Blvd., Suite A
Lakewood, CO 80214-5293
Phone: (800) 245-9081
Website: www.acvim.org

American College of Veterinary Ophthalmologists (ACVO)
P.O. Box 1311
Meridian, Idaho 83860
Phone: (208) 466-7624
Website: www.acvo.com

American Holistic Veterinary Medical Association (AHVMA)
2218 Old Emmorton Road
Bel Air, MD 21015
Website: www.ahvma.org

American Veterinary Chiropractic Association (AVCA)
442154 E 140 Rd.
Bluejacket, OK 74333
Phone: (918) 784-2231
Website: www.animalchiropractic.org

American Veterinary Medical Association (AVMA)
1931 North Meacham Road-Suite 100
Schaumburg, IL 60173
Website: www.avma.org

Animal Behavior Society
Indiana University
2611 East 10th Street #170
Bloomington, IN 47408-2603
Phone: (812) 856-5541
Website: www.animalbehavior.org

ASPCA Animal Poison Control Center
1717 South Philo Road, Suite 36
Urbana, IL 61802
Phone: (888) 426-4435
Website: www.aspca.org

British Veterinary Association (BVA)
7 Mansfield Street
London
W1G 9N
UK
Phone: 020 7636 6541
Website: www.bva.co.uk

International Veterinary Acupuncture Society (IVAS)
P.O. Box 271395
Ft. Collins, CO 80527-1395
Website: www.ivas.org

Orthopedic Foundation for Animals (OFA)
2300 NE Nifong Blvd
Columbus, MO 65201-3856
Phone: (573) 442-0418
Website: www.offa.org

ANIMAL WELFARE & RESCUE ORGANIZATIONS

American Humane Association (AHA)
63 Inverness Drive East
Englewood, CO 80112
Phone: (303) 792-9900
Website: www.americanhumane.org

American Society for the Prevention of Cruelty to Animals (ASPCA)
424 E. 92nd Street
New York, NY 10128-6804
Phone: (212) 876-7700
Website: www.aspca.org

Best Friends Animal Sanctuary
5001 Angel Canyon Road
Kanab, UT 84741-5001
Phone: (435) 644-2001
Website: www.bestfriends.com

Friends of Rabbits
P.O. Box 1112
Alexandria, VA 22313
Phone: (703) 627-7892
Website: www.friendsofrabbits.org

House Rabbit Society
148 Broadway
Richmond, CA 94804
Phone: (510) 970-7575
Website: www.rabbit.org

Rabbit Welfare Association
RWF P.O. Box 603
Horsham, West Sussex RH13 5WL
UK
Phone: 44 08700 465249
Website: www.houserabbit.co.uk

Royal Society for the Prevention of Cruelty to Animals (RSPCA)
Phone: 0870 3335 999
Website: www.rspca.org.uk

The Blue Cross
Shilton Road
Burford
Oxon OX18 4PF
UK
Phone: 44 01993 825500
Website: www.bluecross.org.uk

The Fund for Animals
200 West 57th Street
New York, NY 10019
Phone: (212) 246-2096
Website: www.fund.org

The Humane Society of the United States (HSUS)
2100 L Street, NW
Washington DC 20037
Phone: (202) 452-1100
Website: www.hsus.org

INTERNET RESOURCES

Healthypet
Website: www.healthypet.com
Healthypet.com is part of the American Animal Hospital Association, an organization of more than 29,000 veterinary care providers committed to providing excellence in small animal care.

Petfinder
Website: www.petfinder.org
Petfinder.org provides an extensive database of adoptable animals, shelters, and rescue groups around the country. You can also post classified ads for lost or found pets, pets wanted, and pets needing homes.

Pets 911
Website: www.1888pets911.org
Pets 911offers a comprehensive database of lost and found pets, adoption information, pet health, and shelter and rescue information. The website also runs a toll-free phone hotline (1-888-PETS-911) that gives pet owners access to important life-saving information.

Rabbit Hopping Organization of America (R.H.O.A.)
Website: www.rhoa.tk
This website provides information on how to introduce your rabbit to the sport of hopping. The organization itself is the first of its kind to offer hopping as a sport to all rabbit owners in the United States. Once registered with the R.H.O.A., members will receive a complete set of rules and guidelines pertaining to training and competition.

The Small Animal Pages
Website: www.pet-net.net
This website provides rabbit owners with a variety of pet information, chat groups, humor pages, and links to rescue groups and numerous other rabbit-related websites.

VetQuest
Website: www.vin.com
VetQuest is an online veterinary search and referral service. You can search its database for over 25,000 veterinary hospitals and clinics all over the world. The service places special emphasis on veterinarians with advanced online access to the latest health care information and highly qualified veterinary specialists and consultants.

PUBLICATIONS

Books

Brown, Meg and Virginia Richardson. *Rabbit Iopaedia*, Interpet Publishing.

Davis, Susan E. and Margo DeMello. *Stories Rabbits Tell: A Natural and Cultural History of a Misunderstood Creature,* Lantern Books, 2003.

Fox, Sue. *Rabbits.* TFH Publications, Inc.

James, Carolina. *The Really Useful Bunny Guide*, TFH Publications, Inc.

Kelsey-Wood, Dennis. *The Guide to Owning Dwarf Rabbits*, TFH Publications, Inc.

Land, Bobbye. *The Simple Guide to Rabbits,* TFH Publications, Inc.

Leewood, Hazel. *Pet Owner's Guide to the Dwarf Rabbit*, Interpet Publishing.

Lindsay, Anne. *The Guide to Owning a Rabbit*, TFH Publications, Inc.

Martin, Barry. *Rabbits as a New Pet*, TFH Publications.

Mays, Marianne. *Pet Owner's Guide to the Rabbit*, Interpet Publishing.

O'Neil, Amanda. *Golden Tips for Keeping Your First Rabbit*, Interpet Publishing.

Page, Gill. *Getting to Know Your Rabbit*, Interpet Publishing.

Pryor, Karen. *Don't Shoot the Dog: The New Art of Teaching and Training*, Bantam Books, 1985.

Vernier, Louise. *Your First Rabbit*, TFH Publications, Inc.

Whitman, Bob D. *Domestic Rabbits and Their Histories: Breeds of the World*, Leathers Publishing, 2004.

Magazines

Best Friends
5001 Angel Canyon Road
Kanab, UT 84741
Website: www.bestfriends.com

Friends of Rabbits
Online Newsletter Archive
P.O. Box 1112
Alexandria, VA 22313
Website: www.friendsofrabbits.org

Fur & Feather
Printing for Pleasure Ltd.
Elder House
Chattisham
Ipswich
Suffolk IP8 3QE
UK
Website: www.btinternet.com

House Rabbit Journal
148 Broadway
Richmond, CA 94804
Website: www.psg.lcs.mit.edu

Rabbits Only
P.O. Box 207
Holbrook, NY 11741
Website: www.rabbits.com

The Rabbit Warren
E81B Daniels Road
Shelton, WA 98584
Website: therabbitwarren.tripod.com

Index

Note: **Boldfaced** numbers indicate illustrations.

A

Academy of Veterinary Homeopathy (AVH), 242
acquiring rabbits, sources for, 80–85
activities for rabbits, **220**
adoption, 82, 83
adult vs. baby rabbits, 90
agility, **233**, 233–234
American Academy of Veterinary Acupuncture (AAVA), 242
American Animal Hospital Association (AAHA), 242
American Beveren Rabbit Club, 241
American Cavy Breeders Association, 241
American Checkered Giant Rabbit Club, Inc., 241
American Chinchilla rabbits, 26, 33, 63–64
American College of Veterinary Internal Medicine (ACVIM), 242
American College of Veterinary Ophthalmologists (ACVO), 242
American Dutch Rabbit Club, 241

American English Spot Rabbit Club, 241
American Federation of New Zealand Rabbit Breeders, Inc., 241
American Fuzzy Lop rabbits, 32, 36–37
American Harlequin Rabbit Club, 241
American Himalayan Rabbit Association, 241
American Holistic Veterinary Medical Association (AHVMA), 243
American Humane Association (AHA), 244
American Livestock Breeds Conservancy (ALBC), 25
American Netherland Dwarf Rabbit Club, 241
American Rabbit Breeders Association (ARBA), 14, 81, 198, 241
  breed standards, 26, 28, 30, 32–33
  popularity rankings of breeds, 77
  regarding poisonous plants, 187
  registering rabbit with, 221
American rabbits, 26, 33, 62–63, **63**

American Sable rabbits, 32, 51
American Satin Rabbit Breeders Association, 241
American Society for the Prevention of Cruelty to Animals (ASPCA), 187, 244
American Tan Rabbit Specialty Club, 241
American Veterinary Chiropractic Association (AVCA), 243
American Veterinary Medical Association (AVMA), 148, 243
Angora rabbits, 23, 28, 29
Animal Behavior Society, 243
animal shelters, 83
ARBA. *See* American Rabbit Breeders Association (ARBA)
ARBA Certificate of Development, 28
ARBA Standard of Perfection, 28
ASPCA Animal Poison Control Center, 243

B

baby rabbits. *See* kits
baby vs. adult rabbits, 90
balls as toy for rabbits, 107

bathing, 143
bedding, **102**, 103–105
behavior
  bonding, **144**, 144, **170**
  meaning of specific
    behaviors, 168–169
  temperament, 15–16, 34,
    85–87, 177, 205
behavior problems, 14–16,
  85, **178**
  cannibalism, 206
  chewing, 171–172
  digging, 172, **173**
  hormones, raging, 169
  medical issues and, 169
  nipping and biting,
    170–171
  training and, 179
Belgian Hare, 9, 24, 26, 32,
  52, 52–53
Best Friends Animal
  Sanctuary, 244
Best Friends, magazine, 247
Best of Breed (BOB), 225
Best of Group, 225
Best of Opposite Sex, 225
Best of Show (BIS), 226
Best of Variety, 225
Beveren rabbits, 26, 33,
  64–65, **65**
bill of sale, 89
Black-tailed jackrabbit, 7
bladder stones/sludge, 159
Blanc de Hotot rabbits, 26,
  33, 65–66
Blue Cross, 244
body type profile, 34

bonding, 144, **144**, **170**
breed clubs, 27–28
breed standards, **25**, 26, 28,
  30, 32–33
breeders, 81–82
breeding, **197**, **213**
  breed choices for, 195–
    196
  business of, 197
  considerations, 194–195,
    212
  for improving the breed,
    197–198
  litter size, 202–203
  principles of, 199–202
breeds, 21–77
  characteristics of, 9–10,
    28–35
  creating new, 27–28
  descriptions of, 36–76
  development of, 23–26
  differences in, 28, **29**
  history of, 22–23
  popularity rankings, 77
  rare, 25–26
  recognition of, 28, 30
  regional, 24–25
  types of, 32–33
Britannia Petite rabbits, 32,
  35, 37
British Rabbit Council, 241
British Veterinary
  Association (BVA), 243
Broken color markings, 31
brushing, **136**, 136–137
buck rabbits, 90, 199
bumps and lumps, 162–163

Butterfly markings, 31

C
cages, 98–101
  floor type, 99–101
  indoor, 111–112
  maintenance of, 116–117
  size of, 101
California rabbits, 33, **66**,
  67
cannibalism, 206
carbohydrates in diet, 121
carriers, 92–93
carrying your rabbit, **182**
cats and rabbits, 178–179
cedar shavings, 105
Champagne d' Argent
  rabbits, 25, 33, **67**, 67–68
characteristics of breeds,
  9–10, 28–35
Checkered Giant rabbits, 33,
  35, 73, **74**
chewing, 171–172
children and rabbits, 18–19,
  184, 230–231
Cinnamon rabbits, 33, 68
clubs and societies,
  resources for, 241–242
coat colors, 31
Commercial body type, 34,
  35
Commercial Fur Class, 223
Compact body type, 35
condition, show rabbits,
  225, 226–227
Crème D' Argent, 26
Crème D' Argent Rabbit

Federation, 241
Cylindrical body type, 35

D

Delta Society, 234–235
diet. *See* feeding
digestion, 122–123
digging, 172, **173**
diseases
  infectious, **152**, 153–156
  noninfectious, 156–165
doe rabbits, 90, 199
dogs and rabbits, **176**, 176–178
domestic rabbits, 9
  wild rabbits verses, 12, 80
Domestic Rabbits and Their Histories (Whitman), 246
domestication, history of, **10**, 11–12
Don't Shoot the Dog (Pryor), 246
down hairs, 137
dry foods, 123–126
Dutch rabbits, 32, 35, 37–38, **38**
dwarf breed rabbits, 9, 32, 35
Dwarf Hotot rabbits, 32, 38–39

E

ears
  care of, 88, 141–142
  mites, 142, 157
  tattoos, 221–222, **222**

emergency, signs of, 151
English Angora rabbits, 32, 53
English Lop rabbits, 29, 33, **69**, 69–70
English Spot rabbits, 32, 35, **54**, 54–55
European rabbits, 7, 11
euthanasia, 165
exercise, 16, 188–190
exercise pen, indoor, 107, 109
eyes
  care of, 87, 143
  color, 34

F

fancy rabbits, 14
fat in diet, 121–122
feed containers, 105–106, **106**
feeding, 121, 123, **124**
  amount to feed, 130–132
  carbohydrates, 121
  choices for, 123–130
  diet, history of, **120**, 120–121
  dry foods, 123–126
  fats, 121–122
  fiber, 122–123
  foods to avoid, 129
  fruit, 129–130
  hay, 125–126
  milk formula, 213–214
  minerals, 122
  moist foods, 126–130
  molting and, 138

nutritional needs, 121–123
obesity and, 132–133, **133**
orphaned kits, 214–215, **215**
pellet food, 123–125
protein, 121
scheduled, 130
treats, 131
vegetables, 126–129, **128**
vitamins, 122
water requirements, 126
feeding supplies, 212
female (doe) rabbits, 199
female vs. male rabbits, 90
fiber in diet, 122–123
finding a rabbit, 80, **81**
fleas, 157
Flemish Giant rabbits, 29, 33, 74–75
Florida White rabbits, 32, 39
food labels, 125
foreign breed recognition, 30
foster care, 16
4-H clubs, 81, 230–231
French Angora rabbits, 33, 55
French Lop rabbits, 33, **75**, 75–76
friendly characteristics, 86
Friends of Rabbits, 95, 244
Friends of Rabbits, magazine, 247
fruit, 129–130

Full Arch body type, 35
Funds for Animals, 244
fur
    care of, 89, 136–139
    mites, 157
    types of, 30
Fur & Feather, magazine,
    247
Future Farmers of America
    (FFA), 81

G
gastric stasis, 158–159
gender differences, 91
gestation, **200**, 201–202
*Getting to Know Your
    Rabbit* (Page), 246
Giant Angora rabbits, 33, 70
giant breed rabbits, 33,
    73–76
Giant Chinchilla rabbits, 26,
    29, 33, 76
Golden Glavcot rabbits, 24
*Golden Tips for Keeping
    Your First Rabbit* (O'Neil),
    246
Grand Championship, 226
grazing runs, **110**, 110–111
grooming, **143**
    bathing, 143
    bonding and, **144**, 144,
        170
    brushing, **136**, 136–137
    ear care, 88, 141–142
    eye care, 87, 143
    hand-plucking, 139
    health maintenance, 145

molting, 138
nail care, 139–141, **140**
nose care, 88, 143
orphaned kits, 215–216
sent glands, 143
teeth, care of, 88, **161**
tools, 141
guard hairs, 137
Guide to Owning a Rabbit
    (Lindsay), 246
*Guide to Owning Dwarf
    Rabbits* (Kelsey-Wood),
    246

H
hairballs, 138, 158–159
handling your rabbit,
    182–183
    injuries, 163
hand-plucking, 139
hand-taming your rabbit,
    183–184
hare, snowshoe, 7
Harlequin rabbits, 33,
    55–57, **56**
hatches, 113, 116–117
Havana Rabbit Breeders
    Association, 241
Havana rabbits, 32, 39–40,
    40
hay, feeding, 125–126
hay racks, 106
health
    characteristics of, **84**,
        87–88, **88**
    guarantees, 80, 89
    maintenance, 145

medical records, 89
health care, 147–165, **149**,
    157
    annual exams, 149–151
    illness, signs of, 151–
        153, **156**
    neutering and spaying,
        172–174
    senior rabbits, 165
    veterinarian and, 148–
        149, **150**, 217
health problems
    bladder stones/sludge,
        159
    bumps, 162–163
    dehydration in kits,
        207–208
    emergency, signs of, 151
    gastric stasis, 158–159
    hairballs, 138
    handling injuries, 163
    heatstroke, **162**, 163
    illness, 151–152, **156**,
        157
    infectious diseases, **152**,
        153–156
    lumps, 162–163
    malocclusions, 88,
        160–162
    mites, 142, 157
    noninfectious diseases,
        156–165
    parasites, 157
    pasteurellosis, 154–156
    poisonous plants, 187
    preventing, 159
    pudding stools, 160

red urine, 160
respiratory problems, 105
stress, **164**, 164, 228
Healthypet, 245
heatstroke, **162**, 163
Heavyweight Belgian Hare, 24
hereditary malocclusions, 88
Himalayan rabbits, 23, 32, 35, 40–41
history
of breeds, 22–23
diet, **120**, 120–121
domestication of rabbits, **10**, 11–12
of rabbits, 6–9
Holland Lop Rabbit Specialty Club (HLRSC), 241
Holland Lop rabbits, 32, 41–42, **42**
homecoming, 92–94
hopping and agility, 231–234
hormones, 169
Hotot Rabbit Breeders International, 241
House Rabbit Journal, magazine, 247
House Rabbit Society (HRS), 14, 84, 95, 148, 244
household pets and rabbits, 174–179
houseplants, 187
housetraining, **185**
Humane Society of the

United States (HSUS), 244

I
illness
care of, 157
signs of, 151–153, **156**
indoor
cages, 111–112
exercise pen, 107, 109
housing and accessories, 98–112
indoor rabbits
outdoor rabbits verses, 98
playtime for, 186–188
infectious diseases, **152**, 153–156
injuries, 163
International Veterinary Acupuncture Society (IVAS), 243
internet forums for purchasing rabbits, 85
internet resources, 245

J
jackrabbit, Black-tailed, 7
Jersey Wooly rabbits, 29, 32, 42–43, **43**
judges for show rabbits, 224

K
kindling, 204
kits, 208–209
dehydration and, 207–208
handling, 205
healthy signs, 205–206

orphaned, 210–217
strays, 206–207

L
lactation, 207
large breed rabbits, 33, 35, 62–73
leash training, 190–191
life span, 16
Lilac rabbits, 26, 33, 57
litter, 102–103
box for, 101–102
box training, 185–186
location of hatches, 114, **115**
longhaired rabbits, 137
Lop Rabbit Club of America, 242
lumps and bumps, 162–163

M
male (buck) rabbits, 199
male vs. female rabbits, 90
malocclusions, 88, 160–162
markings and coat patterns, 31
mating, 200–201
Meat Pen Class, 223
medical records, 89
medium breed rabbits, 32–33, 51–62
minerals in diet, 122
Mini Lop Rabbit Club of America, 242
Mini Lop rabbits, 32, 44, **44**
Mini Rex rabbits, 32, 45, **45**
Mini Satin rabbits, 26, 32, 45–46

mites
    ears, 142, 157
    fur, 157
mixed breed rabbits, **91**, 92,
    196
moist foods, 126–130
molting, 138
multiple rabbits, 91–92,
    174–175, **175**
multi-species households,
    175–179

N
nails
    care of, 139
    trimming, 139–141, **140**
National Association of
    Professional Pet Sitters,
    234
National Breeders and
    Fanciers Association of
    America, 26
National Californian Rabbit
    Specialty Club, 242
National Federation of
    Flemish Giant Rabbit
    Breeders, 242
National Jersey Wooly
    Rabbit Club, 242
National Lilac Rabbit Club
    of America, 242
National Mini Rex Rabbit
    Club, 242
National Pet Stock
    Association, 26
National Rex Rabbit Club,
    242

National Silver Fox Rabbit
    Club, 242
nest boxes, 105, 203–204
nesting materials, 204
Netherland Dwarf rabbits,
    28, 29, 32, **46**, 46–47
neutering and spaying,
    172–174
New Zealand rabbits, 26,
    33, 70–71
New Zealand White rabbits,
    28, 29
newspaper advertisements
    for rabbits, 85
noninfectious diseases,
    156–165
nose care, 88, 143
nutrition, 121–123

O
obesity, 132–133, **133**
online training information
    www.clickerbunny.com,
    189
    www.clickertraining.
    com, 189
orphaned kits, caring for,
    210–217
    cleaning, 215–216
    feeding, 214–215, **215**
    feeding supplies, 212
    hand-rearing, **216**
    keeping warm, 211–212
    milk formula, 213–214
    older kits, 217
    veterinarian's and, 217
Orthopedic Foundation for

Animals (OFA), 243
outdoor exercise, 188–190
outdoor housing, **112**,
    112–116
    hatches, 113
    location, 114, **115**
    safety, 115–116
    weatherproofing, 113–
    114
outdoor rabbits, 92, 114
    indoor verses, 98

P
Palomino Rabbit Co-
    Breeders Association, 242
Palomino rabbits, 33, **71**,
    71–72
parasites, 157
pasteurellosis, 154–156
pellet food, 123–125
personality. *See*
    temperament
Peruvian rabbits, 24
Pet Owner's Guide to the
    Dwarf Rabbit (Leewood),
    246
Pet Owner's Guide to the
    Rabbit (Mays), 246
pet sitters, 234
pet stores, 85
Petfinder, 245
pet-quality rabbits, 82, 196
Pets 911, 245
pine shavings, 105
playtime, 186–188
Pointed white color
    markings, 31

poisonous plants, 187
Polish rabbits, 32, 47, **48**
popularity ranking of
  specific breeds, 77
posing, show rabbits, 227
pregnancy, false, 210
protein in diet, 121
publication resources,
  246–247
pudding stools, 160
purebred rabbits, 82, 85,
  91, 92
pygmy rabbit, 7

R
Rabbit Hopping
  Organization of America
  (R.H.O.A.), 245
Rabbit Iopaedia (Brown &
  Richardson), 246
The Rabbit Warren,
  magazine, 247
Rabbit Welfare Association,
  244
Rabbit Welfare Association
  & funds (RWAF), 95
rabbits
  hares verses, 6
  as pets, 14–16, **34**
Rabbits (Fox), 246
Rabbits as a New Pet
  (Martin), 246
Rabbits Only, magazine,
  247
rare rabbit breeds, 25–26
Really Useful Bunny Guide
  (James), 246

red urine, 160
registering rabbits with
  ARBA, 221
rescue groups, 82, 84–85,
  244
respiratory problems, 105
Rex rabbits, 33, 57–59, **58**
Rhinelander Rabbit Club of
  America, 242
Rhinelander rabbits, 26, 33,
  59–60
Roasters and Stewers Class,
  223
roles in human society,
  13–14
Royal Society for the
  Prevention of Cruelty to
  Animals (RSPCA), 244

S
Satin Angora rabbits, 33,
  60, **60**
Satin rabbits, 33, 72, **72**
selection considerations,
  16–19
selective breeding, 12, **13**
Self color markings, 31
Semi-Arch body type, 35
senior rabbits, 165
sent glands, 143
Serres, Olivier de, 23
Shaded color markings, 31
shavings, controversy
  around, 104
shorthaired rabbits, 136–137
show rabbits, grooming, 142

showing your rabbit, 220–
  226
  class divisions, 223
  ear tattoos, 221–222, **222**
  judging, 224–225
  managing a herd, 229–
    230
  organizations for, 222–
    224
  preparation for, 227–228
  qualities for, 223
  registering, 221
  winners, **225**, 225–226
showmanship, 226–230
show-quality rabbits, 82, 85
shy behavior, 177
Silver Fox rabbits, 26, 33,
  72–73
Silver Marten Rabbit Club,
  242
Silver Marten rabbits, 33, 61
Silver rabbits, 26, 32, 48–49
Simple Guide to Rabbits
  (Land), 246
Single Fryer Class, 223
Small Animal Pages, 245
small/dwarf breeds rabbits,
  32, 36–51
snowshoe hare, 7
spaying and neutering,
  172–174
species of rabbits, 7
spraying territory, 90
Standard Chinchilla rabbits,
  33, **61**, 61–62
Stories Rabbits Tell (Davis
  & DeMello), 246

stress, 164, **164**, 228

T
taming your rabbit, 183–184
Tan rabbits, 32, 49–50, **50**
tattoos, ears, 221–222, **222**
teeth, 10
    care of, 88, **161**
temperament, 15–16, 34,
    85–87, 177, 205
therapy rabbits, 234–236,
    235
Thrianta rabbits, 32, 50–51
Ticked color markings, 31
toys, 106–109
training rabbits, 179
    commands and tricks,
        189
    leash, 190–191
    litter box, 185–186

travel checklist, 238–239
treats, 131

V
vacationing with rabbits,
    236, 237–239
vaccinations, 89
vegetables, 126–129, **128**
veterinarian
    checkups, **150**
    locating, 148–149
    orphaned kits and, 217
veterinary and health
    resources, 242
VetQuest, 245
vitamins in diet, 122

W
water requirements, 126

weaning, 90, 202, **208**,
    209–210
weatherproofing housing,
    113–114
welfare organizations, 244
Wide Band color markings,
    31
wild rabbits, **8**
    behavior, 8
    domestic verses, 12, 80
    habitats, 7
    rabbits vs. hares, 6
wild vs. domestic animals,
    12

Y
Your First Rabbit (Vernier),
    246

About the Author

Sue Fox is the author of numerous books on small animals and several breeds of dog. Her home in the Sierra Nevada Mountains of California is shared with a happy menagerie.

Photo Credits